Revealing Antiquity

· 13 ·

G. W. Bowersock, General Editor

The End of the Past

Ancient Rome and
the Modern West

Aldo Schiavone

Translated by Margery J. Schneider

Harvard University Press

Cambridge, Massachusetts

London, England

2000

This book was originally published as *La storia spezzata: Roma antica e Occidente moderno,*
copyright © 1996 Gius. Laterza e Figli SpA, Roma-Bari. English edition arranged
through the mediation of Literary Agency Eulama, Rome.

Library of Congress Cataloging-in-Publication Data

Schiavone, Aldo.
[Storia spezzata. English]
The end of the past : ancient Rome and the modern West / Aldo Sciavone.
p. cm — (Revealing Antiquity; 13)
Includes bibliographical references and index.
ISBN 0-674-00062-5 (alk. paper)
1. Rome—History—Empire, 30 B.C.–475 A.D.   2. Civilization, Western—Roman influences.
3. Europe—History—476–1492—Economic aspects.   I. Title.   II. Series.

DG311 .S35   2000
937'.06—dc21   99-057780

Contents

Preface

This book tackles what is commonly considered a major subject. The reader will judge whether it is a risky choice.

I must confess that although I have often admired and respected their work, I am lukewarm about historians who willingly situate their research at the periphery of events, far from the facts that determined the course of our past, as if these were regions too familiar and well worn to be frequented by true experts.

I have no affection for the old, panoramic mode of historiography, and I am perfectly aware that God is in the details—or (if we prefer) that particle physics teaches us a great deal about the structure of the universe. Nevertheless it must still mean something if a star explodes, especially if we happen to be nearby.

I could not have written this book without two valuable episodes: from 1974 to 1980, I coordinated a seminar on the ancient world at the Istituto Gramsci; and from 1982 to 1993, I edited the *Storia di Roma* series at Einaudi. Sharing the latter enterprise with Arnaldo Momigliano until his death was an unforgettable experience. Two research appointments abroad were of benefit to me in the final stages of writing: one, during the winter of 1993, at the Ecole des Hautes Etudes en Sciences Sociales and the Maison des Sciences de l'Homme in Paris, and the other in the United States during the spring and summer of the same year, divided between Brown University and the Institute for Advanced Study. The least I can do is mention the friends who made these visits possible: Maurice Aymard, Jean Andreau, and Jan Thomas in Paris; Tony Molho in Providence; and Glen Bowersock in Princeton.

Emilio Gabba, Andrea Giardina, and Corrado Vivanto read the entire manuscript, which could have gained even more from their suggestions and advice.

The first two chapters were the subject of three seminars I gave at the universities of Pavia, Ferrara, and Bari. Their final draft makes use of many comments made by the participants.

A.S.

Rome, September 1995

This work achieved its definitive shape in the summer of 1993 at Brown University and the Institute for Advanced Study. For me it has been, from the beginning, an American book. I am therefore particularly glad that, with this translation, it has become one in reality. This was made possible through the help of many persons. Among them, I would like to mention individually Margery Schneider, who has had the ungrateful task of translating my difficult Italian, and Margaretta Fulton of Harvard University Press, who has overseen the entire work with skill and care.

Above all, I am happy to express my thanks to Glen Bowersock. The American version of *La storia spezzata* is dedicated to his friendship.

A.S.

Princeton, October 1998

Introduction

Ancient history is becoming more and more a discipline just for specialists. This transformation is not particularly new, but it is now generally acknowledged to be irreversible and inevitable.

This was not always so. Gibbon's *History* and Mommsen's *Roman History,* and possibly also Rostovtzeff's *History of the Ancient World*—to say nothing of the work of Burckhardt and Fustel de Coulanges—were by no means destined only for the eyes of scholars. They conveyed images of the ancient world that were meant to impress the minds of all cultivated readers of their time. They were designed to provide access to the broad intellectual patrimony of an epoch or a milieu.

Among the preceding generation's authoritative historians of the ancient world, perhaps only Moses Finley really knew how to communicate outside the closed circle of the professoriat. Syme succeeded in doing this occasionally. Momigliano never even tried to do it, since his preferred style was brief and concentrated, and he never watered down his ideas in an expansive treatment. Still, Mazzarino and Dumézil, who possessed first-rate narrative skills, made the attempt.

We could find many explanations for this disposition to stay within one's own confines—something that has the flavor of a renunciation. But it is assuredly also the consequence of the extraordinary increase in specialized research that has overtaken ancient history in the past thirty or forty years. English and American historiography provides telling examples. We allow ourselves to be trapped into minute observation of facts under the influence of ancillary disciplines—philology, archaeology, papyrology, epigraphy, quantitative analysis—which enable us to decipher these new details. And so we run the risk of losing the overall view, as well as our ability to talk about it to a larger public. We no longer ask ourselves general questions; we no longer construct global perspectives. Our images, though they gain in definition, lose proportionately in breadth and depth.

In this book I have attempted to react to this kind of tendency. I have tried to write an interpretative essay closely concerned with a most demanding question: Why did the historical course of the West contain within itself the greatest catastrophe ever experienced in the history of civilization—a rupture of incalculable proportions—the extent of which seems unchanged even if we look at it not as "the end of the ancient world" but as a dramatic transition to the Middle Ages?

The answer involves an inquiry across the boundaries of various disciplines which American readers, and now even European readers, are not accustomed to see brought together: economic history, the history of culture and mentality, social and political history. This approach also imposed a continuous counterpoint between ancient and modern. I have tried to develop the argument in an account that is meant to be read through and not merely consulted. I hope that I have succeeded, without sacrificing in any way what is traditionally and emphatically called scholarly rigor.

Chapter One

A Golden Age

Historical explanations usually tend to assume the form of stories. But the account presented here does not have an official beginning, from a narrative perspective. We can enter into it at various times and places, as if into the path of a long strategic reconnaisance flight describing a sort of ellipse on the map. The way we have chosen to start is only one of the many possible alternatives.

(1)

Around the middle of the second century A.D., in the spring of a year we are unable to name with certainty—maybe 143 or 144, but other dates have also been suggested[1]—a young and talented rhetorician of the Greek language, born and educated in the far-off district of Mysia, in Asia Minor, delivered an oration before the imperial court in Rome that was to find lasting fame. Public lectures were very much in fashion at the time. Their style was prescribed by the level of the audience; and intellectuals liked to show their devotion to the stage, taking pleasure in well-chosen and well-stated words, retracing the ideas of the masters of antiquity at every worldly occasion, whether professional or social.

This brilliant rhetorician was named Aelius Aristides. His invitation to speak had come about through the good offices of his teacher Alexander,[2] who had contributed to the education of Marcus Aurelius and therefore had influential connections.

The speech, "To Rome," was presented in the Athenaeum, the magnificent new building that Hadrian had made the center for the furtherance and study of Greek culture. Today there remains no trace of this structure, which must have been located near the Forum of Trajan, in the heart of the capital.[3] The theme on which Aristides held forth to his audience—which may have included the emperor Antoninus Pius himself—cannot be considered particularly original for its time. The topic was praise of Rome: the character of the city, a comparison with the empires of the past, the richness of its commodities and practices, the quality of its institutions and government. This was, as everyone must have known, a stock subject befitting the occasion: Aristides had been summoned to the ceremonies marking the anniversary of the birth of Rome.

But the rhetorician must have impressed the members of his audience, who were used to distinguishing between the literary decorum of political loyalists and the flattery of the numerous minor figures who frequented the margins of the court, having come from all corners of the empire. We know for a fact that he subsequently had contact with no fewer than three emperors: there is a direct account of his meeting with Antoninus, which surfaced in Aristides' own dream vision, as reported in the *Sacred Discourses*.[4] Later, he met Marcus Aurelius (who was willing to endure long periods of waiting just to be able to hear him speak) and Commodus.[5]

The young man would prove quite talented. His life—divided between illnesses (mostly psychosomatic, some have suspected with good reason),[6] travel, and the constant recording of his own dreams in an immense, 300,000-line[7] nocturnal diary[8] (in that same era, Artemidorus also took great pleasure in gathering and comparing accounts of dreams)[9]—was a prime example of the connection between introspection, investigations of the occult, asceticism, and the disinterested exercise of power, all of which seemed to compensate for the superficial frivolity of the times[10] and which, in the case of Marcus Aurelius, extended to the personage of the emperor himself. Aristides' erudition, combining that of the rhetorician and the philosopher, was linked with a rhetorical movement that Philostratus was to define as the "Second Sophistic"[11]— a current, based on ideas and classicist convictions, that sometimes pedantically affected the old style but at times was more serious and better reasoned. We must consider it one of the most characteristic schools of thought of those decades.

Indeed, if we manage to separate Aristides' speech in Rome from the unfavorable light that its circumstances may project on it (for an encomium of the empire delivered before the court by an ambitious author may not at first sight appear to be an example of moral independence and intellectual autonomy), the text reveals itself to be neither dull nor insignificant. It was not simply a vulgar rehashing of its sources, which modern scholars have carefully identified[12]—Plato, Isocrates, Polybius, Plutarch, and many others. Virtually throughout, its prose and conceptual construction managed to stay afloat in the ocean of literary quotations and commonplaces in which even Aristides sometimes indulged, following the dominant taste of the times.

The speech, rather, arose from a feeling of fullness and civic accomplishment—from the profound conviction that in the deeds of the present time one could discern the signs that an ancient destiny was being fulfilled. Beyond all of the mannerism, this feeling on the part of the speaker affords us true insight into his era.

Aristides was certainly aware of the many doctrines on the universal mission of Rome that were circulating among his contemporaries. At that time, some of them even claimed to find signs of predestination in the name of the city itself: they imagined that by rearranging the letters of the word familiar to everyone, they could discover another word (*amor,* or "love") that was considered allusive and secret.[13] But our speaker succeeded in raising his discourse to a higher level—that of the small circle of the prophets of past events—finding the path to a reading that combined the unpretentiousness of his political allegiance, which he professed without the slightest trace of doubt, with the pride of a man who believed himself capable of explaining to the masters of the world the significance of their own history.

To Aristides, Rome's conquest of a huge empire was an act that completely transformed the atmosphere and social reality of the entire human race. First of all, the lands were made sweeter—this according to a metaphor he used, in a phrase that is stylistically notable ("the whole world has been adorned [by you Romans] like a pleasure garden").[14] A humanized natural world (user-friendly, one could say) now rendered the lives of men pleasant, whereas before there had been only difficult and harsh conditions ("I conceive of life before your time as [. . .] harsh, rustic, and little different from living on a mountain");[15] there was now a multitude of cities ("the seacoasts and the interiors have been filled with cities"),[16] all of them magnificent ("the cities shine with radiance and grace");[17] the countryside was safe ("gone beyond land and sea is the smoke rising from the fields and the signal fires of friend and foe");[18] on the seas, Poseidon "exchanged merchant ships for warships";[19] everywhere there were "gymnasiums, fountains, gateways, temples, handicrafts, and schools."[20]

At the same time, there had been a change in civil and political conditions, thanks to the Romans' universal diffusion of a uniform and rational system of social organization, as a result of which the conquerors were integrated with the conquered, and people were evaluated according to their merit, not their luck or strength ("you have divided into two parts all the men in your empire—and with this expression I have indicated the whole inhabited world—and everywhere you have made [Roman] citizens all those who are the most accomplished, noble, and powerful people, . . . while the remainder you have made subjects and the governed").[21] Where conflicts once raged, now peace was spreading among men ("no envy walks in your empire"),[22] since the Romans saw to it that each person was assigned the position he deserved, not according to a logic of domination but on the basis of a general standard of social and political reasonableness (an exemplary model of order, or *taxis*),[23] which was able to distinguish between those who were worthy of governing and those who could only be governed.

The same idea—the depiction of a total reversal—was reflected in an elaborate cosmological metaphor, at the rhetorical and conceptual climax of the speech: "The poets say that before the rule of Zeus everything was filled with faction, uproar, and disorder, but that when Zeus came to rule, everything was put in order. [. . .] So, too, in view of the situation before you and under you, one would suppose that prior to your empire everything was in confusion, topsy-turvy, and completely disorganized, but that when you took charge the confusion and faction ceased, and there entered universal order and a glorious light in life and government, and laws came to the fore and the altars of the gods were believed in."[24]

It seems clear that what captured Aristides' attention, and what he tried to express by means of effective literary devices, did not have much to do with the greatness of princes and their deeds. Rather, it was the faculty for imposing order and transformation evident in the entire Roman civilization at its height, and its effect on the condition of humanity, that astounded him and elicited his admiration. (Aristides often used the word *oikoumene* ["the inhabited world"] to refer to the world that the Romans had spiritually and materially civilized.)[25] And what impressed him more than anything else was the spread of wealth—we would call it the power of the Roman economy—which he described in a cascade of sights and impressions that underlie the speech. It is stressed at the beginning, in the description that serves almost as a preamble:

> Here [to Rome] is brought from every land and sea all the crops of the seasons and the produce of each land, river, lake, as well as of the arts of the Greeks and barbarians, so that if someone should wish to view all these things, he must either see them by traveling over the whole world or be in this city. It cannot be otherwise than that there always be here an abundance of all that grows and is manufactured among each people. So many merchant ships arrive here, conveying every kind of goods from every people every hour and every day, that the city is like a factory common to the whole earth. It is possible to see so many cargoes from India and even from South Arabia, if you wish, that one imagines that for the future the trees are left bare for the people there and that they must come here to beg for their own produce if they need anything. Again there can be seen clothing from Babylon and ornaments from the barbarian world beyond, which arrive in much larger quantity and more easily than if merchantmen bringing goods from Naxus or Cythnus had only to put into Athens. Your farmlands are Egypt, Sicily, and all of Africa which is cultivated. The arrivals and departures of the ships never stop, so that one would express admiration not only for the harbor, but even for the sea. Hesiod said about the limits of the Ocean that it is a place where everything has been channeled into one beginning and end. So everything comes together here—trade, seafaring, farming, the scourings of the mines, all the crafts that exist or have existed, all that is produced and grown. Whatever one does not see here is not a thing which has existed or exists.[26]

And in Aristides' final remarks, the empire is actually transformed into a magical scene of eternal festivities: "The celebration of national festivals, like a sacred and inextinguishable fire, never ceases, but passes at different times to different people, yet always is somewhere. For now all men deserve this."[27]

The age of the Antonines emerges from this evocative document as if in a state of grace: an era in which the high-minded rule of order and reason, instituted by the demiurgic action of the Romans, was able to develop to its highest potential, bestowing civilization and opulence.

This was an elegant interpretation, in which the classical themes of ancient idealism and rationalism reappeared in conjunction with a political philosophy influenced by Polybius, to which more current observations and analyses (from Dio Chrysostom and Plutarch) were linked. It was a structure whose effectiveness and suggestive power would be difficult to deny, unless some bias against it existed.

(2)

In whose name was Aristides speaking?

It would be a mistake to see nothing more in the mirror of Aristides' elaboration than a reflection of imperial complacency, a learned and careful representation to be placed solely within the iconology of Roman power. This aspect is surely present (Aristides makes use of the same officially celebratory adjectives found on the coins of the period);[28] but the rhetorician's learned prose attests to something more substantial. We can assume that he was expressing—to be sure, in a learned and subjectively filtered manner—a vision that was largely shared by a significant number of his contemporaries, and that thus was rooted much more solidly in the reality of his time than in a stereotype of the court. He gave a voice to all of the minor (and in some cases not so minor) urban elites[29] ranging from Spain to Asia whom the presence of Rome had helped to create or advance, progressively integrating them into a system of worldwide power and entrusting them with ever more important organizational and administrative duties. These groups and social classes, employed to good advantage in Hadrian's constitutional model, left an impressive record of their own civil vocation and public zeal in the thousands of inscriptions and buildings scattered from one end of the Mediterranean Sea to the other.

By the middle of the second century, the members of these classes—dispersed throughout the urban areas of the provinces, and completely assimilated into the equilibria of the capillary organization of the empire—constituted a reservoir of available administrative and political talent, a source of productivity, and an accumulation of wealth. They thus formed the true backbone of the dominant "party apparatus" of the Romans. Aristides' oration represented, first and foremost, a distillation of their feelings—a legacy of ideas and experiences that constituted the mental fabric of the imperial ruling classes, from Britain to Africa.

If we make this attribution, the quality of our interpretation is heightened. In such a markedly apologetic vision, we can now sense—in addition to Aristides' obvious and understandable loyalism—the presence of the considerable self-importance and glorification manifested by important social strata with regard to their role and function. By having Aristides speak in the prestigious Athenaeum, the skillful stage managers of the imperial court avoided limiting the event to a culturally commendable celebration of the majesty of the empire, as the tastes of the moment would have dictated. They also staged a display of the fidelity and unconditional approbation that surrounded the power of Rome on all sides, and that represented the most unequivocal legitimization of Rome's supremacy. Beyond its literary or historiographic value, therefore, Aristides' oration can be analyzed as a document of interest from the standpoint of what could be termed the sociology of culture and consensus. It opens an essentially direct perspective on the ideological convolutions of a process of integration that had no equal in the ancient world. At that time, many believed they were living in a latter-day golden age—just as Aristides had written—or at least in a state of unprecedented well-being and comfort.

(3)

But in order to understand Aristides' assessment in its fullest sense, we must attempt to situate our text against an even larger background. The optimism just described was not the only component of the sensibilities of the era, nor were Aristides' own sensibilities limited to it.

Even as this rosy image was establishing itself among the members of the ruling class of the empire—especially in the provinces and the court, to a greater extent than among the old Italian nobility, which was already beset with difficulties and problems—a veil of uneasiness, perplexity, and anxiety was beginning to fall over the consciousness of many people in these same aristocracies, gradually coming to rest on their souls.

From our vantage point, we can identify some of the elements in this distant welter of emotions. At its center we find something resembling a disjoined, or at least ambivalent, perception of the world. The same reality whose glory was extolled—for its opulence, its self-assurance, its ample opportunities for life and knowledge—assumed quite different contours when it was observed and experienced in the light of a different order of thought: not from a pragmatic or political point of view, but from a religious or metaphysical one. All at once, it revealed itself to be a universe devoid of meaning, from which every trace of the divine had dramatically retreated—a place occupied by a wealthy, refined, but spiritually empty civilization. And the more obvious its material advantages and benefits, the more arid and devalued it seemed. "The majority of humanity owes its knowledge of god to dreams."[30] "Any act is impossible, [. . .] without the consent of God." "Oh where was there help?! Where were the gods?! Was what had happened the last emanation of their power, their revenge and retaliation for their abandonment again by abandoned mankind?!" "The life of the body is entirely a flowing river, the life of the mind is dream and delirium; existence is war and sojourn in a foreign land; fame is oblivion." We can glimpse the elements of a redundant and troubled eclecticism, crystallized into a somewhat feverish Platonism with occasional shadings of Pythagorean contamination (a frequent combination). Also visible are tumultuous readings, a constant drive to look within oneself, into the truth of the "interior soul" (as Plotinus would later call it).[31]

It was widely felt that a relationship with the abandoned gods must at all costs be reestablished. As material and tangible certainties, the vehicles of discontent and deception, fell away, the paths of the occult, astrology, and magic still remained open—as did that of dreams,[32] in which the codices of the unconscious were mistaken for signs of the manifestation of secret presences in mortal souls (in keeping with a long tradition: the relationship between dream and revelation had already been acknowledged in the Old Testament, for example). There emerged a full nocturnal array of "holy men," deemed capable of restoring contact and acting as intermediaries with the supernatural.[33] Without some knowledge of these motifs, it would be impossible to comprehend the life and characters of Apuleius,[34] many of Lucian's figures,[35] the stages of Aristides' own life and his impassioned research on Asclepius (the eternal symbol of healing and magic salvation, unfettered by the practice of medicine and official science),[36] the life of Apollonius in Philostratus' narrative[37] (not to mention many Gnostic doctrines, or the flowering of the hermetic tradition), Artemidorus' catalog of dreams,[38] and even a portion of the reflections of Marcus Aurelius—an emperor who was lonelier than all his subjects.[39] At the very heart of the imperial prosperity, a kind of dark admixture, a zone of entirely new sensibilities, had congealed. If for now the public sphere remained untainted by this impasto, it was already evidenced in the consciousness of some people, and in their literary transcriptions of it.

But we must avoid the danger of an interpretative short-circuit. The existence of this clot of perturbation, deposited in the depths of the mental history of the times, does not necessarily stand in the way of the positive appraisal of the empire's economic and social conditions, which was at least as extensive as any negative one, that we have just re-constructed through Aristides' words. We should not reduce his valua-tion to a mannered apologetic behind which lay an entirely different set of truths. To believe this would be an oversimplification. Both attitudes had equal currency in those years. In the sensibilities of the day, states of anxiety and depictions of opulence coexisted in a relatively precarious equilibrium. The malaise we have noted was simply the indication of a fault line, a new schism between public happiness and private uneasi-ness, which in some cases could even descend into forms of heightened existential suffering. (But the latter, in large part, was destined to fall outside the era's codes of literary communication, which were domi-nated by the constant dissociation between spontaneity and stylistic elaboration, between emotion and *remplissage*. We can therefore only reconstruct them indirectly, by bringing the more remote layers of meaning to the surface of the texts, or through networks of data and biographical evidence.)

Aristides himself is one of the best examples of this kind of appar-ent duality—diurnal versus nocturnal—or at least of the multiplicity of levels in the consciousness of his day. Contrary to what some have claimed,[40] there was neither disjunction nor artificiality in his appraisal of the civilization of the empire; nor is there evidence that his thinking changed over the course of time. His exhausting quest for spiritual salva-tion, so clearly evidenced in the *Sacred Discourses*, in no way detracts from the solidity and reliability of his political assessment of the civil plenitude and prosperity of his own epoch. It was simply proof that per-sonal experience had demonstrated to him the extent to which the for-tunes of the empire might no longer coincide with the internal well-be-ing of her worthiest children.

(4)

Since today we know what was later to ensue, and what catastrophe was preparing to devour that world, we are strongly tempted to interpret this changing stratum of anxiety retrospectively—a stratum whose exact dimensions, in any case, are difficult to measure, given the shortcomings of the available documents—and to read into it something of a mysterious forecast of future events. In an important essay, E. R. Dodds proposed (although with great prudence) this kind of anticipatory interpretation, resorting also to the attractions of Jungian models.[41]

These are fascinating hypotheses. They probe uncertain, ill-defined ground. Is there a history of the unconscious, a nocturnal schema, that is in some way parallel, or somehow connected, to the more visible history of the forms of consciousness and their changes? Can its course be traced by deciphering the states of syndromes or the sequences of symptoms to be discovered in the manifestations of community life and in the literary and artistic products of an era? And what truth is there in the statement that it is not the structure of dreams that is historically and culturally conditioned, but rather the model to which that structure conforms in the awakened consciousness, thanks to the selection and reelaboration of memory?

In our case, however, it is possible to avoid becoming immersed in the confusion of such demanding questions. This is all the more imperative in that the risk of deforming one's perspective is quite real: the far-off observer can be deluded into believing he has uncovered profundity and interconnections where none exist. Perhaps we can more cautiously travel another route.

The key to an explanation lies in considering the public optimism and individual crises of this era to be the mixed result of a perception of reality, which, although fractured, bore the signs of a single mental condition. In order to get to the bottom of this, we must not assign the task of interpretation to two different types of investigation: the political and civil texts to the historians of the economy and society, and the "psychological" ones to the students of mentalities or religion. On the contrary, it is essential that we make every effort to grasp the root they have in common. The starting point—which we have no reason to question— remains the conviction demonstrated by the dominant and intellectually more attentive classes that their lives were immersed in a level of prosperity and material security that had no equal in their experience. But under close scrutiny, this opinion, which permeated the cultural sensibilities of the time, from Pliny and Aristides to Favorinus[42] and up to the great jurists of the imperial council,[43] reveals itself to be rather peculiar and, to us, surprising. It certainly reflected a state of comfort, but one entirely lacking in hope for additional, ever-possible improvements and continuing advancement. These expectations later accompanied the progress of modernity in the Western consciousness, eventually becoming one of its most recognizable mental backdrops,[44] at least from Bacon on, even before the theorizations of the late eighteenth-century and positivist eras.[45] Nor can this void be explained by the absence in ancient times of an enlightened conception of the future. The fact remains that the lack of such a conception was perhaps less complete than some have concluded when making an overly sharp contrast between ancient "cyclicity" and modern "linearity,"[46] although eighteenth-century philosophical subjectivity was the first to identify itself directly with the progressivity of history.[47] Furthermore, what was lacking here was not only faith in the gifts of the future but also simply the impulse to act—the urgent need to perform or function over and above any preestablished limits, which had for so long characterized the heart of imperial rationality (the life of Caesar is a good example) and which we can consider the Roman attitude that comes closest to the usual modern idea of progress.

On this point Aristides was completely silent; this is the most puzzling aspect of the speech. His perspective was entirely concentrated on the present. The future received mention only when he expressed his hope for an indeterminate and static prolongation of the existing time. The world—the Roman Empire—had reached its culmination. Civilization was fully formed and active; it could not go forward from that point. On the horizon of future expectations, change (for the worse) was imaginable, but not progress. Decline was the only possibility, according to the aforementioned cyclical and naturalistic conceptions of time, history, and politics that had conditioned all ancient thinking from Plato to Polybius, and that Aristides did not reject but was simply attempting to avoid.

Advancement of any kind was no longer conceivable. There were no further goals to reach and no conquests to plan—nothing that arms could conquer, nothing that politics could accomplish, nothing that the application of thought and technology could achieve. So much wealth and opulence did not open onto anything beyond itself. The land was already a garden in all respects. (Aristides called it a *paradeisos*.[48] The word, probably of Zend origin, is used in the Septuagint translation of the Old Testament to refer to the Garden of Eden.) It had been transformed and pacified through the deeds and the sound imperial judgment of the conquerors.

But a state of anxiety (as well as a feeling of satisfaction and the growth of a strong sense of restraint) can result from the constant perception of a state of perfection that is unable to break through its own boundaries, especially in an aristocratic culture which had imported from ancient traditions the ideas of civil and military engagement, constant testing, and life as action, and one which continued to prescribe for itself highly competitive and emulative models of behavior.

This is probably what happened. In the minds of the members of these social groups, the awareness of their own prosperity, together with the discovery that civilization had now advanced to unsurpassable limits in mental as well as material and geographic terms—the intuitive feeling that they had arrived at an ultimate point beyond which they could discern nothing but an obscure and latent relationship between sterility and comfort—resurfaced as bewilderment and apprehension. The imminent crisis was neither foreseen nor anticipated in any way, but the effects of an indefinable lassitude of history were coming together. And this was enough to feed a subterranean lake of anxiety. It was a syndrome of boundaries, of limits: what had already been accomplished could be preserved only by enclosing it within fortified walls, removing it from the dreaded retreat of the waves of time.

In the great defensive structures and imposing ramparts that the Roman engineers were building in the same era at the frontiers of the empire—for them, the frontiers of the world (an image similar to the one Aristides used: "you erected [your walls] as far off as possible")[49]—perhaps we can glimpse something more remote than a simple and questionable strategic decision. Those walls reveal themselves as petrified projections of the secret fears of the age—barriers against the worries and anxieties that many people could feel besieging the thresholds of their minds. But the hidden dread that drove them to erect the walls had not yet become a distinct perception of collective insecurity. The perturbations, even when they reached the consciousness of the emperor himself, were fragments that did not fit together into a single picture. Thus, the ramparts and fortresses ("which gleam with more brilliance than bronze")[50] seemed to arise solely from an awareness of the power that had been attained. They were also intended as a challenge.

On the other hand, people's doubts did not necessarily take on the elusive forms that we have been discerning. Prophecies of the fall of Rome, associated with its imperial vocation, had been circulating for a long time—at least since the prediction related by Antisthenes of Rhodes, in Hannibal's time,[51] and repeated intentionally by Phlegon of Tralles in the middle of the second century A.D.

If the history of mankind was viewed as an eternal cycle, then by necessity the decline of Rome was already imprinted on the period of her greatest glory, however indefinitely that decline might be postponed. In Lucius Annaeus Florus' reworking of Livy, done for his own rhetorical and historiographic purposes (an exercise which would have amused Giovanni Battista Tiepolo many centuries later),[52] the entire imperial period, despite all of the apologetic statements, seemed to correspond to the old age of the world—although Annaeus Florus later implausibly adapted his biological schema, modeled on Seneca's,[53] by tacking on a reference to a period of regeneration, which he credited to the reign of Trajan. And the same agitation, the same gnawing feeling, kept reappearing, although within different cultural parameters—the suspicion that within the admirable prosperity of the empire lay hidden a zone of exhaustion, termination, and sterility.

In a chapter near the end of our account, we shall return to this mental state, which will be referred to here as "the end of time." For the moment, it is enough to have explained why this mood did not dilute the force and credibility of Aristides' vision. On the contrary, this state of mind permits us to assess the speech more accurately, and to understand it for what it was: a description of an era that, in the rhetorician's firm belief, was an age of splendor—but that was portrayed, it might be said, while he held his breath. Now, however, we must make a long leap, in order to compare Aristides' views with those of two others—analogous to his, but much closer to us.

Chapter Two

Why Not Then?

(1)

The first truly modern interpretation of the age of the Antonines (and the entire principate) did not take shape until the end of the eighteenth century, although humanistic circles had already developed serious philological and antiquarian interest in the history of imperial Rome.

By this time, the observers were located far from their object (more than 1,600 years had passed), and their viewpoint was very different from that of Aelius Aristides. Their eyes were now used to observing quite different landscapes: liberty in England, the Enlightenment in France, science in Scotland. The setting had been transposed from the Rome of Antoninus Pius to the London of George III, the Walpoles, and the Pitts, and to the calm shores of Lake Geneva, where Voltaire and Rousseau spent their time. These surroundings and these years provided the backdrop for Gibbon's *Decline and Fall of the Roman Empire*.

In spite of the many differences, it was as if time had come to a halt. In Gibbon's new reconstruction, the second century reappeared on the scene illumined by the same light. Every detail resumed its original place: the splendor of the city and urban life, the scholarship of the institutions, the safety of the provinces, the intensity of commerce, the prosperity of the citizens, the quality (it could be said) of community life. The images of modernity and those of antiquity, fashioned through Aristides' lens, shaded into one another to the point of becoming intermingled.

The first three chapters of Gibbon's majestic fresco preserve intact Aristides' representation of a charmed era. In literary terms his account is memorable—from the famous first lines ("In the second century of the Christian era, the Empire of Rome comprehended the fairest part of the earth, and the most civilized portion of mankind")[1] to the strong and compelling conclusion: "If a man were called to fix the period in the history of the world during which the condition of the human race was the most happy and prosperous, he would, without hesitation, name that which elapsed from the death of Domitian to the accession of Commodus."[2]

But Gibbon had knowledge of something that Aristides could not have foreseen: the violent end that this world was to meet. He was perfectly aware of the difficulties (to which Peter Brown later playfully alluded)[3] of commencing the history of a "decline" by describing a "golden age." For this reason, he carefully inserted observations and elements that would mitigate for the reader the effect of so much admiration, without actually altering its boundaries. His writing is rich in nuances and shading, irony and deliberate ambiguity; the narrative modalities he employed were among the most impressive of eighteenth-century English prose, sometimes bringing Sterne's cleverness to mind.[4] It is not surprising, then, that shortly after the sentence cited above, as if to comment on the use of the adjective "happy," he added a rapid but biting observation on the "instability of a happiness which depended on the character of a single man,"[5] thereby unambiguously distancing himself from the absolutism of imperial Rome. (In any case, criticism of the despotism of the princes had appeared recurrently in modern historiography long before the Enlightenment, as early as Leonardo Bruni.)[6]

In the same way, we should not be surprised that Gibbon elsewhere called the second century an "age of indolence,"[7] thereby including in his schema an attribute of collective psychology which, despite its unavoidable lack of precision, turned out to be extraordinarily acute (as we have just seen).

This subtle equilibrium, which managed to attenuate previous assertions without obscuring them, succeeded in achieving a remarkable effect that further enhanced the contiguity between the modern reconstruction and the image presented by Aristides' oration: it imbued Gibbon's portrait of the second century with the same simultaneously diurnal and nocturnal patina that was discernible in Aristides' rendering, once his political opinions were properly situated against the background of the sensibilities of his era. What for contemporaries was a vision of suspended splendor resurfaced in Gibbon's work with a combi-

nation of colors that reproduced the ancient tonalities. Its luminosity
was veiled by a sort of historiographic "melancholy" (a term Gibbon
himself used)—the kind that might be felt by someone appreciating the
perfection of a landscape with the knowledge that a landslide is about to
obliterate it.

Nevertheless, for Gibbon the age of the Antonines remained the culmination of the Roman Empire. Even when, after the French Revolution, he toyed with the idea of a different beginning for his account,[8]
the substance of his opinions remained unchanged. In an early essay,[9]
Arnaldo Momigliano hypothesized that Montesquieu should be considered the source of the points of emphasis in Gibbon's assessment,[10] and
that, later, Condorcet was the commentator for whom the contradiction
during the Enlightenment between ideological hostility toward all des-
potic regimes and the defense of the age of the Antonines was most obvious.[11] But the *Considérations* does not contain much evidence to support Montesquieu's influence, and the reference to Condorcet is likewise
difficult to explain.

Actually, on this point Gibbon should be seen as the creator rather
than as the inheritor of the tradition. Close examination reveals that his
propensities were based on ways of thinking that were different from
those in the sources usually attributed to him. What fascinated him,
more than the genius of the emperors and their skill as rulers (as in
Montesquieu's brief comments), were the same characteristics that attracted Aristides: the solidity and richness of texture of the society and
urban life in that remote era—in a word, civil society, not the high
offices of the imperial government. Gibbon's perspective was the same
as our ancient rhetorician's, notwithstanding his entirely modern analytic talents. And if we wish to trace the sources of inspiration for this
kind of scenario among the authors who form the background of the
History, Hume and Adam Smith come more readily to mind than their
French contemporaries.[12]

In any case, it is certain that Gibbon was familiar with Aristides. His
library on Bentinck Street contained a copy (in Samuel Jebb's edition,
still cited later by Dindorf),[13] and his Greek was good enough to read it
accurately. Moreover, Aristides was not a neglected author in those days:
Jacob Reiske—the learned German classicist whose work Gibbon knew

well—had just written that Aristides' orations constituted a resource of greatest importance for the knowledge of the Roman Empire.[14] Gibbon quotes "To Rome" twice in the first three chapters of the *History*.[15] It thus seems quite possible that some of its antique tints found their way into the modern composition, and that hidden threads connect Aristides' meditation and the Enlightenment of Gibbon,[16] through their common exaltation of a world seemingly brightened by an incomparable rationality.

This might already be sufficient. But perhaps we can take another route to explain the light in which Gibbon flooded his golden age, and to reinforce its meaning further.

The covert objective of drawing parallels between the Roman and the British empires permeated the writing of the *History*. Shortly after the publication of the first volume—in February 1776, just a few months before the outbreak of the American Revolution—with England embroiled in its ordeal on the far side of the Atlantic, this comparison emerges unmistakably in the text of a letter in which Gibbon complains to his dear friend Deyverdun that "the decline of the two empires, Roman and British, proceeds at an equal pace."[17] His remark combines scientific study and political preoccupations; its irony is cloaked in uneasiness.

The *History* contains nothing so direct or explicit.[18] Nevertheless, it is not unreasonable to believe that in Gibbon's depiction of the consummate achievements of the age of the Antonines—in addition to the influence of Aristides, ancient sources, and modern authors, as well as the melancholy retrospectiveness of the account—lay signs that his affections had found a new object. His regrets and "nostalgia" (a word which had only recently come into use) were apparently transferred to that admirable far-off age. But in truth these feelings were directed at a different empire—one which was closer and quite precious to him, and whose imminent future he incorrectly believed to be imperiled.

(2)

Let us move from the American and French revolutions to the Russian. With a remarkable symmetry of dates, the two masterpieces of modern historical writing on the Roman Empire accompanied (and in their own ways reflected) the beginning and the end of the age of revolutions in the West.

About 150 years after Gibbon's *History* appeared, a troubled exile fleeing his country (Russia, in the throes of civil war) wrote his life's work. *The Social and Economic History of the Roman Empire*, by Michael Rostovtzeff, was published in English in Oxford in 1926.[19] Between the two works lay the void created by Mommsen, who had conceived his *Römische Geschichte* around 1848 (another era of revolutions) but had decided not to write the section on the Roman Empire. This gap was only partly filled by his book on the provinces (which appeared much later, in 1885) and by the various manuscripts (very recently published) containing the notes of his students.[20]

In Rostovtzeff's work, an enormous mass of literary, archeological, epigraphic, and numismatic information constantly sustains the warmth of the evocative and precisely delineated scenarios. To encounter them is like immersing oneself in the conceptual and visual plot of great paintings such as Giorgione's *Storm* or Vermeer's *View of Delft*. And in one of them—perhaps the most deeply felt and shared—the age of the Antonines appears again.

The style of historical writing and the cadences of the narration are different from Gibbon's,[21] but the charm we have come to recognize remains intact here. We are once again transported to the same landscape: an empire of a thousand cities, distinguished by the admirable vitality of its urban centers, from the most modest to the most wealthy; by the wise and prudent power of its government; by the strength of its professional army, composed of faithful soldiers; and especially by the prosperity of its exemplary economic and civic life.

Thus, Aristides occupied a clearly privileged position here: there is virtually complete harmony between the ancient orator and the modern historian. Rostovtzeff considered Aristides' speech a document of prime importance for the reconstruction of the second century. He believed unconditionally in its complete reliability and defended its importance with conviction, making it one of the foundations of his account. In a close paraphrase of the Roman speech, he wrote: "The first impression [. . .] is overwhelming. Never before had so considerable a part of Europe, Asia, and Africa presented an aspect so civilized—so modern, one might say—in its essential features. Some of the cities were large, some were small; some were rich and luxurious, some poor and modest. But all of them had this in common: they exerted themselves to the utmost to make city life as easy and as comfortable as possible."[22]

There could be many explanations for Rostovtzeff's enthusiasm, as for Gibbon's. Perhaps it is a continuation of the pro-Antonine tradition of the eighteenth century[23]—although it is somewhat difficult to find evidence of any propensity for Enlightenment thinking in Rostovtzeff, if we bear in mind his skepticism about the possibility of limitless progress for modern civilization. (At most, his might be considered a historical rationalism strongly colored by pessimism. And it must be noted that Rostovtzeff was careful not to cite Gibbon on the subject of the second century, and that there are only three references to the *History* in the whole work, none of them on matters of importance.)[24] Or else, we can simply conclude that Rostovtzeff, a fugitive from Lenin's Russia, was stirred by Aristides' depiction of a prosperous and peaceful empire ruled by wise and virtuous princes, who were able to promote self-government and the well-being of their citizens without incurring the risks that attend a violent popular democracy.

However, Rostovtzeff's account of the second century did far more than simply evoke Aristides' speech, and it even went well beyond Gibbon's description. The Russian's investigation was rooted in the progress of classical studies made in the nineteenth century and the first twenty years of the twentieth, progress that made more in-depth research possible and allowed for a much more clearly defined range of observations. It should thus not surprise us that, like Gibbon, Rostovtzeff did not hesitate to introduce—with prudent realism—passages that were decidedly inconsistent with his thesis: the depopulation and economic crisis in Italy, the intolerably high cost of Trajan's wars, the problems posed by many provinces. He went so far as to state that even during the charmed reign of Antoninus, "we must not exaggerate the wealth of the empire: there were factors which undermined it even in times of complete peace."[25] He used the same descriptive mechanism that Gibbon did, albeit on a more complex historiographic level: the negative elements effectively completed the picture, without giving the lie to its overall direction. And although Rostovtzeff's *Social and Economic History* served to consolidate the interpretative schema which held that a number of the

characteristics of the impending crisis were already present and opera-
tive by the middle of the second century, the shadows they cast did not
prevent him from maintaining that the reign of Antoninus marked the
period of the most widespread social, economic, and civil development
in the ancient world.

For Rostovtzeff, moreover, the second century was also the period in
which Roman society showed its most marked "modernity"[26] (a word to
which we will return later) and in which its mature civilization seemed
to be most similar to our own. The notions of proximity and absolute
comparability with the Europe of his own day (which Gibbon must have
shared, otherwise his opinion that life in those days was the best possible one would have made no sense) now found more precise definition in Rostovtzeff's hypothesis that real economic and social contiguity—scientifically demonstrable and historically proven—existed
between the ancient and the modern.

About 1,800 years after it was formulated, what might be called "the
Aristidean model" of the second century received further, and resounding, confirmation. The passage of time, and assessments by new observers of the progress of modernity, seemed to enhance the fascination
of the model and its fundamental principles, rather than to repudiate
them.

(3)

But the exceptional longevity of this image and the attraction it exerted
in such a wide variety of contexts cannot by itself be taken as evidence of
its trustworthiness. There is no doubt that thorough verification of the
values embraced by Aristides' speech would require extremely careful
measurement of the accuracy of its descriptions against the actual conditions in the empire, to the extent we are able to ascertain them.

Nevertheless, even the most severe critic must yield in the face of the
indisputable soundness of at least one aspect of Aristides' vision, and
this kernel of certainty has probably helped ensure its fortune. There
may be various reasons for taking exception to the quantitative information presented in the speech (the wealth of the second century was
not so conspicuous, the well-being of the people was not so widespread,

the cities were not so magnificent as he claimed, and so forth). But there is no reason to question the accuracy of the qualitative relationships between the elements under consideration. Above all, we have no reason to dispute the proposed scale of the comparisons between past and present.

The interconnections that Aristides discovered among a set of phenomena (public peace, the regularity and security of commerce, the quality of urban life, the "worldwide" circulation of ideas, people, and resources) whose happy combination defined the character of the era for him are capable of standing up to any criticism. And the terms of the historical comparison that he made would likewise remain unchanged. Considered from the point of view of the global diffusion of civic and economic growth (rather than according to the intensity of the growth region by region), this era was—undeniably—without parallel in the ancient world, and represented a high point that was never surpassed.

The importance of this fact is absolutely paramount, bringing up a major historical problem that will be central to our account: what Arnaldo Momigliano called "the question of the continuity of European history."[27]

This path also leads to Rostovtzeff. Contemplating the heights that the empire had attained, the Russian historian, in the tormented conclusion of his book, posed a question that must have troubled him (or so we imagine): "Why was the city civilization of Greece and Italy [. . .] incapable of creating conditions which would secure for the ancient world a continuous, uninterrupted movement along the same path of urban civilization?"[28] "In other words," he continued, "why had modern civilization to be built up laboriously as something new on the ruins of the old, instead of being a direct continuation of it?"[29]

This alone would have sufficed. But in 1946, exactly twenty years later, in a brief essay on the decline of the Roman Empire that perhaps did not attract the attention it deserved, F. W. Walbank took up the same theme in almost identical language, and furthermore connected it explicitly with Aristides' second-century interpretation (although he was inclined to discount Rostovtzeff's faith in the Roman speech). "What we must ask is: Why within a hundred years did this vigorous and complicated structure [the principate of the Antonines] cease to operate as a going concern? Why has there been not a straight upward line of progress from the time of Hadrian to the twentieth century, but instead the familiar sequence of decay, middle ages, renaissance and modern world?"[30]

Let us pause for a moment. We must do our best to restore to these questions their original freshness by raising them again silently within ourselves. We should try to reconstruct the intensity of the problems that they elicit by disengaging them from the tangle of issues in which they were buried (and where in truth their own authors had concealed them): the ocean of various topics, opinions, and periodizations that we encounter from schooldays on when we speak of the "end" of the ancient world.

At least after Gibbon, historians have wondered why, beginning with a certain period, around the third century A.D., the Roman Empire—as a unitary and "worldwide" structure—had begun to collapse. Whether they used the word "decadence," as was common at one time,[31] or avoided it, as was the preference later on, the essence of the question did not change. They were always seeking sound reasons for the fact that a civilization and its organization—in the social, economic, political, and cultural senses—had disintegrated and vanished, instead of perpetuating itself. These attitudes unwittingly reproduced the same static manner in which the ancients, as we have discovered, thought about the destiny of Rome before the crisis. Just as Aristides could not envision any future that was not a fixed projection of existing circumstances, modern historians considered the collapse of the imperial structure from only one point of view: as the interruption of a state of affairs which, under less unsettled conditions, they implicitly supposed would have been able to continue indefinitely. As we read in a well-known book, "When everything is taken into account, we may ask ourselves how the empire could have held out so long, and we cannot but admire the obstinacy with which it resisted its destiny."[32]

More recently, the field of observation has shifted and become more fertile. Attention has now moved from why the empire did not last to how the crisis, as it proceeded, gave more or less ephemeral life to a complex transitional society which is usually called "late antiquity." This is an entirely new universe, one which deserves thorough investigation in which simplistic and teleological explanations have no part, and complete acknowledgment of its autonomy. It is a universe where fossilized or defeated figures lived alongside forms that were scarcely delineated, fluid, mobile, feverishly mutating, full of promise. But although this change of perspective has produced results of great value[33] (especially for the history of cultures and mentalities)[34] whose significance for the renewal of the study of antiquity cannot be overestimated, it tends to overshadow an essential point. By concentrating on the formative processes of the world of late antiquity, and on the inextricable interconnections between the old and new that accompanied them (especially in the eastern regions), some of these studies ended up more or less explicitly proposing the idea of a gentle and almost imperceptible transition between the empire of the second century and the Europe of the early Middle Ages, thereby downplaying, even if unintentionally, the disruptive and catastrophic aspects of the changeover, at least as they were present in western Europe.

In two possibly overrated essays, Henri Pirenne had prepared the ground as early as the first decades of the twentieth century:[35] "In 600 the physiognomy of the world was not different in quality from that which it had revealed in 400."[36] I doubt that Gregory of Tours or Gregory the Great—and along with them the whole roster of terrorized and distressed humanity, exhausted by pestilence and famine, whom they put on view—would have shared this opinion; or that even one of the twenty thousand souls (give or take a few) lost in the solitude of the ruins, to which the population of Rome was reduced, would have agreed— a population which in the first half of the fifth century, although by then drastically reduced, still numbered in the hundreds of thousands. Not to mention the tacit arbitrariness in Pirenne's choice of date: the year 400, when the empire was already in a state of crisis, despite the ephemeral successes of the fourth century—shortly after Ambrose described as "cadavers" the once opulent cities of the Po Valley he crossed as he traveled along the via Emilia.[37] So why not compare the second century with the sixth or the seventh, and claim that the empire of Favorinus' day was similar to the Italy of Paul the Deacon, or that the economic situation portrayed in the legal analyses of Julian or Celsus or in the stories of Lucian or Aulus Gellius anticipated that of the chronicles of Jordanes? Or simply that the Rome of Ammianus Marcellinus[38] was substantially unchanged from the city of Boniface V and Leo II? Or that Liutprand's "anti-Roman" invective reflected the teachings of Augustine, professor of rhetoric in Milan?

We should admit that this reconstruction is untenable.

Let this be quite clear: more than a century of discussions and controversy has shown that every one of the "continuist" hypotheses can find many elements of justification in historiographic work. From the limited point of view of our species, time appears first and foremost as continuity. The movement of history is always sustained over long spans of time, and never completely wipes out anything, except through very slow processes. Beneath every rupture—from the Neolithic "revolution" to the Industrial Revolution, not to mention more recent political upheavals, from 1789 in France (as has been clear since Tocqueville) to 1917 in Russia (as we are now realizing)—we can discover the threads that wove it together and that connected even the most startling innovations with their immediate or distant past. But the patient and indispensable research (much of it in vogue among historians today) that attempts to expose the presence of forms that survived between late antiquity and the early Middle Ages—in the institutions, in the cities or in the countryside, in daily life, and most important in the mentalities, where, between paganism and Christianity, the search for God cast a shadow on every internal experience—can be truly meaningful to us only if it does not in any way obscure the significance of the structures that were shattered. And if it does not neglect the fact that the extent of the catastrophe is the only thing that renders precious to us the rediscovery of the network (quite often subterranean or marginal) that had managed to survive under the debris.

With their questions, Rostovtzeff and Walbank succeeded in reopening the whole discussion. By placing the subject of the transition to the Middle Ages in parentheses, so to speak, they stressed the aspects of rupture and discontinuity that were indelibly introduced into the history of Europe by the fall of the Roman Empire. But they accomplished much more: they proposed a way of thinking that revealed vistas of great interest. They no longer asked *why* the empire had not been able to survive in the West, or *how* the society of late antiquity had been created, but instead set out to discover why this world, *before* the crisis, had not proven capable of developing in a different direction. The hypothesis of a decisive change was introduced into the interpretation. The reference (which we might also consider a historiographic provocation) to the plausibility of a direct line between ancient and modern civilizations had no other purpose than to suggest in a rapid way that the collapse should not be considered the inexorable destiny of the Roman Empire, but that the Roman system, given the end result, might perhaps have been able to arrive at different outcomes, even some that might have had closer correspondences with modernity.

To pursue this line of thought, we must be able to perceive the value of an important priority. An explanation for why Roman society failed to rise any further once it had reached the peak of its development, why there was no transformative impulse of the kind that Pirenne identified in Europe after the year 1000,[39] must be a prerequisite for analyzing the ensuing collapse of Rome and its particular characteristics. This entails an investigation of the structures and events that prevented the formation of stronger evolutionary ties and rendered the end of the ancient world an epochal period in the history of the Western world—to some extent, the original genetic code of the modern period. In areas where the catastrophe did not occur, or did not wreak the same amount of havoc—in the eastern and non-European parts of the empire—the course of events assumed a different profile. To be sure, it would be superficial and simplistic to interpret the entire history of Byzantium in the sixth to fifteenth centuries as simply the extreme protraction of a long period of stagnation, but it is undeniable that the continuity in the East brought stability to features and characteristics that were entirely different from those that the crisis imposed on the West.

Thus, when Rostovtzeff and Walbank raised their question ("Why has there been not a straight upward line of progress from the time of Hadrian to the twentieth century?" in Walbank's words; and "Why had modern civilization to be built up laboriously as something new [. . .] instead of being a direct continuation of it?" as Rostovtzeff put it), neither was inventing an improbable historical situation. Nor were they devising some kind of "counterfactual" history, as some would claim. Instead, they were performing a kind of conceptual experiment that brought them right to the heart of the history of Rome and the history of Europe. They had unburdened themselves momentarily from the weight of past events, and had mentally returned to the era of the

Antonines at its peak. Their research had liberated them from the stubborn and widespread prejudice that a material civilization, insofar as it is "ancient," must necessarily be "primitive." They had succeeded, rather, in restoring the image of a world of extraordinary maturity. They had rewound the film of history to that point. Before their eyes arose the reconstructed *tabula rasa* of a future that had not yet been determined: the course of European history could have taken other paths. Once this void can be imagined and this artificial suspension introduced into the course of events, a new scenario, with all its vast possibilities, is illuminated. Now the emphasis is no longer the ancient one, concentrated on the "duration" of the empire or the "causes" of its decline, but rather on something that can be present only in the modern consciousness: its failure to develop, the potential transformations that went unrealized, just when the first signs of this evolution seemed most clear.

Considering the levels of growth and sophistication that Roman society had achieved, why was it impossible for Europe to take a different route toward modernity, if, much later, at the end of the Middle Ages, the economic conditions were quantitatively comparable to those of the ancient era? Why was a changeover consisting of uniform and gradual steps impossible, in place of the devastating dissolution that made necessary a new, laborious beginning, arising from a much lower threshold than the one that the Romans had previously reached, in both quantitative and organizational terms? In other words, what separated imperial antiquity so irremediably from European modernity?

This new perspective was dynamic, not static. Roman society was no longer measured against the yardstick of its hypothetical survival in the state it had attained, the indefinite continuation of its existence (as Aristides had hoped and Pirenne was to repeat). Instead, the crisis was incorporated into a path of development that could have led Roman society to something other than its destruction.

Rostovtzeff and Walbank (the latter perhaps even more than the former) thus attempted to construct a completely new conceptual design. However vaguely, they had sensed the existence of something like an "evolutionary fork in the road" in the history of the Roman Empire: in their view, this was the real pivotal moment that determined the now-familiar sequence of events in the history of Europe: the end of the ancient world, the barbarian West, the Byzantine empire, the Middle Ages, the

Renaissance, and the modern age. And they tried to say—if only in a flash—that at the origin of this course of events, which we now take for granted and consider "natural," there is a historiographic knot that we have still to untie: the real meaning—for moderns—of a course of events that came to a full stop instead of taking flight.

Why is it impossible to trace a direct line between the civilization of the second century and our own? Why instead was there a rupture that was unparalleled in the entire history of the West? Why did the social and economic textures of the empire come unraveled down to its smallest elements between the sixth and the seventh centuries—its inhabitants dispersed, its great workshops shuttered, its market mechanisms for mass consumption dissolved, its cities decimated?[40] Some have said that our perspective would be different and clearer if we examined the question from a "Germanic" rather than a "Mediterranean" point of view. But there is no truth to this: we cannot comprehend the encounter between Romania and Germania in the early Middle Ages without taking into account the disintegration of the empire in the West. Some have claimed that in certain provinces—Africa, for example—the status quo remained the same for much longer and nothing definitive happened during those years. This may be true. But in the meantime, what took place in the heart of the western part of the empire—in Italy, Gaul, and Spain? Why did it take more than a millennium for the economy of Europe once again to reach quantitative levels comparable to those of the Roman Empire? And finally, why do our present-day forms of social, productivity-oriented, and technological organization derive more from the collapse of the Roman system than from the growth that had marked its development?

(4)

The rupture that determined the course of European history can also be examined from the medieval standpoint. The urban and commercial revolution that took place between the eleventh and thirteenth centuries restored to the city its privileged role in European events after a long period of eclipse—and not only in terms of economic and social history, if we consider the development of Italian culture or the birth of the university. Roman civilization had also been an essentially urban phenomenon. At first sight, then, it might seem that after an interruption of several centuries, a link of some kind had been restored, and progress could pick up again from the point where it had been interrupted.

This, however, would be a superficial impression, admissible only as a hasty approximation. To be sure, there were many cases of urban continuity between late antiquity and the early Middle Ages, especially in northern Italy and southern France, as far north as Lyons, where colonization and urbanization by the Romans had reached its greatest intensity. There, the architectural complexes and networks of roads that survived from one era to the other could be considered evidence of unitary development.

But apart from this very tenuous contact (which we could also call fragile uniformity), the reality was very different. The cities now taking shape—both those that were completely new (like those in northern Europe, and like Venice, Ferrara, and Amalfi in Italy) and those that were located on preexisting Roman and early medieval sites (Padua and Milan, for example)—represented a completely new point of departure. The models of institutions, urbanism, and economic production now being formed were fundamentally different from those of the ancients; and the continuity of topographic features (if it existed at all) served only to emphasize the historic and functional discontinuities. A city is not only stones[41]—it is also flesh and ideas; and first and foremost, it is a state of mind.[42] When the medieval revival refashioned preexisting materials and components, it inserted them within completely new frameworks. In many ways, the European cities of today represent the direct continuation of their medieval contexts, but their relationship with their Roman predecessors is virtually solely archeological in nature. The Roman cities ended up literally under ground because of the disproportionate increase in stratification and the long-uncontested pressures of nature: they were buried by the violence of history. What has survived from ancient times is only the continuity of their location and, sometimes, imprints left on the terrain (which may also, with some effort, be seen in the countryside)—an everyday experience for inhabitants of France and Italy.

Moreover, it is not only a question of urban history. The recovery in Italy and Europe between the twelfth and fourteenth centuries, which marked the true beginning of the new era in the West, did not in any way resemble the civilization of the Roman Empire. The same Italian humanists who, as late as the end of the fifteenth century, formulated and executed the literal and figurative rebirth of the classics, lived in surroundings that were not in the slightest reminiscent of those of the Romans. They themselves were aware of the remoteness of the world they lovingly evoked—so much so that the impetus spurring them toward the past sprang precisely from their subtle reelaboration of this perceived distance. From then on, the gap between the humanists' representation of the cultural exemplarity of the ancient world (their admiration was never transformed into identification or repetition, but incited them instead to "conversation or competition")[43] and their portrayal of the remoteness of all aspects of the economic and social conditions of the ancient world—the disjunction between the continuity of ideas and the discontinuity of material things—was to be a constant in the cultural development of modern Europe.

It would certainly be inappropriate to say that the complex course of events in the economic and social history of Western Europe from the late Middle Ages to the Industrial Revolution followed a straight path, unless it is viewed as a single very long period. We must avoid lending a teleological tone to our interpretation. The new route was also marked by a variety of compromises, fiascoes, failures, and slumps:[44] first in Italy, which led to the definitive shift of the center of economic and technological innovation to Northern Europe, and later in Spain, Portugal, and Holland. But however far-reaching these crises may have been, they remained local in nature, and their severity was eclipsed by that of the collapse of Roman society after the second century. In comparison with this event, on the whole the path leading from the beginning of the second millennium to the present seems relatively straight; this time the journey would not be cut short.

Thus, we can see that the essence of the problem is no different when we consider it from a viewpoint closer to that of the modern day. So what exactly was the historical thrombosis which took place at the zenith of the ancient world—a crisis that the West would need more than ten centuries to recover from completely, and that would give rise to a civilization developed on completely different foundations from those that had collapsed?

In the writings of Rostovtzeff and Walbank, the echo of this question blurs and fades away unanswered. Rostovtzeff's hypothesis (which, like his book, is well known) linked the decline of the Roman Empire to the inability of the ruling classes to integrate the entire provincial population, not just the elites, into their superior civilization, and to the struggles of the masses—which ended in generalized and bleak barbarization—to obtain equality by force, the only possible means. This debatable (and much debated) interpretation was obviously influenced by the events of the 1920s in Russia and Europe. In any case, it led to an explanation of the "causes" of the crisis, without devoting any more than momentary attention to an analysis of why Roman society had come to an abrupt halt. As for Walbank, the problem simply never came into his field of vision. His research, although rich in observations and valuable ideas, does not help us to make significant progress.

To solve the problem they raised requires an unusual approach to the subject: an appraisal of the institutional, mental, and material components of the hegemonic Roman system and its economy, conducted from a dynamic and evolutionary point of view that examines its potentialities, characteristics, and attitudes. True comprehension cannot come from focusing on the age of the Antonines alone; it is not sufficient to look to a later period, such as the third century. Aristides' era allows us to phrase the question correctly, but not to resolve it. By that point, the empire had the weight of history behind it, limiting its future to a very narrow set of possibilities. By that time, the branch of the fork—if there had ever been one—that might have led away from the crisis proved to be definitively blocked off. We must return to an earlier period, when Roman society still possessed expansive force and had not yet reached its enervated culmination. It is there, in the dynamics of its structures and the relationships among its constituent parts—in the modes of production, technology, labor, consumption, social groups, mentalities, political machines and their effects—that we can discern the pattern that will reveal the secret and the destiny of this world.

Chapter Three

The Hidden Form

(1)

The task we have assigned ourselves is anything but simple. The route immediately leads to treacherous terrain, which is inevitable when matters relating to the history of the Roman economy are brought up for discussion, as we are now preparing to do.

Despite the tremendous growth of economic historiography in the course of the twentieth century, it cannot be said that this young and successful discipline[1] has quite managed to cross the threshold of studies of the ancient world.[2] Noteworthy progress has been made in recent years, thanks especially to the contributions of anglophone historians and to new archeological research.[3] Nevertheless, establishing the legitimacy of economics as an "official" specialization in ancient studies is meeting with difficulty. Until recently, only a small number of truly important studies had been completed, and the efforts of the few scholars who were writing on the subject often remained marginal compared to their other interests.[4] It was as if the topic itself, when all was said and done, concealed within it—along with its indisputable magnetism—a kind of intrinsic precariousness, an evanescence that discouraged more direct approaches.

The reasons for such persistent evasion are not easy to determine. The most common explanation, which has long been in circulation and continues to be presented in various forms, originated in the defenses and skepticism of positivist attitudes, which, although out of fashion, still have many strings to their bow. According to this explanation, the difficulties are due almost exclusively to the gaps and lacunae in the available sources, which, as far as economic circumstances are concerned, offer a mass of information that is so incomplete as to render impossible any truly exhaustive investigation. If we moderns know little about the matter, the responsibility lies entirely with the ancient documents.

Not long ago Moses Finley demonstrated that convictions of this kind, if they are idly repeated, take on the characteristics of sheer prejudice. "Grousing is not good enough," he wrote. "In the end, therefore, our problem is less one of devising new and complicated methods . . . than of posing the right questions."[5] Nevertheless, as Finley himself was well aware, neither a subtle approach nor a correct methodology is capable of rescuing research on ancient economies from the state of undeniable inferiority with which we must contend if we wish to proceed with our investigation.

Yet the nature of the obstacle is different from what is commonly believed. In attempting to construct a reliable account of the economic history of Greece and Rome, we realize that the greatest impediments are not created by the well-known absence of statistical series, the lack of quantitative parameters that are so fundamental to the study of other eras, or the truly labyrinthine number mazes that ancient authors so often present when they engage in sums and calculations. Beyond these murky areas, which modern critics already appreciate, and with which in many cases they are learning to contend, there is something more deep-rooted blocking our view. It is a barrier that not only concerns the informational content of the sources, but also works at a profound and global level.

The writings of the ancient West do indeed lack precise data on economic history—but a lot more is missing as well. What is absent is any evidence that the economy was perceived as a distinct sector of human activity and social life. There is no sign that the ancient world identified the "economic sphere" as a network of events, circumstances, causes, and effects which could and must be united in a single framework and be explained in accordance with their principles. This serious void points up what might be called the dissonance between our questions and the condition of the documents that economic historians must often resign themselves to facing, as Carlo Cipolla has observed.[6]

We can leaf through and classify as much as we like the few surviving texts in which the ancient world consigned its least fragmentary reflections on subjects related to the modern, late eighteenth-century concept of economics, or which seem to touch on it, at the very least: Aristotle's *Politics* and the fifth book of his *Nicomachean Ethics;* Xenophon's *Economics* and the peripatetic *Economics* of Pseudo-Aristotle; the Roman treatises on agriculture by Cato, Varro, and Columella (the corresponding Greek texts are lost); and the observations of Pliny in *Historia naturalis*—to mention only the best known of them.[7] We should also note that in these works, which vary in their origins, intentions, and degree of speculative discernment, we sometimes seem to come across—in some lexical contiguity, perhaps, or in an analytic segment that could hint at a latent but unexpressed category of concepts—the incunabula of some of the great economic discoveries of modern thought. In one isolated passage, we can even find (with a certain measure of excitement) the two magic words *oikonomia politike*.[8] It would take about two thousand years for them to appear again together—first in 1615, in Montchrétien's *Traicté de l'oeconomie politique*[9] (which, I believe, was the first book to have the two words in its title), then in the terminology of the physiocratic *économistes* of the eighteenth century.

But in the case of each of these classical examples, the more successfully it seemed to plant the seed of a science which developed later, the more inevitable the disappointment which closer examination produces. None of these works contained the slightest insight about how an economic system might function or how one could conceptualize the organization of the subsistence of a city or a population—and their wealth.

To be sure, there is no lack of clues describing the material conditions of society and its environs (we have just encountered some very important ones, in Aristides' speech), or suggestive comments on subjects like household administration or farm management, the result of experience acquired at the time by the ranks of enthusiastic farmers and assiduous merchants. And we can find elements of something that might be considered "social anatomy" in, for example, Aristotle and in the Roman jurists—evidence of their exceptional analytic talents. In reading attentively the thoughts of historians from Thucydides to Sallust and Tacitus and of jurists from Servius to Ulpian,[10] we find interpretations that attributed certain events to generically "economic" causes (for example, the relationship between wealth and military conquest, or between law and the development of production).

Recognizing this potential does not solve our problem. We must admit that the ancients lacked the basic perspective which would later make possible the major advances of modern economic thought. They lacked a vantage point—typical of the physiocrats and later utilized to even greater effect by Adam Smith and the classical economists—from which they could have traced in economics the outlines of a unitary system. Such a vantage point would have allowed them to examine an economy as an organism regulated by scientifically describable laws—a sort of "natural order" analogous to the one perceived in physics or astronomy. The simile (well established in the ancient world at least from Aristotle on) that likened the body politic to the human body did not go so far as to include economic processes in its metaphorical space. In contrast, in his *Tableau économique* Quesnay clearly had in mind the model of the circulation of blood in the body (Harvey's *Exercitatio anatomica* dates from 1628),[11] and probably that of Newtonian mechanics as well.

The ancient word *oikonomia*—composed of *oikos,* or "house," in the sense of "accumulated property," and a second morpheme, derived from the root *nom,* which we must translate as "administration," "regulation," or "organization"—allowed for no such allusions. It simply designated the "operation or administration of the household" (as in Pseudo-Aristotle's *Treatise*), or the "orderly arrangement of parts" of something in particular—for example, the cosmos, in Chrysippus,[12] or a poem or rhetorical treatise, in Quintilian.[13] Nor did other Greek or Latin words or expressions fill the gap. In fact, as Karl Bücher had already observed at the end of the nineteenth century, there are no Greek or Latin terms to refer to the fundamental concepts of modern economic analysis, familiar to us through our intense, if recent, use of them: "production," "circulation," "consumption," "capital," "revenue," "investment."[14] What is more, in these languages the word "labor" does not even exist in the widest sense (and the one most used by moderns): that of generic human activity which transforms environment and reality—the abstract "labor" of Smith, Ricardo, and Marx.

(2)

To perceive this gap is to make possible a further discovery. For a long time, the economy of the Greco-Roman world seemed (and largely continues to seem) to be a hidden continent because it presented itself that way already, as a nebulous and opaque form, to the eyes of the ancients, or disappeared altogether.

Our difficulties deepen a long-extant shadow. The sequence of relationships and events that determined the availability of goods and resources unfolded invisibly in that world, following rhythms that appeared obscurely automatic, perceived only through the most obvious and least specifically "economic" of connections and causalities. It took the triumph of capitalism to bring economics fully (or at least partly) into view and surround it with endless spectacle and discourse.

If Greco-Roman civilization has for so long remained closed off by the moderns in an image of perfection that was detached from the foundations of its real life; if we have for so long preserved a vision of it in which politics, knowledge, passions, characters, arts, and institutions seemed to be crystallized in the void of a pure play of forms; if this culture continues to be portrayed as a charming stylistic perfection suspended outside of history—this deceptive isolation (which is the source of the idea of "the classical") has not simply been the result of a deformation of perspective that began with the Renaissance. The modern interpretation was merely the reflection of an attitude rooted in the ancient mentalities—an inveterate condition, an imprint that informed the creation of every piece of writing and every image (and, it may be added, every object) through which these civilizations still speak to us, and hide from us.

This condition is not easy to describe. It was the expression of an important element of the inner nature of Greek and Roman aristocrats, which will be discussed below. Here let us note its most evident feature: the perception that the zone of contact between nature and organized human labor—the sites, in the workshops and in the countryside, where virtually all social wealth was generated—was a kind of dead zone for human civilization. It was a "dark hole" of community life, recognized as a basic and immutable necessity, but something to which it was altogether pointless to devote any higher form of thought. This deep-seated attitude actually bordered on repression.

In this gray area, the incontrovertible experience of the ancients seemed to confirm that no productive activity of any consequence could take place without being engulfed and contaminated by the degrading debasement of slave labor, even though it was considered indispensable and entirely "second nature." Indeed, Greek and Roman society seemed to be further evidence of this: the more the world of cities and prosperity progressed and gained strength, the greater the need to increase the range and depth of its undergirding of slaves, to the point where a considerable part of the whole social fabric became involved. "The number of slaves was directly related to the levels of civilization and wealth."[15]

The individual exertions of the free peasant, who made a living through cultivating his own land, were the only way to escape this damnation of material labor and ascend to a less humiliating status. But the exit hatch was very narrow. In the idealization of agricultural labor (to which our discussion will return), the productive aspects remained in the background. Emphasis was placed on the belief that daily association with the land created a particular moral type, which was held up as an ethical and civic model. This idea was portrayed in various ways: the virtuous example of the farmer-citizen-soldier of the first Roman republic, which would later appear in the nostalgic apologies of writers from Cicero's time to Trajan's; or the fascination of Virgil's gentle and contemplative pastoral life; or the ideological glorification of the wise owners of *villae*, at the economic high point of Roman Italy.

What are the origins of such radical forms of exclusion, which condemned the whole universe of production to marginality, or even banished it from ancient culture? This question will be answered near the end of our account. In the meantime, let us begin by looking in two directions.

An observation from what might be called economic anthropology opens the first line of inquiry. In ancient societies, in order to ensure a standard of living that went beyond the mere survival of the producers, and to achieve significant margins of accumulation, labor—especially of an agricultural nature—must have been performed under unusually harsh conditions. In the history of the Roman economy, this threshold was crossed in the third and second centuries B.C., when farming shifted in focus from small peasant properties, and cultivation at the subsistence level by individual families, to plantations with intensive and specialized cultivation, or large estates with heterogeneous crops. To appreciate this transformation, we need only consider the layout of the areas designated for the daily life and repose of the teams of slaves on a farm in Etruria or Latium, areas which archeologists have restored with impressive precision;[16] or recall the prescriptions of Cato[17] or Columella.[18] These writers considered it entirely normal for slaves to work all day long in chains under strict surveillance, to be deprived of even the slightest privacy, and to be fed the minimum quantity necessary to restore their forces; treating them otherwise required making an exception.

This harshness was not peculiar to Roman civilization or even to slave-holding societies. It could be found in many preindustrial societies (and others besides). If we could graph the levels of suffering caused by labor in different eras (overlooking the fact that these comparisons would be quite risky, since the quality of pain changes over time), it would be clear that entire generations of peasants in medieval Europe and even English laborers at the beginning of the Industrial Revolution also paid a high human price. But it was only in the ancient West—both in Athens and in Rome—that circumstances came together in a decisive way. The intensification of the pressure on productive work—pressure which was indispensable if whole social classes were to come into existence unimpeded by the necessity of providing for their own sustenance—was accompanied (for various reasons, which were almost always military in nature) by a very strong bias toward slave labor.

Thus was established a kind of permanent short circuit between the increased social weight on labor and the spread of its institutionally coercive nature. This was a combination which was both extraordinary and deadly. It crushed the world of production (whether based on slaves or on the free labor that never completely disappeared)[19] in a suffocating and inexorable vise. Moreover, another element contributed to the gravity of the situation: the relationship, always near the breaking point, between the pressures of demography, the growing needs of the nonproductive but socially dominant classes, and the paucity of technological innovation. In the empire of the first and second centuries A.D., millions of men and women (from a variety of social conditions, ranging from the urban elites, to the armies lined up on the frontiers, to the crowds who thronged Rome and the other big cities of the empire) were permanently exempt from productive labor. For those who were charged with the task, simply feeding these masses was a challenge that bordered on the impossible.

When Aristotle, in the famous introduction to the *Politics*, made his distinction between someone who is a "freeman" and a "master by nature" and someone who is a "slave by nature,"[20] he was not simply confirming the nature of an institution that sustained all of civilization before his eyes; he was establishing the terms of a social division of labor that linked slavery indissolubly with production. (According to Aristotle, a slave is a person who "uses his body as an instrument of action," whereas a master is a person who can "govern using his intellect.") This attests to the existence of a total scission—not only between liberty and slavery, but also (as we shall see) between production and intellect, and between culture and material labor.

To be sure, not all slaves toiled in farming, mining, or manufacturing. Especially during the Roman age, careful attention to their abilities and talents (of which the surveys of jurists and the typologies of agricultural administration are faithful records) enabled the most capable to be assigned to higher tasks and functions, which could include management of an entire plantation, or even a position at the imperial court. Their occupations brought them satisfaction, profit, and comfort. But in return, as if in compliance with a secret equilibrium, the position of free laborers employed in production was almost always murky and irremediably marginal.

We could say, at this point, that all agricultural and manufacturing labor of a subservient nature—whether slave labor or not—contained such a heavy burden of discrimination and oppression, and was conjoined so forcibly with compulsion without consensus, that it was very difficult to include it in the moral universe and the mental sphere of vision of the higher classes. Its harshness and coercive nature were measured on its own peculiar scale of consistency: ethics and intellect were allotted no part in this lowly and degraded world.

As the republic was coming to an end, Cicero provided an exemplary illustration of this degradation, reflecting and confirming a centuries-old principle that was to resonate throughout the history of the empire. "The work of all hired men who sell their labor and not their talents is servile and contemptible. The reason is that in their case wages actually constitute a payment for slavery. [. . .] All mechanics work in contemptible professions because no one born of free parents would have anything to do with a workshop."[21] And Seneca, citing Posidonius in his *Letters,* divided the arts into four categories: "mean and vulgar, recreational, educational, and liberal." He went on to specify that those in the first "are proper to artisans: exclusively manual, they are used for material matters in life, and they exhibit neither dignity nor decorum."[22] Again in the fourth century, Libanius felt the need to state this admonition: "an artisan should never be treated roughly by a youth dedicated to *paidea.* The youth should learn to live in peace with these people, and never be considered unworthy of the praise of those who earn their bread through the work of their own hands."[23]

Other examples could be cited; the long tradition of common sense brings clearly to light a unique cultural paradox, which evolved during the whole classical period in the Occident. This particular type of productive mechanism, which resorted so regularly to slavery as to make it the model par excellence of dependent labor, was so violent that although it made possible the formation of complex and brilliant civilizations, it could not be accepted by these same cultures under any terms other than total obscurity. It was banished beyond the boundaries of the universe of sociability and culture which it nevertheless played a role in preserving, reduced to being considered an unpleasant necessity of nature, of no value and with no hope of improvement.

Thus, the entire realm of labor was enclosed in a shell of ethical and cognitive indifference, in which any kind of inequality was admissible because nothing that happened there fell within the purview of reason and sensitivity. Instead, all was consumed in a circuit of deterministic materiality, where men were reduced to objects devoid of existence beyond what they produced for others. It was acceptable to exert any kind of pressure on them, while at the same time affirming the dominion of the "civil" world and its laws. Only the thinking of the Roman jurists had reason to stray from this principle, at least in part (and we shall see why below).

This radical banishment was characteristic of the Greek and Roman civilizations; it was the somber underside of their magnificence. In its own terms, it had no equal in the modern Western world—not even the slave-holding societies of the New World, where aberrant forms of Christian racism manifested themselves in areas of both English and

Spanish domination (one need only think of the *indios,* considered to be soulless animals according to the improvised battlefield theology of the *conquistadores).*

Perhaps modern observers have also been deceived by this reticence and silence which was so foreign to them, and which led them on many occasions to conclude that slavery represented a negligible phenomenon in the total picture of classical societies. If ancient culture did not concern itself with it, why should we? What seemed to be simply a commonsensical attitude was actually a gross error of judgment that served to perpetuate the ancients' concealment unconsciously and without explanation. But the true state of affairs would have been clear to any observer of modern slaveholding systems: in all cases on record, the presence of the extended practice of slavery leaves an indelible mark on the entire social, cultural, and mental framework of the environment in which it develops. Nothing there can function independently any more. During his travels in America, Tocqueville wrote vivid pages on this process of contamination. They constitute the outline of a veritable anthropology of slaveholding societies, which has validity for the entire history of the Western world.[24]

But the colonies of North America before the Declaration of Independence, and the United States prior to the Civil War, offer a stark contrast with Rome: the presence of slave labor was not at all taken for granted and accepted as "natural" by the collective consciousness. Indeed, slavery was considered a thorny ethical and social problem, and was invariably accompanied by a considerable mass of justificatory literature, aimed at protecting it from the expected objections and attacks (to which in fact it was continually subject). The pamphlet written in 1701 by a certain John Saffin of Boston[25] can probably be considered the first of these not very enlightened prose pieces. A constant stream of them were in circulation during the next century and a half (and not only in the South), and the flow continued until the end of the Civil War. Their reasoning is not difficult to summarize: it ranges from statements of the most obstinate racial prejudice (which occupies a significant portion), to invocations of the Holy Scripture, to the overtly propagandistic idealization of slavery, shown in contrast to the newfangled misery of the working classes. The satirical cartoons published in *Punch* between 1840 and 1860 acted as a biting iconographic counterpoint to this comparison.[26] But even at its most extreme—in the doctrine of "positive good," for example, which claimed that slavery, far from being a lesser or inevitable evil, was absolutely and positively beneficial, for both masters and slaves[27]—it was always in a fundamentally defensive position. In modern societies, there were economic and ethical alternatives to the institution of slavery, even where it was holding its ground with the greatest tenacity. The outside world, which had taken a different path, was bearing down on it.

In Greece and Rome, no analogous ethical or economic justifications were to be found. Slavery had no need for them in these civilizations. Isolated polemicists were the only ones to contest it on all counts;[28] but although their observations may have been acute, they found no favor. The presence of slavery was overwhelming. Its mechanism had an all-encompassing validity. More than a "peculiar institution,"[29] it seemed to be a universal system.

(3)

But we can also look in a different direction to explain why the ancient economy was invisible.

It disappeared in the cultures of the era not only because their vision was congenitally distorted, but (also) because in their world the "economic" sphere—in the discrete and distinguishable form in which it regularly appears to the modern eye—was never truly operational. If the capacity to see it was lacking, it was (also) because the object itself was absent.

Of course, in every society there has existed (and how could it have been otherwise?) an ever-changing nexus of the conditions of survival, which provided a context for the exploitation of nature, the organization of productive labor, and the availability of resources. But the linkage was given by the uninterrupted presence of elements unrelated to the economy, such as military events, the political redistribution of wealth, climatic and environmental equilibria, and the abundance or scarcity of slave labor. The modern worker is "created," so to speak, by the system of production, and without it would not exist as a worker. The slave, on the other hand, was defined as such apart from the work he performed, because of ties of personal dependence that had noneconomic origins. In short, his identity as a slave preexisted whatever productive activities he might carry out, and his work played no more than a secondary role in determining his place in society. It is only by coming to a retrospective and substantive understanding of the combinations of uninterrupted changes of scene that it is possible to isolate the elements that constituted the course of the economic process as a whole. To study ancient economies is to search for a hidden and evasive form. Hesiod was correct: in this world, "the gods keep hidden from men the means of their survival."[30]

The need for this support, which always tended to envelop economic phenomena in a layer of actions and relationships of other kinds, never decreased. At no moment in its history was the Roman economy able to stand on its own two feet. It was never capable of triggering the mechanisms of smooth financial and technological self-sufficiency that, in the form of capitalism and the Industrial Revolution, succeeded in "liberating Prometheus" in the modern world. This incapacity did not apply only to the most archaic settings, where the dissolution of economic mechanisms into social functions of a different kind is easiest to observe. Indeed, the more the ancient economies embraced relatively complex forms of commercial activity (as in the case of Rome and, in some respects, Athens), the less independent they were. They were increasingly subject to noneconomic institutions and events (wars of conquest, political redistribution, slavery) which had major effects on their identities and trends.

(4)

Thus we must ferret out a multiform and hidden reality: connections, proportions, relationships constructed and experienced by the ancients of which we are able to trace the signs, even though they remained largely unconscious of them. It is like entering into a more remote and secret stratum of their history.

The density and characteristics of such an unusual inquiry must inevitably have an effect on its telling. Anyone who believes that an investigation focusing on the economic history of Rome should conform to the same standards of reconstruction as histories of modern (and medieval) economic systems would have to abandon the project at the outset: it would be impossible to achieve this kind of result.

We must recognize that there is no single way of presenting economic history. There are several standard modes (and variations of these modes) of approaching the history of industrial economies, and the history of medieval economies as well. But these should not presume to be considered the general criteria of legitimacy for all studies of economies of other periods or regions. Just as each system has its own rules of operation, it also has its own code of description.[31] The problem is recognizing it, not measuring its distance from a nonexistent universal model.

In this sense, Andrea Giardina's objection that no all-inclusive interpretation of the Roman economy can properly be considered "economic history" (in the usual sense of the term)—that study of the Roman economy is, rather, a particular version of "social history"[32]—proves in many respects to be particularly astute. Indeed, it would even be arbitrary and strained to refer to the Roman "economy," strictly speaking. If we continue to do so here, it is only because of lexical convention; but it should be evident that the word "economy" as it is used here has a very different meaning from the modern one that is so familiar to us. It serves solely to designate a system of relationships involving various levels, and an intrinsically multiform network of problems and events.

Chapter Four

Optical Effects

(1)

In the closing years of the nineteenth century and the early decades of the twentieth, an impassioned debate unfolded in Germany that signaled the first genuine modern interest in the economies of the ancient world. Its outcome is far from decided; indeed, it seems to have resurfaced with renewed vehemence in recent debates—for example, between Andrea Carandini and Moses Finley, and between Carandini and C. R. Whittaker.[1]

Although the polemics actually began thirty years later, their origins lie in the essays of J. K. Rodbertus, published in the years 1864–1867.[2] These studies opened the way to the works of Karl Bücher, which were published beginning in 1893.[3] The essence of the thesis propounded by these two authors would later (in an expression destined to meet with success) come to be known as the "primitivist" interpretation of the ancient economies.

At the time his ideas were taking shape, Rodbertus was witnessing the great expansion of European capitalism in the 1850s and 1860s—not only in England and France, but also in Germany and in Austria. What he envisioned was a rigorously gradualist philosophy of universal economic history—one he shared with Friedrich List and Bruno Hildebrand, the founders of the so-called historical school of economics (and he perhaps had a direct influence on Hildebrand).[4] For this reason, it seemed to him that the only way to arrive at a credible reconstruction of what he called "the economic life of classical antiquity" was to emphasize its dramatic backwardness, compared to the production, commerce, and finance of the modern era. The dominant form he traced in the evidence of antiquity was the *oikos*: a self-sufficient family unit, enclosed within the estate of a lord. It served as the basic and exclusive cell in a world of "domestic" autarchies,[5] devoid of trade and markets.

In truth, even for Rodbertus the *oikos* was a sort of ideal model whose precise historical identity had rather vague outlines, despite its tendency to be associated with the major slaveholding properties of the Roman era. The term was used to define, in a conceptual sense, the structures and basic functioning of a natural economy lacking commercialization and any significant circulation of money and goods. It served as the quasi-symbolic record of specific productive and social conditions that modern progress had virtually eliminated.

Bücher's research placed even more emphasis on the ideal type of the *oikos,* placing it in a full and ambitious interpretive context. For the first time, studying the economy of the ancient world was deemed worthwhile for its own sake, and this activity came to be organically linked to the ethnographic investigations of primitive societies that were flourishing at the time. In the background lay the theory of the "stages" of economic development, which was the cornerstone of the historicism of the *Nationalökonomie.* Even though Bücher could not characterize the civilizations of classical antiquity as primitive societies, their economies nevertheless occupied an early position along the linear path he considered to be the one true road to modernity. The closed model of the *oikos* remained indisputably at the center of the economic history of Greece, Carthage, and Rome, although it was integrated with the concept of "urban economy" in descriptions of the life of the great imperial cities. The importance and influence of commerce and monetary circulation continued to be overlooked, for the transformations of money and commodities were not included in this world.

The one-sided nature of this thesis—which in many respects was truly extreme, despite the corrections and attenuations that Bücher (who had no formal training in either Greek or Roman studies) inserted in subsequent editions of his most important work[6]—engendered such negative reactions from scholars in the field that eventually it was completely overturned. These were the golden years of ancient studies in Europe, and nothing, it seemed, was able to withstand the fervor for research.

Indeed, that was exactly what happened. And Eduard Meyer and Mi-

chael Rostovtzeff came to be the protagonists of the predictable reversal
of fortune: they shaped what would later be called the "modernization"
of the economies of antiquity.

Momigliano's observation—that Meyer was one of the few German
historians of the late nineteenth century whose scholarly education was
almost entirely free of Mommsen's influence[7]—helps us to understand
the origins of Meyer's unique "modernism," which actually was quite
different from the "modernism" of Mommsen's *Römische Geschichte*. We
can complete the picture by adding the other pillars of Meyer's education: the teachings of Leopold von Ranke, and an interpretation of
Hegel's thought that was at the very least conservative, if not frankly re-
actionary and exaggeratedly worshipful of the state.[8] Perhaps he could
have avoided his most glaring distortions, or at least mitigated the ex-
tremism of his convictions, if he had filtered his ideas through studies
more juridically oriented toward the constitutional aspects of the reality
of Roman politics, or through a less polemical attitude toward the liberal features of society and the state—that is to say, Mommsen's own
world. But none of these even came close to influencing him. On the
contrary, he was dominated by an almost obsessive rage against the historical school of economics that had inspired Rodbertus and Bücher.
Thus, Meyer was able to persuade himself that the enthusiastic and
complete approval of classicism necessarily went hand in hand with the
unreasoning exaltation of the "modernity" of that world. Since all of the
differences melted away, he could view the ancient economies as being
completely developed in the industrial and capitalistic senses and, more
important, as having the character of pervasive totalizing states. All
traces of the primitive system of the *oikos* and the extended natural
economy were gone. Meyer found it unnecessary to use specific conceptualizations in describing the conditions in Greece and Rome. To
him, terms such as "factory" and "workers" were perfectly appropriate,
as was the claim that ancient and contemporary economies were utterly
identical.

The reasons for Rostovtzeff's positions are less easily explained. For
him, as for Meyer, the modernization of the ancient economies ran
parallel to his own conservative political orientation. Given the cultural climate of the first two or three decades of the twentieth century,

we might conclude that the convergence of their ways of thinking was no coincidence. One possible area of common ground was that neither understood the historically determined character of modern European economies, which they had projected instead into a timeless eternity. (In contrast, the school of *Nationalökonomie*—like Marx's research, although with different methods and objectives—had tended to historicize completely the various economic systems, both ancient and modern.) But we must remember that, at the time, even some scholars who were inspired by Marx—although not ones known for their sophisticated interpretations—chose to modernize the economies of the classical period. Robert von Pöhlman[9] and even Giuseppe Salvioli[10] are good examples. It would be wrong to search for strict symmetries and correspondences.

Rostovtzeff's talents and educational background were, however, quite different from Meyer's, as was the nature of his approach toward historiography, and he advanced his conclusions by other means. His vision of modernization was derived from an empirical conception of the modern economy rather than from a precise theoretical conviction; he distrusted all economic doctrines, not just Marxism. His vast knowledge of antiquity brought him in contact with immense quantities of data, which clearly demonstrated the complexities of the civil textures of ancient Greece and Rome. In the face of this wealth of evidence, Bücher's hypotheses revealed all of their reductiveness, and a modernizing interpretation must have seemed to Rostovtzeff the only one that properly respected the integrity of his material.

The admirable series of frescoes that Rostovtzeff laid out in the two volumes of his *Social and Economic History of the Roman Empire*[11] is entirely infused by these currents of contemporization: he saw no need to posit any qualitative discontinuity between classical and modern economies, or between the European and (even) the American economies. The differences, if any were to be found, were merely quantitative. It was probably under the influence of a similar suggestion, evoked by the visionary force of his scrutiny, that the problem posed by the lack of continuity (which we have just mentioned) became apparent to him—as if in a flash. If the ancient world had already taken, so to speak, the same route as the modern world, then why was it that "modern civilization had to be constructed as a new entity [. . .], instead of being its direct continuation"?—a good question, but one that was most likely prompted by a misleading comparison.

The importance of Rostovtzeff's imposing works certainly helped to make his opinions influential. But as early as 1925, when Friedrich Oertel asked whether "we should consider the ancient economy highly developed, or, instead, think of it as primitive,"[12] his doubts had an almost entirely rhetorical value, and his "positive" response, favoring the modernist thesis, was largely discounted. Shortly thereafter, in 1932—despite the long-standing repute of an excellent work by Max Weber,[13] which went in an entirely different direction, and despite the important studies along the same lines published by Johannes Hasebroek[14] (one of Weber's students)—Rostovtzeff could claim with good reason that the old hypothesis of the *oikos* no longer had supporters.[15] A few years later, the copious (indeed, copious to a fault) research of Fritz Heichelheim, published in 1938, seemed to be a definitive confirmation of the scope of the victory.[16]

(2)

What, beyond Rostovtzeff's own prestige, swept the field in this debate? This question is not difficult to answer. Both orientations—especially in their more radical formulations—actually arose from the same historiographic shortcoming (although it assumed two opposite positions). Both sides were inspired by their perception of the same reality: the explosive capitalist expansion in Europe and America at the end of the nineteenth century and the beginning of the twentieth, at the close of the late nineteenth-century depression. Viewed in the mirror of the new economic regime, the whole world seemed truly in motion. The pressured atmosphere of the contemporary scene may even have given rise to more specific historiographic research into the material basis of ancient societies. Despite making new viewpoints possible, the reverberations of the present day also impaired the clarity of the studies' perspective. In both modes of reconstructing the past—whether modern forms were indiscriminately projected back in time, in order to fill in all of the most important phases of the history of Greece and Rome, or whether the ancient world was seen as totally detached from modern developments—the same basic motif kept reappearing. This was the writers' inability to define an undisturbed relationship between the consuming presence of the economic life of their own day, and the conditions of an ambiguously remote past, whose mode of production they sought to trace for the first time. It was the impossibility of avoiding the optical illusions caused by excessive proximity and excessive distance. Both answers, in the very fact of their drastic incompatibility, revealed the same frenzy, which condemned them to equal implausibility. Both were attempting to sever the knot with a single blow by imposing one single answer: the ancient and the modern were either totally assimilated into each other or totally distinct, with no points of contact; in the latter case the two economies would be lodged at the extremes of a rigid periodization.

With this in mind, it is understandable that the modernist hypothesis was destined to prevail. Of the two, it was the one that allowed for the formation of more familiar insights, required less conceptual effort (at least at that time), and seemed to be more compatible with the new masses of data (archeological, numismatic, papyrological, and epigraphic) that specialists in their zeal were constantly unearthing. Rediscovering capitalism seemed easier than ignoring it.

But the victory proved more fragile than it had appeared at the end of the nineteen thirties. To be sure, the original versions of the opposing arguments—as Bücher and Meyer had represented them—no longer had their advocates. In the research of recent decades, the problems seemed at first to be different: heated clashes over methodology and ideology, especially on the role of slavery in the Greek and Roman societies (an issue which a whole strain of historiography, from Ulrich von Wilamowitz-Moellendorff[17] to Eduard Meyer himself[18] to Werner Wilhelm Jaeger,[19] had deliberately attempted to suppress), and on the validity of a firmly continuist interpretation of their economies (which was at the heart of Finley's thesis). But the old questions eventually reemerged, although clothed in different forms. They persist to this day, an unresolved accumulation of doubts and uncertainties. No discussions on the economic history of Rome have completely managed to avoid resuscitating these old dilemmas in some way—especially the studies connected with the wave of neo-Marxism in Italian classical studies in the 1970s and 1980s, and the work of British classicists like Moses Finley and his school. And today, Finley's continuism—which, because of its indisputable success, Keith Hopkins has ironically dubbed the "modern orthodoxy" of historiography[20]—can truly be considered the belated revenge of the primitivists.

There is, in fact, another explanation for this tenacious vitality. More than a debate between two historiographic orientations, it involves a fundamental characteristic of the world we seek to describe.

"Primitivism" and "modernism" can be considered something other than two different research perspectives. In their own way, they reflect a profound aspect of the reality they are investigating: the intrinsically "dual" nature of the ancient economies—especially that of Rome—and the double image they continue to project to the modern observer. It is only by fully recognizing this division from the outset that we can transcend the partial truth of the two hypotheses and reconcile them in a single more mature and convincing interpretation.[21]

Chapter Five

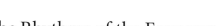

The Rhythms of the Economy

(1)

When did the imperial economic system take shape?[1] How far back must we go to paint a complete picture?

Let us consider the period between the first part of the third century B.C. and the middle of the second century A.D.—from decades just before the First Punic War to the time when the echoes of the last important conquest, Trajan's Dacian campaign, had just died out. Examining such a long stretch of time is necessary, in order to reveal the underlying structure of the historical issues under consideration here.

We will not explore the variety of phenomena and conditions that determined the superficial contours of the entire economy of the empire. Recent archeological and epigraphic research has resulted in a wealth of data that provides a more accurate vision than that of Rostovtzeff's era, and at times produces close-up descriptions of unexpected vividness. Using these bits of evidence, we can reconstruct the changing organization of production and society in many urban or rural microcosms of the immense panorama of provinces, from Britain to the threshold of the North African deserts, from Spain to Mesopotamia: the everyday reality and the material civilization of millions of men and women from generation to generation and from century to century.

In our account, the term "Roman economy" has, so to speak, a concentrated and synthetic meaning. It refers specifically to an original and stable combination of characteristics (which we call a "system"), with the history of Rome as its locus of genesis and success, which was then projected—through a complex web of relationships between the center and the periphery—onto a setting of multicontinental dimensions (although Rome never attempted to standardize the variety of modes of production that coexisted within the empire, remaining satisfied with ensuring their reciprocal compatibility and establishing a network of contacts between them).

The period under discussion begins with the formation of the original nucleus of this system, and ends with the first signs of its collapse. A history of the economy of the archaic period, which immediately precedes the one we have chosen to treat, would lead us far from the path we wish to follow.

As already mentioned, in the first centuries of Roman history neither human labor nor the availability and arrangement of resources in the community were regulated by mechanisms in which it is possible to trace a specifically "economic" aspect. All of material life was steeped in forms of production and redistribution, as well as of cooperation and exchange, in which other social ties predominated. Modern economic functionality—and, to some extent, the more mature forms of ancient economic functionality as well—always tends to have "single-strand" activities. Every activity associated with it fulfills a single objective: the greatest gain with the least expense. Archaic societies, on the other hand, are intrinsically "multi-strand" oriented.[2] In a relationship of exchange, for example, the partners are not only buyers and sellers of goods, but, quite often, kinsmen (actual or potential) first and foremost, or allies, or clan rivals, or ritual or battle companions; or many of these things at the same time. In every transaction, a bundle of expectations and interests came into play that could never be reduced to pure economic quantification.

At the heart of archaic Rome, the kinship network held an absolutely dominant position. It determined aristocratic distinctions and served as the foundation for connections in the community. It was the source of positions of military and religious power (the selection of kings and priests) and of modes of ritualizing the sacred and magical, which played an essential role in the collective mentality.

Kinship groups were also the units of production in the city. The land was divided up among them through practices that historians are still debating, but in which we can trace models of distributive egalitarianism, perhaps the reflection of unconscious atavisms. Work, which was performed within these units, evolved according to an imprecise division of time periods, duties, and hierarchies—a division that was determined as much by the will of the heads of families as by the needs of the group. By the ninth century, a maze of shops, sanctuaries, roads, and fords covered the middle and lower valleys of the Tiber, and served—along with the mechanisms of an "administrative economy"—to channel supplies and trade (of salt, wood, and costly manufactured items).

In the sixth century B.C., the presence of the Etruscans in Rome began to change the archaic characteristics of the framework, creating less fragile social differentiations, an elementary "political" organization, and more impressive accumulations of wealth among the patricians. Evidence of each of these phenomena was reflected in the original nucleus of the Servian Constitution, and has surfaced in very recent archeological discoveries. The Servian reforms were built around the relationships (simultaneously military, economic, and institutional in nature) among soldiers who made war, citizens who voted, and landowners who grew crops—connections destined to last, as the multiple meanings of the Latin word *centuria* clearly reflect. The term can signify a military unit, a voting unit in an assembly, or a unit of land.

The hundred-year crisis that accompanied the end of the monarchy and the birth of the republic—continuing throughout the obscure fifth century B.C., which was dominated by the dispute between the patricians and the plebeians—engendered a long period of impoverishment and regression. Rome was paying the price for its exit from the Etruscan orbit after the fall of the Tarquins. But the expansion quickly resumed. Republican institutions became well established, and the patrician-plebeian compromise allowed for the creation of a new coalition of mixed aristocracy, which was the final step in the formation of a fully individualized economy. The result was the "economic constitution" of the republican *polis:* a network of small landholders—at the same time farmers, citizens, and soldiers—guided by a sober and severe class of nobles. This was the original stratum of Roman society in the era before the conquests, and it served as a foundation for all future developments.

The situation remained stable until the middle of the third century B.C., just before the beginning of the first war with Carthage. At that time, in connection with the resumption of strong expansionist thrusts both toward the north and, especially, toward the areas of southern Italy colonized by the Greeks, numerous elements that were to mark a turning point in the life of the community made their appearance in Roman society. They soon determined the basic characteristics of the mature

Roman imperial economic system, which took shape after the Second Punic War with the transformations of the second century B.C.

(2)

We can identify at least five areas of innovation, from which there was no turning back.

First of all, there was a rather noticeable increase in trade, both within the republic and over long distances, which was accompanied by the formation of new social classes with specifically mercantile interests, and by the accumulation of a substantial amount of commercial capital. The early political division within the mixed patrician and plebeian nobility was the most evident sign of this change. Two groups arose out of this class during the third century B.C. The first, pro-mercantile and expansionist, was openly interested in reinforcing the Roman presence, first in southern Italy and later overseas, in Sicily and the Mediterranean. The Scipios emerged as its leaders of greatest prestige at the time of the Second Punic War. The other group, more traditionalist, continued to believe that Rome's future lay in preserving a tighter community of small peasant landholders within more modest geopolitical boundaries. At the end of the century, Quintus Fabius Maximus, known as "the Delayer," consul five times and dictator twice, was one of its most ardent supporters.

The increase in trade, now apparent throughout the Mediterranean (as is well documented by the conditions of the treaties between Rome and Carthage that preceded the Punic Wars), had an immediate influence on the highest levels of the republic's institutions. In the middle of the third century B.C., soon after the conquest of Sicily, a new magistracy was established to adjudicate cases between foreign citizens (merchants, evidently), or between Romans and foreigners in Rome, on questions which we would classify as those of "commercial law." In a short time, this jurisdictional activity, which was a profound innovation with respect to the juridical traditions of the city, led to the creation of a new set of regulations, later called *ius gentium*, which was observed in all business transactions between Rome and the Italic and Mediterranean populations—as distinct from the older *ius civile*, which was jealously reserved for Romans alone.

Linked with the mercantile expansion, the diffusion of Roman coins, used most noticeably for trade in the Italic area as early as the end of the fourth century B.C., reached considerable levels. By the close of the century, the system in force during the Second Punic War led to stabilization in the use of bimetallic bronze and silver coins. It was only later, at the end of the republic, that this model was integrated with the minting of gold coins.

At the same time, in the late third century there was a no less important transformation in the modes of agricultural production and rural life in Latium, Campania, and Etruria. From the end of the First Punic War, a mass of slaves unprecedented in the Western world was regularly utilized in the new aristocratic landholdings which had resulted from the Italian conquests. It would be impossible to provide an authoritative estimate of their numbers—despite the many discussions of the few, highly unreliable data found in the sources—or to determine their growth patterns with any certainty. But on the whole we can consider the orders of magnitude that P. A. Brunt reconstructed to be fairly plausible: he conjectures that about 100,000 slaves were captured during the First Punic War, and that by 225 B.C. there were about 600,000 slaves in Italy, out of a total population that could not have been much greater than four million.[3]

Finally, we note a continuous increase in population,[4] and a transformation in the architectural texture of the city. According to census data, which can on the whole be considered fairly reliable, the population of Rome went from 166,000 male citizens in 340–339 B.C. to about 300,000 in 252–251, before the sharp drop recorded in 247–246 produced by the bloodshed of the First Punic War. Some observers have judged the estimates of the increase excessive, given the hemorrhage in the population prompted by the migration of Roman citizens to the newly founded colonies. The debate centers on the number of citizens between 336 and 323: total population figures of 130,000, 150,000, and 250,000 have all been proposed. But information on the Roman water supply implies a sudden rise in population during the period 312–273 (coinciding with the construction of the first two aqueducts, the Aqua Appia and the Anio Vetus). This increase in water use was matched only by the one of 144–127, more than a century later.

The physical layout of the capital was transformed as the population

grew. The Comitium and the Forum were redesigned. A new dwell-
ing-type was spreading: organized into groups of houses and shops,
built in the ever more vertical configurations that technical advancements in construction were making possible. It is estimated that around
the year 270 B.C. the population of Rome reached 200,000.[5] The early
nucleus of the imperial city was taking shape, transforming the old
proto-republican structure with new uses of land and space which indicated that a more complex social stratification (along with the new
needs that accompanied it) was now firmly established in the urban
context.

The evidence we have presented could be deemed sufficient—but
there is more. Ancient historians were already aware that the early decades of the third century B.C. were a time of significant economic transformation. Corroboration for this assertion lies in the terse but quite effective appraisal of the effects of the definitive Roman conquest of the
Sabines, vanquished by Manius Curius Dentatus in 290 B.C. "It was then
that for the first time the Romans became aware of wealth, when they
conquered this population," we read in a brief passage from Quintus
Fabius Pictor that Strabo transcribed (perhaps through the mediation
of Polybius).[6]

Two comments are in order. First of all, Fabius linked the new wealth
of the Romans to their success in war, immediately revealing the evidence of a relationship whose significance we will soon assess: the connection between economic growth and military conquest (of land, but
also of slaves, precious metals, and other resources). Second, he spelled
out the consequences of this victory from the standpoint of what we
might call behavior and mentality: it was only then that the "Romans"
(we must interpret this word as signifying the new patrician-plebeian
aristocracy) "became aware" of wealth, and perceived the changes it
brought to collective practices. The history of the third century consists
not only of economic transformations, major military encounters, and
pronounced internal political disputes, but also of changes in ideas and
social styles. The parameters and values of the entire aristocratic culture of the first republic, the culture that had accompanied the patrician-plebeian compromise, were altered. It began to separate its own
self-image and objectives from the needs and hopes of the world of
small landholders, who until that time had formed the military and

political backbone of the city, but for whom (paradoxically) the very frequency of wars was causing ever greater difficulties.

The explication of the later date we proposed to conclude the period under examination—the mid-second century A.D., where our account began—requires less commentary. Here, in counterpoint to the final campaigns of military conquest (for example, the Dacian campaign, which is depicted in the series of reliefs carved in the panels that spiral around Trajan's Column), the splendor of the urban aristocracies of Spain and the Orient and the spread of unprecedented prosperity began to be infected by economic stagnation, financial exploitation, impoverishment, and (as we have seen) feelings of internal uneasiness that it would be impossible to overlook. At the same time, the decline in Italian agricultural production was becoming irreversible.

(3)

Within this span of time, when considered in its entirety the history of the Roman economy—like that of all preindustrial economies—appears to be a series of set scenes moving quite slowly, sometimes accelerating a bit, but never involving any sudden or wrenching perturbations or abrupt changes in condition. There is surely a subjective element in our sensitivity to this slow pace, prisoners as we are to ever increasing tempos of activity, and conditioned as we are to perceive economic history (and other kinds of history) as if it were caught up in a perpetual whirlwind. But the slowness we notice is also a real phenomenon, which we cannot simply attribute to our subjective viewpoint as observers: it is an intrinsic relationship between the length and the form of events that marks the entire economy of Rome (and is one of the standard elements in every continuist interpretation). In particular situations—after the devastation of the Second Punic War, for example, or as a result of the great oriental campaigns of the second century A.D., or after the Social War, the formation of the "municipal system," and the conquest of Gaul—we are certainly able to distinguish more rapid changes. But in each case the stimulus was stifled by the presence of a hard kernel of resistance at the heart of the event, which tended to counteract the pressures of transformation with an obstinacy never found in modern societies, whose survival depends on their periodically exercised willingness to revolutionize the bases of their own existence. The strength of this constraint makes it necessary for our interpretation to be particularly cautious. Modern economies, precisely because of their conspicuously dynamic nature, regularly go through phases of disequilibrium of varying duration and degrees of intensity, and tend to assume—for reasons related to the interactions among the different elements—an aspect of discontinuity and oscillation, which is particularly evident in the medium term. To explain these phenomena (we are not talking about the possibility of predicting them), and to distinguish manifestations of genuine economic trends from more unavoidable, structural, or systemic episodes, economic theory has devised ever more sophisticated and penetrating analytic methods, chief among these being the numerous varieties of the rigorous and complex "theory of economic cycles."[7]

In describing the economy of Rome, we can rely on nothing similar. Indeed, despite a few preliminary attempts,[8] we must abstain from almost all of the formulas, both verbal and mathematical, that economic historians of the modern era are accustomed to employing so abundantly. Over long time spans, we can identify periods of expansion or recession, which were almost always linked to situations or events outside the scope of economics in the strict sense of the term (wars, conquests, or catastrophes, for example). In some cases we can distinguish relatively brief periods when the signs of a concentrated expansion were particularly distinct, or when an especially severe recession, strong enough to be considered a true structural collapse, was taking place. But we cannot expect to be able to link these periods to one another using the syntax of leaps and pauses, and peaks and valleys, that we need to describe modern economies effectively. In short, we can recognize secular trends, interspersed with more intense episodes, but the rhythms of this history make it impossible to describe cycles. And the very concept of growth, which is so familiar to us, can be properly used only if we succeed in investing it with meanings that are very different from those to which we are accustomed.

In the early years of the fourteenth century,[9] before the plague of 1348 had killed approximately one quarter of Europe's people, the population of the continent was about 80 million. By 1700 it had already reached 115 million, and by 1900 it had grown to 285 million. According to a hypothetical but reasonable estimate, in 1300 more than 80 percent of the active population was involved in agriculture (a ratio that, as we shall see, was fairly close to that of the Roman Empire in the first two centuries A.D.). In 1700 the proportion was still over 70 percent, but by 1900 it had dropped sharply to 50 percent. Despite the urban and demographic revolutions of the eleventh, twelfth, and thirteenth centuries, by the year 1300 there were still no more than six cities with populations greater than 100,000 (in the Roman Empire of the second century A.D. there were probably seven: Rome, Carthage, Alexandria, Antioch, Ephesus, Pergamum, and Apamea). In 1700 there were twelve (London, Paris, Milan, Venice, Naples, Rome, Palermo, Madrid, Lisbon, Amsterdam, Vienna, and Istanbul), but by 1900 there were 125. In 1300, the per capita consumption of iron was between 0.5 and 1.5 kilograms; in 1700, it was between 1.1 and 2.0 kilograms; by 1900, it had increased to 80 kilograms.

Over time, the ancient economies experienced no changes that were even remotely comparable. But the idea of growth (and its theoretical elaborations)—from the early "growth models" of Adam Smith and David Ricardo[10] to the sophisticated analyses of the twentieth century[11]—is the offshoot of these more recent leaps and reveals its own origins. Its meaning incorporates the experiences of gradual progression and sudden surging—both the concept of irresistible linear growth and the fluctuations, spurts, and sudden changes of speed that break up the smooth course of development. It represents the conceptual projection of tremendous historical accelerations, and reflects the coexistence of the increasing imbalances and reciprocal dependence among regions in a world that is becoming ever smaller and more interconnected (in the twentieth century, the median per capita income in advanced countries reached an order of fifteen times that of remote areas).

Therefore, it is not only a question of the word that we choose to use. What is at stake—and bears attentive oversight—is the power of analogy of the ideas that the words call to mind.

Now that we have realized that the dynamics which characterize industrial modernity are, as we can see today, extraneous to Greek and Roman economic forms, we understand why contemporary scholars—of whom Finley was the first—have been so insistent in advancing markedly continuist hypotheses in their analyses of these systems. Even when they do not say so explicitly, these commentators base their arguments on their observation that ancient economies were uniformly incapable of transformative accelerations.

But the correct identification of a single characteristic, no matter how important it may be, does not guarantee that all theses built on it will be complete and persuasive. In the meantime, it is necessary to provide an explanation of the origin and the causes of this barrier. We need to understand which constraints in the imperial system of Rome functioned to prevent the triggering of some kind of dynamic that may have been comparable, not necessarily to modern growth situations, but at least to conditions of growth in preindustrial Europe (as was evidenced, for example, in Italy, France, Holland, and Germany between the late Middle Ages and the seventeenth century). This problem brings us back, in another way, to the central point in the questions posed by Rostovtzeff and Walbank. It is a knotty perplexity in which all of the continuist interpretations become entangled.

Yet even the existence of this barrier does not compel us to believe that the ancient economies were immobile systems that were all substantially equivalent to one another (as the continuists often tend to think) or cohesive units lacking noteworthy internal distinctions, or that they were incapable of producing economic well-being in certain (admittedly limited) cases, and even true opulence, although under very special circumstances. If we adopt the parameters utilized for preindustrial modern and medieval societies (which make use of approximative transpositions, with no pretense of precision) and apply them to an area and a time period like the Mediterranean in the final eight centuries B.C. and the first two centuries A.D., we can easily hypothesize that there were quantitative imbalances between "wealthy" and "poor" geopolitical areas approaching a ratio of one to three, or even, in particular circumstances, one to four or five. These variations are quite significant, if we keep in mind that even small differences in the availability of resources, with a proportional increase in the margins of available surpluses, could be enough—and, in the case of Rome, soon were enough—to bring about considerable changes in the mechanisms of the distribution of wealth, and to have social and cultural consequences of great importance.

Chapter Six

Dual Equilibria

(1)

Compared to the rhythms of the economy, those of the political scene of the same period appear much more agitated (lightning-swift military campaigns, conquests of vast territories, successful and victorious alliances)—to such a degree that, in retrospect, very often it is believed that an irreversible destiny was at work. A spectacular sequence of events blended military talent and efficiency, administrative skill, and governmental inventiveness in a unique combination. Hard on the heels of the political and military events came major institutional changes and significant transformations in the ruling classes: the crisis of the republic and the emergence of the principate of Augustus and then of Hadrian; the decline of the old senatorial oligarchy, which yielded to a new, more extensive aristocracy, flexible and diversified, both in Italy and in the provinces.

The rapid changes in politics, the slow-moving pace of the economy: the overall movement was like an ocean of waves with longer and more even currents coursing through its depths. Up to a certain point, the disparity in rhythms was absorbed physiologically. But later, once the critical threshold was reached, it would become deadly. We will return to this topic below.

In the economic history of the empire, all movement seemed to be concentrated at the two ends of the process: at the time the system was being formed and growing most actively, and during the period of its dissolution. This characteristic makes it possible to take in the contours of the whole picture in a single glance. A many-layered image with strong contrasts takes shape.

The economy of Rome is best described as an agrarian-mercantile system based on slavery, whose three most important components—agriculture, slaves, and the circulation of commodities—were directly dependent on the imperial and "worldwide" configuration of their political context.

All output was essentially agricultural in nature; moreover, agriculture left its mark on urban and rural manufacturing activities as well. Despite its strong dependence on climatic and meteorological variables, agricultural production in Italy and the more advanced regions (Sicily, Spain, the southern part of Gaul, Egypt and northern Africa, Syria, and Asia Minor) managed consistently to achieve considerable surpluses, which were reserved for long-distance commerce.

Merchant trade, supported by the widespread circulation of money and substantial capital, encompassed the entire Mediterranean. It created an economic arena in which the intersection of supply and demand, as well as the trends of the inflation curve, determined pricing and price fluctuations, by means of mechanisms that are reminiscent of aspects of the late medieval economies of Italy and northern Europe—although in Rome and other major cities of the empire, sophisticated mechanisms of "administrated trade" were to a large degree successful (for mostly political reasons) in supplanting the spontaneous operation of the laws of the market.

The social classes involved in this economy of exchange—whether as owners of land, workshops, and slaves, or as holders of commercial capital, or as consumers in a position to support the most sustained and best-defined share of the demand—were the very same ones who were at the highest levels of political power and cultural influence. Because of this, in ancient literary documents we see that the mercantile shell which protected and enhanced the lives of the elites in the archipelago of their cities had the effect of covering up and concealing from our eyes the density and the dimensions—if not the very existence—of the entire portion of the empire that did not depend on the mercantile system for its survival.

This is a dangerous distortion that can lead to entirely arbitrary conclusions. Indeed, this problem has regularly plagued many of the accounts of the modernists, which Finley has properly showered with sarcasm.[1] The reality was quite different. Even in the most advanced regions, the mercantile economy coexisted with an extensive zone of natural or subsistence economy, consisting of farmers who consumed crops that they cultivated, or of very small-scale local trade, none of which created any appreciable "trading profits" (to use Fernand Braudel's expression).[2] This cluster of social and economic relationships existed alongside the more evolved forms, and included within its orbit the lives of entire populations, whose history grew cold and faded away,[3] immobilized in the fundamental repetition of a cyclical pattern that was resistant to growth.

Slavery always served as the basis of mercantile production. The widespread presence of great quantities of slaves is documented in almost all of the major areas of agriculture and manufacturing, although we must keep in mind that a large number of prisoners, especially in Rome and other parts of Italy, were used for housework and nonproductive activities.

Massive amounts of wealth—collected in almost all cases through imposed taxation—were regularly transferred from the more wealthy peripheral regions to the center, according to the model Keith Hopkins has effectively outlined.[4] Correspondingly, commodities were constantly exported from these same regions to Rome and Italy and (less intensively) to the furthest reaches of the empire, where the armies protecting the borders were garrisoned. The profits that were realized in the provinces helped to create the liquidity necessary to pay the taxes, and in this way equilibrium was restored.

The heterogeneity of the form of economy we are describing is striking. On the one hand, it seems to be a typical example of a "traditional" agricultural society:[5] its productive structure is dominated by agriculture, the natural economy occupies a large sector, and manufacturing is on the whole weak and secondary. But the numbers do not add up properly. The "worldwide" dimensions of the empire are not consonant with this image of backwardness. Other factors must have been present, if we are to explain the well-developed circuit of taxation and trade, supported by appropriate levels of supply and demand, that succeeded in regularly transferring many millions of sesterces in capital and tens of thousands of tons of goods from one end of the Mediterranean to the other. And in its turn this large-scale commerce relied upon a production structure based on true slave-labor plantations, where the work (not only in agriculture but also in the skilled trades) was performed according to elaborate and shrewdly conceived parameters. Our entire interpretation is thus moving toward a state of uncertain and contradictory ambiguity—the same one we saw reflected in the opposing visions of the primitivists and the modernists.

But the difficulties will melt away if we can renounce the search for a single unique characterization—one that, historically and economically, does not exist. What is more, we must understand that the essential nature of the system dwells precisely in its lack of homogeneity. It very nearly approaches what modern theorists call a "dual economy":[6] a system whose very survival depends on the separation of its two basic levels, which, even as they exist in the same time and the same place, function entirely independently of each other, although they are subject to constant cross-pollination and integration.

There is a major distinction to be made, however. In modern examples (always drawn from situations of underdevelopment), the balance between the two strata—the natural economy and the exchange economy—tends to be unstable: either they are in a constant state of disequilibrium, or they can reach equilibrium only at the extreme margins. Sooner or later, the more advanced and dynamic side—when it emerges and takes root, often through external influence—succeeds in gaining the upper hand, eroding the space of the other side and reducing it to a historical fossil of decreasing relevance.

In Rome this did not happen: the "archaic" and the "advanced" forms were stabilized. The latter, although it expanded, did not prevail over the former; and both coexisted compatibly for a long time. The stability of this combination was, in fact, the dominant feature of the imperial economy.

Such a strongly marked duality should not surprise us. Major unresolved polarities, which in many ways remain inscrutable to us (as Andrea Giardina has noted),[7] are characteristic not only of the economy but of the entire history of Rome. For example, the ethnic isolation—to the point of banishment—of the originality and superiority of the Roman and Latin component with respect to the rest of Italy (and the world), but at the same time the Romans' seemingly unlimited capacity to absorb and assimilate different peoples and cultures. Likewise, their unparalleled and long-cultivated zeal for domination and imperial exploitation in contrast to their talent for building a network of regionally autonomous structures and their tendency to develop a policy, unequaled in the history of the Western world, of transferring power and responsibility to the local ruling classes by means of the judicious granting of citizenship. And the massive use of slaves, at levels never before reached, was paired with the very widespread practice of enfranchisement—which gave any master, by means of his voluntary and irrevocable decision, the power to transform at a single stroke any slave (who was until that moment a mere object or tool) into a citizen of the hegemonic community. In these contrasts the force of the contradictions was not a paralyzing one, or at least it did not have this effect at first: it did not lead to the reciprocal undoing of both sides. On the contrary, it succeeded in triggering in unforeseeable ways—at least up to a certain point—the creative and combinatorial capacities of the opposites that were confronting each other.

(2)

From a quantitative standpoint, the dualism of the levels was not in equilibrium. In the empire as a whole—and also in Italy alone—the subsistence of the majority of the population usually depended on the consumption of items that did not enter into the newly established commercial circuits and that were not the output of production processes oriented toward the creation of commodities.

At the risk of a certain measure of approximation, we can state that this more backward arena included the economies of all of the internal and mountainous areas of the Italian peninsula and the provinces—from the Apennines to the Pyrenees, the Balkans, and Anatolia. It also included the subsistence-level lives of the poorest classes, wherever they were (except in Rome and partly in the other major cities of the empire). On the other hand, economies largely based on systems of markets and trading played a leading part in the condition of the landowning classes, no matter how modest, in the coastal centers of Italy, Sicily, southern Gaul, Spain, and almost all of the Middle East; and the situation of the highest and most Romanized classes all over the empire is apparent in the functioning of economies broadly involved in fixed networks of trade and exchange. It is unlikely that peasants along the Danube, in the Po Valley, or in northern Gaul, shepherds in Samnium or Lucania, or urban proletarian families living on the outskirts of cities like Pompeii,

Italica, or Athens consumed goods produced beyond a range of several
miles from their homes. But the "invisible hand" of the large-scale market regulated virtually everything that touched the daily life of a Trimal-
chio and the thousands of others like him from one end of the empire to
the other (for this literary character created by Petronius is the embodiment of a sociological type), or a senator in Rome, or a large landholder
in Carthage, or a simple physician in Antioch, or even a slave at the imperial court.

We must be careful not to distort the actual state of affairs here. To
suggest that a unitary representation based on the concepts of "natural
economy" or "subsistence economy" can depict environments and social
classes that had no real contact with one another, located in areas consisting of hundreds of thousands of square kilometers, in very diverse
anthropological and cultural settings, is simply to yield to our own desire for systematic abstraction.

The localities we are associating with one another are all quite heterogeneous—within the Italian peninsula alone, not to mention the rest of
the empire—and correspond to specific historical circumstances that
are not easily assimilated. Their homogeneity lies solely in the fact that
they were all excluded from the large-scale circulation of commodities
and that their material requirements consisted of essential necessities—
plain food, very simple clothing, rough tools, rudimentary housing—
which they procured outside the market system. If we consider the economic geography of the territory, the empire was actually finely dotted
with closed and isolated microsystems, whose size and demographic
composition varied according to the history and physical configuration
of the settlements.

Yet it is also possible to make an overall appraisal of these economic
conditions from a different perspective: the sufficiency of what was produced. In the first century A.D., the empire comprised more than four
million square kilometers, along an axis of five thousand kilometers
stretching from Britain to the Black Sea, and contained an immense
wealth of natural resources. A reasonable estimate of the population living in these territories at that time does not exceed 50–60 million:[8] approximately that of present-day Italy, and much higher than the population of Europe in the year 1000 but far lower than that of Europe in
1500. (The median population density was about fifteen per square kilo-

meter, but its distribution was very irregular: at that same time, about one million people lived in Rome alone, and about six to eight million in Italy.)

Thus, the portion of this population which relied for its subsistence on the movements of the natural economy lived in conditions of poverty that we can scarcely imagine, despite the undoubtedly favorable relationship between men and the potential resources in their environment. There were chronic problems of undernourishment, with food supplies remaining just above—and sometimes, tragically, below—the levels necessary for survival. Infant mortality was very high (excluding the more advanced areas, it has been calculated that 30 percent of all infants died before reaching their first birthdays, and another 20 percent died before reaching the age of ten). Generations of men and women, in regions well within the boundaries of the Roman Empire, lived with extremely precarious food supplies and poor sanitary conditions, deprived of information from the outside, virtually rejected from history.

Of course, these conditions, considered globally, were not unique to the Roman world. We also find them in the history of medieval Europe, and even in a segment of modern history, although with some major variations. But in the case of the Roman Empire, both the length of time that has intervened and the distortion of the sources (both textual and archeological) on which we depend lead us to overlook them more readily than the consideration of other eras would permit.

It was only on this ocean of scarcity—where the unending, repetitive triggering of a short circuit that was not only material but also social and mental linked productive backwardness with the poverty of consumption, thereby rendering all growth impossible and thwarting the conditions that would have premitted the development of any less subordinate culture—that the delicate but tenacious system of mercantile production and large-scale trade we have just discussed was sustained, as if it were floating in suspension. Its slenderness was inversely proportional to its visibility.

Chapter Seven

The Roman Miracle and
Imperial Rationality

(1)

Let us take a step back and focus once again on Rome in the early third century B.C. The dispute between the patricians and the plebeians had come to an end, and the compromise that was giving life to the new republican aristocracy had fulfilled its promise. After the passage of the *lex Ogulnia,* a law that in 300 B.C. opened the most exclusive priestly colleges to plebeian families, and the *lex Hortensia,* which in 287 decreed that resolutions adopted by the plebeians had the same force as deliberations voted by the *comitia centuriata,* almost no trace of the ancient patrician privileges remained. The patrician-plebeian aristocracy, composed of those who had attained the curule magistracies, had a stable place in the political limelight—and this would remain the case until the civil war. It was a somewhat narrow elite, but one that was not entirely closed off; at least until the middle of the century, not only were many "new men" admitted to it,[1] including Quintus Publius Philo, Manius Curius Dentatus, and Gaius Fabricius Luscinus, but they also played an important role. It was only later, not before the Hannibalic War, that the entry restrictions which characterized the rest of the history of the republic[2] would go into effect: the evidence shows that between 191 and 107 B.C., only three consuls came from families whose members had not already held this position; moreover, two were sons of praetors and the third had a close friendship with Scipio the Younger. (Later on, the situation changed to some extent: between 107 and 44 B.C. eleven "new men" became consuls,[3] including Marius and Cicero. But the *ancien régime* was already breaking up.)

Rome, unlike Athens, was never a "democracy," even in the ancient meaning of the word. Rather, in the fourth and third centuries B.C. it was a "soft" oligarchy—the famous "mixed" constitution extolled by Polybius[4]—which managed to avoid clashes between the nobles and the common people (clashes of the sort that occurred in Athens or medieval Florence), until after the Gracchi it was transformed into a violent factional government.

The aristocrats did not yet possess conspicuous wealth, in the form of either land (which constituted the only true wealth of the community) or personal property. Livy recounts that when, in order to fulfill a vow after the conquest of Veii, the Romans were supposed to make an offering of gold to Apollo that was commensurate with his magnificence, they could not find a sufficient quantity either in the treasury or in the market. They were forced to take up a collection among all of the Roman matrons, who handed over their jewels for the purpose.[5] Territorial limitations made it impossible for large estates to be formed. It is estimated that throughout the whole fourth century B.C. the area of Rome was about 6,000 square kilometers, for a population of adult male citizens numbering no fewer than 150,000 and (as we have seen) no more than 250,000.[6] The economic differences, therefore, were not very large: the ratio between the two extremes of the economic scale was probably no greater than twelve or fifteen to one. But by the end of the republic—when the triumvir Marcus Crassus enjoyed a fortune exceeding 7,000 talents,[7] or a little less than 200 million sesterces—the ratio had grown astronomically, to 5,000 or 10,000 to one.

In terms of social makeup, the republic consisted of a modest community whose members were all simultaneously small landholders, peasant farmers, citizens, and soldiers. Around them a class of merchants and speculators was just beginning to take shape, but it would not play a truly important role until the middle of the second century B.C. The economic and military-political structures appeared to be integrated in a single civic mechanism: there could not have been full-fledged city dwellers (and soldiers) if there had not been farmers (and landholders). Individual acquisition of a parcel of land, which was the most important prerequisite for any person's productive labor, was not only a necessary economic condition but also a necessary institutional one. There was a kind of original citizenship, whose indispensable natural foundation (the land, which served as laboratory, medium of work, and ready supplier of food and raw materials) was combined with a set of historical elements, both social and political (the organization of the city according to property and wealth) and familial and cultural (kinship ties, religion, and respect for tradition, with their redistributive atavism).[8] The passage of time did not alter this picture, and urban life was a fitting example of what Karl Polanyi would call the institutional "embedding" of the economy: a mode of production not centered on itself, but inextricably sustained by external and independent community support.[9]

Though we aim here to describe this situation as it actually was, free of any hint of nostalgic overestimation that would inevitably falsify its contours (as was the case in many of our sources—for example, the preface to Cato's treatise on agriculture,[10] or Pliny's *Historia Naturalis*,[11] with its account of the good old days when senators and military commanders farmed the land with their own hands), it is difficult to deny the particularly unified and cohesive nature of this reality. Thanks to this foundation, the city was able to withstand the political and military strife of the fourth and third centuries B.C., and embark on its first strong expansionist thrusts toward the south and north, which lasted until the First Punic War. It was the Servian legacy of centuriation, inherited from the Etruscan monarchy, adapted, then transplanted into the heart of the republican system, which was most successful at a time when its most strictly military aspects (its original starting point) were virtually obsolete.

The way such a society would function in political and economic terms has been described—virtually x-rayed—in a passage that counts as among the most important in nineteenth-century ancient studies. Inspired by a meditation on Berthold Georg Niebuhr, Karl Marx wrote:

> The commune—as state—is, on one side, the relation of these free and equal private proprietors to one another, their bond against the outside, and is at the same time their safeguard. [. . .] Concentration in the town, with the land as *territorium;* small agriculture working for direct consumption; manufacture as domestic side occupation of wives and daughters (spinning and weaving) or, independently, in individual branches only (*fabri* etc.). The presupposition of the survival of the community is the preservation of equality among its free self-sustaining peasants, and

their own labor as the condition of the survival of their property. They relate as proprietors to the natural conditions of labor; but these conditions must also constantly be posited as real conditions and objective elements of the personality of the individual, by means of personal labor. [. . .] The individual is placed in such conditions of earning his living as to make not the acquiring of wealth his object, but self-sustenance, his own reproduction as a member of the community; the reproduction of himself as proprietor of the parcel of ground, and, in that quality, as a member of the commune. The survival of the commune is the reproduction of all of its members as self-sustaining peasants, whose surplus time belongs precisely to the commune, the work of war, etc. [. . .] Property is *quiritorium,* of the Roman variety; the private proprietor of land is such only as a Roman, but as a Roman he is private proprietor of land.[12]

The dominant theme of this analysis brings to light an important element, clarifying the nature of the subsequent transformation that occurred in the third and second centuries B.C. The proto-republican community could survive only so long as it managed to avoid any alteration of its initial condition. It was locked into its original framework: it endured so long as it remained a group of small landowners whose social inequalities were not an obstacle to their basic homogeneity. It had to sustain itself without changing and without growing. The only possible goal for the basic cycle of production—the agricultural exploitation of the land—was to maintain its existing contours unchanged, leaving it in its primitive state: the same state of self-sufficiency of those landowner-peasant-farmer-citizens that later admirers were to transpose into an ethical paragon of unity, sobriety, and rigor.

This condition of relative equality was, in turn, the result of a specific historical development: the social clashes of the fifth century, which ended in 387 B.C. with the conquest of the territory of Veii and the creation of four new tribes. That annexation had made possible the large-scale political redistribution of land to the plebeians, which had given rise to the model of the small rural landholding—the "seven *iugera*"—about which Varro, Livy, and Columella were still writing.[13] This formed the heart of the popular acceptance of the patrician-plebeian compromise. During the entire fourth century B.C., the equilibrium that had been achieved—and ratified legislatively in 367 by the *lex Licinia*, which limited the right of patricians to occupy the "public land" not assigned to plebeians—effectively became the economic constitution of the society, a presupposition that became entirely entrenched. The abolition of enslavement for debts in 326 B.C. was further confirmation of this tendency. The body of citizens was constituted by "the relation of these free and equal private proprietors to one another." Community life was based on the possession of land and the work of farmers. Indeed, even the patrician-plebeian aristocracy was assessed according to the same measure, despite the fact that because of individual circumstances they might enjoy the use of more land and resources (domestic animals, supplies, tools, slaves, or small hoards of silver and bronze) than they needed for the purposes of pure self-sufficiency. The connection between the political structure and the economic order was airtight. Every possible variation in the configuration of the social fabric was precluded (a phenomenon that Weber perspicaciously but incorrectly labeled "yeomanry preservation.")[14]

To be sure, a trading network did exist, even over long distances, and there were also artisans, merchants, and marketplaces. Rome already had a conspicuous place in the maritime circuits of the central and western Mediterranean: the second treaty with Carthage, drafted in 348 B.C.,[15] is manifest evidence of this. But the amount of trade did not make it possible to accumulate significant quantities of goods or money, and it was not large enough to generate ways to increase the value of the investments that might have broken through the traditional boundaries.

When the changes began, sometime after the year 300 B.C., they did not come about through the internal evolution of the existing state of affairs. The transformations were not the effect of a new balance of production in the countryside, or of technological advances, or of greater functionality in the marketplace. We can also assume that in the long run the system would eventually have altered on its own. But the turn taken by events makes it impossible to prove this. From a certain moment on, the force of the transformations set in motion from the outside—the economic results of the conquests—upset the old order entirely. The innovation was a consequence of war, and the extraordinary advancements of the military system now began to occupy our field of vision completely.

(2)

From the conquest of Veii in 387 B.C. to the fall of Taranto in 272 B.C., Rome's expansionist impulses—directed above all toward the southern part of the peninsula—knew no interruption. The republican war machine was ironing out the kinks in its workings before the decisive test: the engagements with Carthage in Italy, Africa, and Spain, and on the Mediterranean. We can locate the critical point of the period in the years between 338 B.C., when Rome imposed the dissolution of the Latin league, and 290 B.C., with the campaign of Manius Curius Dentatus against the Sabines and the territories beyond, as far as the Adriatic (the events to which Fabius Pictor referred). The exploitation of the conquered territories—well documented by the evidence about the foundation of Latin colonies (of which there were eleven in the years 334–298 B.C.),[16] the formation of new tribes,[17] and the deduction of Roman colonies—inevitably modified the old terms of production and the "egalitarian" structure of agrarian relationships. Beyond a certain threshold, the acquisition of new lands was no longer regulated by the distribution mechanisms imposed by the struggles of the plebeians, and new forms of land concentration began to be developed; the path to villas and the large estates of the senatorial aristocracy, and to the new forms of property produced by the "municipalization" of the second and first centuries B.C., was now laid out. The agrarian landscape of Roman Italy was about to assume its mature and best-known contours, made familiar to us by long tradition, both literary and topographic.

According to reliable data, which date back to K. J. Beloch's estimates,[18] the territory under Rome's control tripled in size in the years 336–280 B.C., going from about 5,700 to more than 17,000 square kilometers. There was another spectacular increase shortly thereafter,[19] in the years before 265 B.C., when an additional area of 9,000 square kilometers was conquered and occupied, in large part by Roman citizens as the spoils of war (through both individual land grants and the establishment of new colonies). The time that the community devoted to war—"surplus time," relative to the time devoted to agricultural production—achieved something that the time devoted to "labor" in the strict sense of the term had not: thanks to the resounding success of its performances, it broke the institutional, material, and mental bonds that had confined the republic to the economic (and political) model of self-sufficiency and small rural landholdings. The Romans began to realize that war was the most efficient of all productive activities, and that the war machine was the best means of acquiring new wealth; from the perspective of the ruling classes, military logic and sheer acquisitiveness went hand in hand. Even on a more modest scale, this had been the case from the outset. The connection between military events and agricultural circumstances is already evident in the early social struggles of republican Rome; clear traces of it remain in the writings of Livy and Dionysius.[20] In the history of Rome, victory in war suddenly appears to be the true—and presumably indispensable—catalyst for all economic growth.

The payoffs of the military campaigns were not limited to the annexation of new lands. From the third century B.C. on, they also created the availability of a labor force which for a long time seemed inexhaustible—namely, slaves. According to Livy's account, in the years 297–293 B.C. alone, as many as 61,000 people were enslaved, in a period in which the adult male population of the republic could not have been much greater than 260,000.[21] It is not difficult to imagine the devastating impact of these masses on the old systems of domestic organization of farm labor. From then on, finding the proper balance between the abundance of land and the abundance of slaves was the main problem of Roman landowners, as well as a classic theme in writings about aristocratic agronomy.

And there were still more benefits of war, including the conquest of almost every kind of article or commodity that the ancients identified as wealth: from precious metals mined in Spain (the silver deposits near Carthago Nova—the modern Cartagena—at the time of Polybius yielded 100,000 sesterces a day and employed 40,000 laborers, almost all of whom were slaves), to the various goods confiscated as legitimate booty, to the enormous quantity of money paid in reparations by the Carthaginians after the Second Punic War (almost 27,000 talents in a fifty-year period, or something in excess of 640 million sesterces). (To comprehend the enormity of this amount, we need only remember that the largest private estate of the imperial era known to us, that of Cornelius Lentulus, a senator who died in 25 A.D., came to less than 400 million sesterces.)[22] Entire libraries could be included in the booty, as happened in the case of that of the Macedonian king Perseus, which after his defeat at Pydna was brought to Rome at the order of Lucius Aemilius Paulus, then used by the circle of Scipio Aemilianus.[23] Rome had never seen such a large number of books in a single collection; and their sudden availability made it possible to read (and transcribe) works that influenced all of the culture of the late republican era.

These new opportunities transformed the economic behavior of the aristocracy. When, in 221 B.C., Quintus Caecilius Metellus, who was to become consul in 206, made a celebrated funeral oration in memory of his father, Lucius, who had been consul in 251 and 247, the metamorphosis had already been achieved. As we read in Book 7 of Pliny's *Historia naturalis,*

> Quintus Metellus, in the panegyric that he delivered at the obsequies of his father, Lucius Metellus the pontiff—who had been Consul twice, Dictator, Master of the Horse, and Land-Commissioner, and who was the first person who led a procession of elephants in triumph, having captured them in the First Punic War—has left it in writing that his father had achieved the ten greatest and highest objects in the pursuit of which wise men pass their lives; for he had made it his aim to be a first-class warrior, a supreme orator, and a very brave commander, to have the direction of operations of the highest importance, to enjoy the greatest honor, to be supremely wise, to be deemed the most eminent member of the senate, to obtain great wealth in an honorable way, to leave many children, and to achieve supreme distinction in the state.[24]

The bond between the nobility and the peasant farmers was now dissolved: a true aristocrat was recognizable as such for having found a way to accumulate huge wealth, to which there was no limit. The magnitude of his fortune was a tangible sign of his preeminence, no less so than his military exploits, his wisdom in civil matters, and the consulships he held. The ancient public vocation of the nobility was beginning to be shaded by overtones and ambitions that modified its conduct and attitudes.

Nevertheless, it was expected that the wealth of the aristocrats would be acquired "in an honorable way" (according to Pliny's transcription of Metellus). As if in a flash, the outlines of a new polarity appear here. This polemic jab, which, although fleetingly mentioned, is so unequivocal, marks the very clear delineation of an early contrast. On one side, there was the manner in which the more prudent members of the nobility were to acquire wealth from then on: through property-based individualism, the wise accumulation of agrarian revenues, and the vigilant use of slaves. On the other side, there was a more unscrupulous mode of behavior, common to the aristocratic circles that were ready to free themselves from the ancient models (a few notable examples being Gaius Terentius Varro, consul in 216 B.C., Publius Rupilius, consul in 132 B.C., and Marcus Licinius Crassus, consul in 70 B.C.). They emulated practices learned from the emerging classes—speculators, profiteers, merchants, *argentarii* (a kind of primitive banker), *publicani* (tax contractors working on behalf of the government)—who were the direct offspring of imperial expansionism. The history of the second and first centuries B.C. spotlights them in their ascent to social success. It was a group which, without daring to clash openly with the nobility (in fact, it never did), circled around them with feverish activity, as if subtly laying siege to them, always hoping to emulate them and join them, often trying to turn their disputes and dispositions to its own advantage. This was a gallery that also included notable figures who, in the third to first centuries B.C., were depicted in a number of literary works, from Plautus' comedies to Cicero's orations, not to mention the hundreds of late-republican inscriptions that still preserve fragments and mementos of their careers and exploits.

But revenues from agricultural enterprises remained the socially preeminent form of wealth. Matters never reached the point of a true "class" dispute between the entrepreneur-merchants and the rentiers, as was to happen so many times in late medieval and modern Europe—in Italy, France, and England. The primacy of the landed aristocracy was never under attack. Any other kind of wealth merely endowed its owner with a transitory and ambiguous status. It was an intermediate step before reaching ownership of land—the only kind of property that provided remuneration in the form of prestige and power. We shall soon return to the topic of this one-dimensional nature of the summit of the social ladder—a constant in the history of Rome.

In addition, the new classes were not the ones who took up the cause of expansion and economic growth. In point of fact, the great senatorial families managed to remain firmly in command of the conquest of Italy and the Mediterranean, skillfully linking agrarian interests and commercial speculations, and transforming themselves in less than a century from a small-scale rural noble class to a wealthy and cosmopolitan imperial aristocracy. At the same time, as soon as they could, the contractors and merchants invested their profits in land, the first rung on the aristocratic ladder to which they all aspired.

In the years 219–218 B.C. Gaius Flaminius, a noble who still sided with the small rural landowners during his censorship (he had been consul in 223), persuaded an obscure plebeian tribune, Quintus Claudius, to bring to a vote—which was successful despite strong opposition—a plebiscite prohibiting senators from owning ships whose tonnage was greater than 300 *amphorae* (about 7.5 tons—very small dimensions, even for ancient shipbuilding).[25] In other words, they were forbidden to carry on commercial activities in their own names. The same regulation (or one that came right after it with the same intent)[26] also banned senators from seeking public contracts. These might seem to be antiaristocratic provisions, aimed at preventing the nobility from extending its control over the new areas of economic life in the republic. But we must not be misled: though important, these were merely formal constraints. They gave legislative form to a line of social demarcation between the "orders" (the nobles and the rest), but they did not establish a true economic barrier between the classes in the modern sense of the term.

Indeed, it is quite possible that the purpose of the law (the stricture was reproposed at the end of the republic, though it had become totally useless)[27] was not actually to prevent aristocrats from growing rich through the profits of speculation and commerce; to get around the prohibition, all they had to do was conduct their business through clients and straw men—as they were already doing, and as they would do countless additional times. Rather, as Filippo Cassola correctly noted,[28] the law was intended to prevent large merchants and profiteers from obtaining the higher magistracies and becoming members of the senate so long as they held their current positions in society—that is, unless they had already converted their profits into landholdings. We should not read into the actions of Flaminius and his followers the intention of making a frontal attack on the nobility—or of drastically reducing the number of those eligible to take advantage of the commercial opportunities and speculative offerings provided by the expansion. Instead, it contained the idea—which would prove to be entirely felicitous—of strongly preserving the aristocracy's link to an "agrarian" conception of wealth, and probably of blocking the overly rapid political ascent of magnates who lacked ties with the rural world. Whether the plan could actually succeed in furthering the lot of small country landholders (as Flaminius had in mind), by keeping the nobility close to them in some way, is an entirely different matter: the decline of the rural plebs proved to be inexorable. Even the far more ambitious attempt of the Gracchi a century later did not succeed in slowing it down.

It is difficult for us to determine the extent to which the new classes of merchants and entrepreneurs corresponded with the members of what was later to be called the "equestrian order." (The expression is found for the first time in the writings of M. Junius Gracchanus, a scholar who lived from 150 to 54 B.C. and was later cited by Pliny.)[29] In any case, it must be said that the term alluded much more to a juridical and political condition than to an economic one. And if we try to impute too uniform and homogeneous an identity to these groups, we risk distorting their natures and roles.

Beginning in the second half of the third century B.C., thanks to the systematic exploitation of the conquered territories and regular tax collections, a veritable river of wealth began to flow into Rome. By the second century B.C., it had reached dimensions long unequaled in the history of the Western world. The organization of the imperial territories beyond the ancient confines of Italy (more or less from Emilia to Calabria) into "provinces" was a masterstroke of brilliant administrative improvisation on the part of the nobility, which tradition gradually codified into government procedure.

Thus, the republic was in a position to measure the effects of a form of economic growth which, although familiar to empires in all eras, reached, in the case of Rome, its most spectacular level of concentration. Unprecedented in the intensity and duration of its accumulation of agrarian and mercantile wealth, it was based on successful military conquests and on the resulting forced redistribution of wealth and labor (in the form of slavery). It was a true economic miracle, and it had no rival in the ancient world. Any Roman calculation of production and rational management of farms or businesses always took into account their ultimate dependence on the military advantages of conquerors—in terms of slaves, land, taxes, and commercial routes.

Military plunder turned out to be the sole mechanism for the self-support that the Roman economy managed to build. The circuit from war to conquest to wealth and back again to war soon became the true driving force of the entire system: a spiral in which every military campaign was simultaneously cause and effect, premise and consequence, as the cycle repeated. War became the preferred means by which politics supported the economy.

Military activity required time and work; second only to agriculture, it was quantitatively one of the most important occupations of adult Roman men. In the years 225–23 B.C.—the period of greatest expansion—the army employed about 13 percent of the male population, and 30 percent at peak times. According to Keith Hopkins' calculations, this means that 84 percent of the seventeen-year-old recruits were called up for five years, or 60 percent for seven years, or 44 percent for ten years, or 28 percent for sixteen years.[30] Given this situation, there is no point in wondering—as many modern historians have—whether the Roman idea of imperial expansion implicitly contained any awareness of the notions of acquisition and purely "economic" interests.

From its origins, the aristocracy of Rome was a warlike aristocracy. As far as we go back in time, this characteristic is constantly present. The political and military instability of archaic Latium—a frontier area, a land of luxuriant forests (still mentioned by Theophrastus)[31] and dangerous swamps, a place of combats, soldiers of fortune (especially Etruscan ones), and clashes between different ethnic groups—can serve as a partial explanation for this remote attitude, and may have fostered a social selection that reinforced it. It is difficult to go any further back; we are already in the zone of uncertainty where historical research on the origins of a tendency turns into the identification of an anthropological pattern (rather than a genetic imprint).

It is probable that the motivation inciting the Romans to war and expansion was grounded in their almost obsessive need for security—the legacy, transformed but not eliminated, of their ancient apprehensions, which more recent dangers had revived. The republic had long had to contend with the old "fear of the Gauls" and "fear of the Carthaginians."

Within the skillful and efficient design of Polybius' narrative, written in the years after 146 B.C., in Roman history the passage of time was synonymous with the acquisition of space. And Polybius was convinced that from 220 to 168 B.C.—the most crucial period of his account, dating from just before the Second Punic War to the Macedonian disaster at Pydna—Roman leaders had progressively executed their plan for world domination, thus making possible the creation of a truly "universal" history in the end. "But ever since this date history has been an organic whole, and the affairs of Italy and Libya have been interlinked with those of Greece and Asia, all leading up to one end."[32]

Polybius intentionally used a Thucydidean pattern, putting it into action in a much larger setting: behind the formation of every great power, there must have been an unwavering desire for conquest.

More than two thousand years later, we find ourselves posing this problem in substantially the same terms. From the early years of the second century, between Zama and Pydna, and shortly thereafter with the almost simultaneous destruction of Corinth, Carthage, and Numantia at the two extremes of the Mediterranean, something had changed in the mechanisms of Roman expansionism. The urge to make war a routine undertaking now took priority over attaining the original objective. The relentless search for safe areas, both on land and on sea, gave way to a different impulse. Conquest became a kind of collective conditioned reflex. It was seen as worthwhile for its own sake and self-justified in the mentality and the ethical and political systems of the entire society. It was valued not only among the aristocracy (the pursuit of "praise" and "glory" that William Harris discusses at length),[33] but also among the lower social strata—the masses who increasingly contributed to the army, which was now in the process of professionalization. (From late-republican Rome to the United States today, imperial military forces made up of professionals have always tended to become armies of outcasts, kept in line through merciless discipline meted out by low-level parvenu officers.)

The complete incorporation of the province of Sicily, and the definitive occupation of Spain and Cisalpine Gaul to the Po and beyond, had opened new perspectives for Roman colonization. The horizons expanded from the coasts toward the interior regions. The time was ripe for the aristocracy's decision to assume the irreversible characteristics of the drive for worldwide domination and exploitation.

The profits from the empire conditioned the social history of Rome during the last two hundred years of the republic. In Athens during the second half of the fifth century, domination of the seas contributed to the maintenance of the democracy. In Rome, the empire definitively separated the aristocracy from the people, destroyed the small rural landholdings that dated from its origins—crushing them with the weight of the needs of war and competition from the farms that used slave labor—and caused extensive unemployment, which was to reach major dimensions in the big cities (where the underprivileged from the country sought refuge). On the other hand, it was successful in broadening the opportunities for promotion and personal advancement with an intensity unknown to the rest of the ancient world, and, above all, in forming new property-holding classes everywhere—both in Italy and in the provinces—which pledged their fidelity in exchange for peace and prosperity. Moreover, it made possible the creation of a network of public assistance, especially in Rome, which enabled the new urban proletariat to survive at least—and not always in misery, compared to the prevailing standards of living.

The equation between victory in war, the acquisition of land, and improvements in the conditions of fairly broad strata of society was substantiated throughout the entire history of Roman expansionism. But the political philosophy and the strategies professed by the elite often revealed that they had only an implicit and piecemeal appreciation of this relationship for various reasons—because of their mentality or culture, or because of the structure of the economic cycle. But it would be wrong to take their silence or reticence (in any case the lack of any kind of clear focus) for a complete lack of awareness or for an inability to register the phenomenon. Common sense told the Romans that new wealth was the "natural" outcome of skillfully waged wars and the subjugation of the defeated, in the same way as properly utilized slaves were the "natural" source of labor in the country; for a long time, these facts appeared so obvious that they were not worth expending many words on. According to the thinking of the leading classes, which was largely shared by the majority of the population, the suitable use of war and slaves fell within the guidelines of a military and profit calculus that had long been in practice. In the history of Rome, economic interests had soon taken the shape of imperial rationality, in which they had also learned to conceal themselves.

> In fact, the Romans have one inveterate motive for making war upon all nations, peoples, and kings: namely, a deep-seated desire for dominion and for riches. Therefore, they first began a war with Philip, king of Macedonia, having pretended to be his friends as long as they were hard pressed by the Carthaginians. When Antiochus came to his aid, they craftily diverted him from his purpose by the surrender of Asia, and then, after Philip's power had been broken, Antiochus was robbed of all the territory this side of Taurus, and of ten thousand talents. [. . .] Do you not know that the Romans turned their arms in this direction only after Ocean had blocked their westward progress? That they have possessed nothing since the beginning of their existence except what they have stolen—their home, their wives, their lands, their empire? Once vagabonds without fatherland, without parents, created to be the scourge of the whole world, no laws, human or divine, prevent them from seizing and destroying allies and friends, those near them and those afar off, weak or powerful, and from considering every government which does not serve them, especially monarchies, as their enemies. [. . .] The Romans have weapons against all men, the sharpest where victory yields the greatest spoils; it is by audacity, by deceit, and by joining war to war that they have grown great. Following their usual custom, they will destroy everything or perish in the attempt.[34]

And again, with a shift of time, setting, and author:

> But there are no other tribes to come—nothing but sea and cliffs and these more deadly Romans, whose arrogance you cannot escape by obedience and self-restraint. Robbers of the world, now that earth fails their all-devastating hands, they probe even the sea. If their enemy have wealth, they have greed; if he be poor, they are ambitious. Neither East nor West has glutted them; alone of mankind they covet both want and wealth with the same passion. To plunder, butcher, steal—these things they misname empire. They make a desolation and they call it peace.[35]

Two mortal enemies of Rome are speaking here. The first is Mithridates, in a letter to Arsaces, the king of Parthians; the second is the British chieftain Calgacus, in a speech to his troops before battle. Because they are hostile to Rome, they express a perception of reality turned on its head—so completely inverted that it projects an aura of total estrangement—with respect to the imperial point of view. Polybius, Aristides, and Favorinus would have been horrified.

These speeches were not at all authentic, however. They were sheer invention on the part of two Roman historians: Sallust, in the case of Mithridates, and Tacitus, in the case of Calgacus. Their accounts had no documentary reliability. Every reader of the era knew very well that there was no plausible way to explain how the (hypothetical) letter of Mithridates had ended up in Sallust's hands, or how the words of Calgacus had been repeated to Tacitus (and by whom?). Beneath the fragile veil of narrative fiction that overlaid it, this inversion of perspective, so harshly displayed, was therefore an intellectual exercise on the part of the Romans themselves, and must have been perceived as such by its contemporaries. Both examples contain the same violent attack, which through its simulation of the mind of the enemy, nullified the identity that the empire had constructed for itself through centuries of elaboration. It was a devastating critique, joining forceful intelligence with raging spirit. It lucidly highlighted the connections between war and money, conquest and plunder, economy and politics throughout the whole history of Rome, and intuited the implacable rhythm of wars ("by joining war to war," as the expression states literally: wars that produce wars).[36]

Does this represent the thinking of Sallust and Tacitus? Was this their idea of the empire? It is impossible to say. All we can state with assurance is that these literary constructions undoubtedly reflect their authors' aesthetic pleasure in successfully imitating the thinking of the enemy. The two historians were certainly mindful that the Romanization of the world had much more complex effects, and we can properly consider them exponents of a responsibly pro-imperial culture. Both reflect anxiously on the relationship between conquest and moral decadence— each in his own way and according to the problems of his own day—the "democratic" Sallust, who perhaps was a partisan of Ventidius,[37] and Tacitus, the supporter of Trajan. And the passage from Sallust presum-

ably contains an echo of the "anti-imperial" and "Asiatic" prophecy related more than a century before by Antisthenes of Rhodes. ("I see coming from Asia bronze-breasted forces and kings allied with one another
and peoples of all kinds to go against Europe, and the din of horses and
the sound of lances, and bloody massacre, and terrible pillaging, and the
debris of towers, and the demolition of walls, and the unspeakable devastation of territory."[38] Here, the dominion of Europe and Rome are one
and the same.) But in the studied elaboration of this brutally inverted
language—which was transmitted from Sallust to Tacitus, and which
links "empire" and "plunder" with the force of an irresistible mental and
linguistic automatism—it is impossible not to detect traces of some
kind of background ideology that went beyond the mere personality of
the two authors. Not a contradiction, in the modern dialectic sense of
the term, but rather the traumatic perception of the inevitable presence
of evil in the creation of empires—another echo of Thucydides, and at
the same time the first contact with what was turning out to be a less
laudable aspect of Roman history. And, significantly, it is only behind
the veil of a fictitious attribution—which mediates between the crude-
ness of the analyses and their true authors—that the economy finally
and suddenly seems to hold the explicit key to explaining the events of
the empire. It is portrayed as having a "diabolical" character, in which
the virtuousness of the conqueror is contaminated by business and
profits. In order to be expressed completely, this mode of thinking had
to be hidden behind the foreignness of an "other"—that is, behind the
façade of the condottieri of implacably inimical peoples. The old aristocratic mentality, which had become the imperial conscience, continued
to repress this kind of explanation for the basis of its own deeds.

But an inverted and foreign image was still able to reveal a truth, however partial. For the ancients, this could turn up in dreams and omens,
or sometimes in the calculated chaos of the festivals. In writing, the immediate source of the words had to be the mouths of the enemies, for
they were the only ones capable of illuminating, through the force of
their marginal and unshared reasoning, the dark side of the greatness of
the masters of the world.

Chapter Eight

Nobles and Merchants

(1)

The sea was the principal protagonist of ancient commerce, and the rivers and winds along with it. Water was the only possible means of conveying large quantities of bulk goods over long distances. "On ships with swift sails he often traveled the great sea"[1]—thus speaks a merchant in a precious epigraph in Brindisi (to cite one example chosen at random from many). And we read in Plato, "People sail for their own gain."[2] The "soft" technology of maritime transport (hulls, sails, rudders, knowledge of winds and currents) won out over the "hard" technology of overland transport (wheels, carts, yokes and beasts of burden, and difficult and costly road-building).

Here again, the ancient economy seems to have been more dependent on geography and anthropology than on history. Its mercantile side involved the coastal areas almost exclusively, linked to the distant Mediterranean relationship between men and the sea. When, from the end of the second century A.D., the axes of the empire shifted—the west (in demographic terms as well) toward the interior of Europe, and the other side toward Africa—the commercial networks were thrown into disarray: the fragile threads of large-scale exchange tended to break (though we must not underestimate the persistence of Mediterranean trade in late antiquity and the high Middle Ages), and the traditional dominance of agrarian relations began to take on overtones of feudalism.

With a river and a ford close by, and the sea and a port not much farther west, Rome enjoyed a privileged location. The city reaped profit from it at an early date, beginning with the archaic era; and it is indisputable that without the Tiber and Ostia, the whole course of Roman history would have been different.[3]

Nothing reveals the intensity of long-distance trade in the centuries of imperial expansion like underwater archeology. The coastal depths of the Mediterranean are an extraordinary involuntary museum of the material civilization of Europe: ships from the days of Augustus or Hadrian lie close to Venetian or Spanish galleys, medieval furnishings, and airplanes (Spitfires or Savoia-Marchettis) from World War II. Sand and rocks a few dozen meters underwater still preserve an incalculable number of Roman relics: hulls, often well preserved, nautical equipment, amphorae, a great variety of objects. This should not surprise us, for shipwrecks were a frequent event in ancient navigation. The technology of the times did not endow shipping with a high degree of safety. All it took for disaster to strike was a sudden storm, an unbalanced load, a minor oversight (not to mention pirates, at least in some eras).

Often it is possible to group by age—at least according to century— the remains of ships that have been located (about eight hundred so far, mostly off the Italian, French, and Spanish coasts, where the most careful searches have taken place).[4] If—in the absence of other plausible reasons to explain an increase or decrease in shipwrecks—we take the number of wrecks remaining from a period to be an indication of the number of voyages made during that time, we can describe a curve which, although it may not represent the absolute level of maritime traffic at this time, at least points to the fluctuations in the total number of sea voyages from one century to the next.

The results of this calculation show that the greatest concentration of the remains of Roman ships can be traced to the four hundred years extending from the second century B.C. to the second century A.D., with the highest density found in the middle of the period. After these four hundred years came a sudden drop (which is unlikely to have been fortuitous) corresponding to the crisis of the third century A.D. When Aristides claimed to be astonished that the sea was able to contain all the ships overflowing with goods that plied its waves in his day, his literary hyperbole was expanding on an actual fact: never before had the Mediterranean been so full of sails.

The merchant vessels of the ancients attained considerable capacity.[5] From the first century B.C. on, the usual dimensions were about four hundred tons: as far as the era of the Antonines is concerned, this statement is confirmed by a very precise text of the jurist Cervidius Scaevola[6] a few decades after Aristides (not to mention the archeological evidence which also supports it). And there is also the boat that Lucian describes: "What a huge ship! A hundred and twenty cubits long, the shipwright said, and well over a quarter as wide, and from deck to bottom, where it is deepest, in the bilge, twenty-nine. [. . .] She was said to carry corn enough to feed all Attica for a year."[7] Even the shipyards of Genoa and Venice in the fifteenth century did not build larger cargo vessels.

Obviously, not all markets were supplied by sea; we must also look at modes of land transport. The Romans were great road builders, from the famous via Appia—still extolled by Procopius in the sixth century A.D.[8]—to the via Ignatia, which extended eastward to the shores of the Bosporus, to the via Domitia, going west from Provence to Cádiz. But their use was essentially military. Actually, commercial land traffic was slow and expensive, suitable only for short distances; a cart pulled by oxen could rarely travel at more than three kilometers per hour, even on good roads. Cato tells us that the price of a certain item (an oil press) went up by about 60 percent because it had to be transported over a distance that could not have been much more than a hundred kilometers.[9] The situation did not improve with time. From Diocletian's edict on prices, at the end of the third century, we learn that the cost of a cartload of grain doubled after about four hundred kilometers of hauling, and that it was less onerous to ship foodstuffs clear across the Mediterranean than to transport them several hundred kilometers by road.[10] (Keith Hopkins has calculated that it may have cost as much as sixty times more to transport goods by land than by sea.)[11]

Even in the absence of banking and credit circuits comparable to those of the late Middle Ages, the commercial networks were supported by the ample circulation of money, which brought under a single regime if not the entire empire at least all of its wealthiest regions. A comparison of the data obtained from discoveries of coins in far-separated areas, from Britain to Syria, makes the existence of a pattern of uniform connections quite plausible. If we agree with the conclusions of Keith Hopkins[12] (which were based on Michael Crawford's numismatic research),[13] we can estimate that the number of silver coins in circulation in the period 80–50 B.C. must have been close to 500 million *denarii* (or 2 billion sesterces), a considerable amount in many respects. In all probability, this liquidity kept increasing, at least during the first century A.D.

Not all of these assets were used for the direct financing of commerce, and we cannot calculate precisely the velocity of their circulation. Nevertheless, there was enough liquidity to sustain a flow of trades that encompassed the entire imperial society. The hypothesis—propounded recently and supported by evidence which, although circumstantial, is still persuasive and elegant[14]—according to which generalized taxation fostered the growth of commerce should be considered valid in its broad outlines, at least in the long run. Indeed, the wealthiest provinces—from Spain to Egypt and Syria—were strongly urged to export their products in order to obtain enough money to meet their tax debts, although these were not very burdensome. In turn, the imperial government employed the proceeds of the tax collections to fulfill, also by means of the marketplace, its obligation to aid and manage the military and bureaucratic structures (when the direct transfer of contributions in kind was not sufficient), particularly in Italy (in the capital), and in the bordering provinces, where the largest part of the army was stationed.

A stable commercial network presupposed fairly widespread demand. Who, then, were the Roman consumers who depended on long-distance trade? Which items were desired? And what types of goods were available?

City dwellers were the primary consumers: residents of Rome first and foremost, then those of Carthage, Alexandria, Antioch, Ephesus, and other urban centers in Italy and the empire. Markets in antiquity—like their medieval and premodern counterparts—were always an urban phenomenon. As in all preindustrial societies, foodstuffs (grain, wine, and oil), the only products of truly mass consumption, were most in demand. If we assume that more than 80 percent of the labor force was permanently employed in agricultural work, and that a sizable portion of the overall yield was specifically reserved for the subsistence of farm workers, we can deduce that not more than 30 or 40 percent of the output—let us call it the "gross internal agricultural product" of the empire—was available for commercial use (an amount from which we must subtract the portion used for payment of taxes in kind, and the not insignificant amount used in growing certain crops—corn and cereals, for example—which was "reinvested" in the form of seeds). According to a hypothetical but reasonable estimate, this means that short-range commerce—the "elementary markets" of which Braudel speaks[15] (where products from the surrounding countryside were traded in a nearby city or small town)—must have involved at least one million tons of food-stuffs per year. And medium- and long-distance trading—which involved the large coastal cities for the most part—accounted for no less than 400,000 tons of produce, which can be valued at about 200 million sesterces, if we take the price of wheat, the most important commodity, as the point of reference. (It fluctuated around three sesterces per *modius,* that is, per 6.55 kilograms—a value that remained relatively stable during the first and second centuries A.D., not including the costs of transport.)

The share of the market occupied by manufactured goods was much smaller. Even if at the height of Roman Italy we can suppose that up to 30 percent of the labor force (which would be a record level for preindustrial societies) from Campania to the Cisalpina was employed in nonagricultural activities (such as handicrafts, slave workshops—both in the cities and in association with the *villae*—the extensive manufacturing of the Flavian and Hadrianic eras), in the empire as a whole the median could not have exceeded 15 to 18 percent. The products most in demand were amphorae for wine, table pottery (the so-called *terra sigillata* or "sealed earthenware," "black-glazed" ware from Campania, or "red-glazed" ware, usually from Arezzo), oil lamps, architectonic terracottas and other construction materials, textiles and hides for clothing, tools, implements, and various wooden, bronze, and iron objects. (The archeological remains of Pompeii offer a virtually complete selection of these.)

(2)

We see their Houses and Lodgings tolerably furnished, at least stuff'd well with useful and necessary household Goods: Even those we call poor People, Journey-men, working and Pains-taking People do thus; they lye warm, live in Plenty, work hard, and (need) know no Want. These are the People that carry off the Gross of your Consumption; 'tis for these your Markets are kept open late on Saturday Nights; because they usually re-

ceive their Week's Wages late. [. . .] In a Word, these are the Life of our
whole Commerce, and all by their Multitude: Their Numbers are not
Hundreds or Thousands, or Hundreds of Thousands, but Millions; 'tis by
their Multitude, I say, that all the Wheels of Trade are set on Foot, the
Manufacture and Produce of the Land and Sea, finished, cur'd, and fitted
for the Markets Abroad; 'tis by the Largeness of their Gettings, that they
are supported, and by the Largeness of their Number the whole Country
is supported; by their Wages they are able to live plentifully, and it is by
their expensive, generous, free way of living, that the Home Consumption is rais'd to such a Bulk, as well of our own, as of foreign Production.[16]

In this passage, which dates from 1728, still a few decades before the
great leap of the Industrial Revolution, Daniel Defoe depicted contemporary English commerce and the demand that stimulated it. Its features were Mandevillean: the first edition of the *Fable of the Bees* had
been published in 1714; the second would come out in 1729,[17] one year
after Defoe's essay. The coloring of Defoe's style could be described as
Hogarthian. His description might appear too optimistic, especially in
its appraisal of the conditions of the workers, who were about to endure
more than a century of suffering—the "social catastrophe" referred to
somewhat excessively by Karl Polanyi,[18] who saw it as the inevitable
result of the "satanic mills" he cited from Blake's verse.[19] In any case,
Defoe was purposely exaggerating, because we know that he tended to
heighten the economic advantages of widespread demand that was supported by fair salary levels. But the fact remains that he depicted a scene
that was anything but imaginary: in this century of great change, even
before the years that would give rise to the industrial transformation,
"when the servant-girls at the inns [could be] mistaken for ladies of condition, being very neatly dressed,"[20] the working class and the lowest levels of the urban bourgeoisie were now considered capable (and not by
Defoe alone) of consuming a broad variety of goods, in direct correla-
tion with the regularity of the salaries they earned. The demand they
created in the marketplace was deemed essential to the total wealth of
the country.

In the Roman world, even in the period of greatest mercantile development, we would not have found anything similar. But we must be cautious here, for the differences between the two eras were qualitative even

before they were quantitative, and did not exist only during the period approaching the Industrial Revolution.[21] In fact, the entire history of the late medieval and modern economies consisted of a series of changes which had transformed the means of production and distribution before they could succeed in expanding the overall quantity of available commodities beyond the Roman levels.

At the center of the European innovations was a different concept of the productivity of labor, linked to the virtually complete disappearance of slavery and the progressive strengthening of a labor-force market that was unknown to ancient societies: in Tudor England, more than half of all families probably received at least some of their income in the form of wages;[22] and this was certainly the case in the Hanseatic cities at the beginning of the seventeenth century.[23] A whole group of transformations was taking place: improvements in technology, institutions, laws, financial administration, and credit management; changes in mentalities and in the "capitalist" and productive role of urban centers. But it was only after the launch of industrialism, when the transformations were complete, that these discrete yet connected phenomena could be fully reflected in the form of an increase in the available quantities.

If we do not concentrate our attention on this qualitative leap—from slave labor to wage labor—we risk losing sight of the fundamental dissimilarity of the ancient and modern economies. When this happens, we are forced to deduce the differences from hypothetical scraps of quantitative data; and as a result we end up undervaluing the capacities of the Roman system (according to well-founded statements by Andrea Carandini[24] against Moses Finley and Richard Duncan-Jones), or believing that there were no differences at all. But the fact is that if the quantitative levels of their output were equal (for clarity, the term "gross national product" could be used here), or even if Rome still held the lead, the qualitative innovations in the more advanced European economies—in Italy, the Hanseatic cities, Flanders, and southern Germany—must be considered, from the late Middle Ages on, an unquestionable advantage.

Until at least mid-seventeenth-century Amsterdam, so expertly described by Simon Schama[25]—the city of Rembrandt, Spinoza, and the great sea-trade companies, the product of the Dutch miracle and the first real "globalization" of the economy—or, at the latest, until the Spanish empire of Philip II, the total wealth accumulated and produced in the various regions of Europe reached levels that were not too far from those of the ancient world. Nevertheless, from the twelfth century to the fourteenth the Italian economy of the urban revival and the "commercial revolution" was based on cultural, productive, and mercantile realities that were entirely different from those in ancient Rome: the Florence of the Bardi, the Peruzzi, and the great commercial and financial companies, the city that made it possible for the *Decameron* to be a kind of "mercantile epic,"[26] showed no resemblance to the Rome of Crassus or Sextus Clodius Phormio. And there was no disturbance among the plebs of Rome comparable to the Ciompi rebellion, which bore the early but unmistakable signs of class struggle—although a long time would pass before the results of the change could fully express the potential of the differences they were producing. It was only in the final, decisive transformation in England, which apparently exploded in the space of a few decades, that all of the innovations which had accumulated through centuries of growth and experiments (and also failures and crises) were ultimately translated into a spectacular quantitative leap.

When David Landes writes that the material existence of an English person in 1750 was closer to that of Caesar's legionaries than to the conditions under which that Englishman's own great-grandchildren would live,[27] we should not accuse him of exaggerating; otherwise, Gibbon's implicit comparison of the prosperity of the empire under the Antonines with that of his day, near the midpoint of the eighteenth century, would be thoroughly incomprehensible. But neither should we interpret Landes' opinion as an assertion that economic history had been frozen for a millennium. Rather, it should be understood as pointing to the extreme margin, where certain aspects of material life had indeed remained unchanged yet concealed impressive transformations. Under this uniformity was the coiled spring of a transmutation which, after long incubation and compression, was now on the verge of exploding. The world in which such comparisons were still possible was about to disappear forever. A great metamorphosis was on the point of obliterating it, incinerating it in a tremendous acceleration. In 1760, England still imported no more than 2.5 million pounds of raw (or semimanufactured)[28] materials for its cotton works, the cradle of the Industrial Revolution. Just one generation later, in 1787, the total had reached 22 million pounds. The later amount bore no relationship to any previous order of magnitude; but the earlier amount was not at all out of line.

Yet the range and capacity of the Roman commercial networks, even those from the period between the late republic and the early principate, should not be exaggerated. It is certain that the move toward mercantilization was a constant factor over the long term. But we can never be too cautious in evaluating the available data. First of all, we must keep in mind that these circuits were mostly used for the agricultural production of foodstuffs, not for manufactured goods. This is different from the situation in advanced economies, where an ever-increasing percentage of trade consistently involved the industrial sector (indeed, by the second half of the nineteenth century the level had reached about half of the total world commerce). Furthermore, we should not forget that the written sources—whether literary or epigraphic—transmit only the testimonies, reflections, and habits of the small number of people who were the most economically and socially advanced in the empire: the tip of the iceberg, where life was lived at the limits of what the whole system made possible. We must, therefore, avoid confusing consumption paid for by commodities and money with needs that were satisfied through other processes of distribution (and production)—both outside Italy or far from the big cities, and in Rome itself.

Moreover, we must also distinguish the presence of commodities and merchants in the Roman Empire from the institutionalized existence of markets of the modern sort, with their specialization and fluctuating prices, and, even more so, from that of an interdependent network of markets. The latter is a phenomenon that was not totally unknown in the Mediterranean of the Romans (for example, in the case of grain, wine, and slaves), but after a period of expansion during the late republic, its dimensions became fixed. (In short, Braudel is certainly more useful in interpreting this state of affairs than Karl Polanyi,[29] but his theories should be employed with caution.) And we must bear in mind that in addition to markets, mechanisms for the "administrative redistribution" of resources, which were dependent on the direct intervention of government power and the bureaucracy, operated on a large scale (and their importance grew over time). Many of Rome's food-supply needs were satisfied by this means.

In purely quantitative terms, all of the cities in the empire consumed a great deal: grain (as we have already discussed), wine, and oil. It is likely that the inhabitants of Rome in the first and second centuries A.D. drank no less than 1.5 million hectoliters of wine of varying quality per year, a level of consumption far exceeding 100 liters per capita. (In fourteenth-century Florence, consumption ranged from 248 to 293 liters.) Demand for wine in Rome was met almost entirely through the mechanisms of the open market.[30] This was not true of the demand for grain, which was fulfilled in part through *gratis* distributions. (In Augustan Rome, for example, a total of 200,000 people received 80,000 tons of grain per year. A special prefecture for the food office administered the program.) In any case, the various means of supply had to provide for a median individual consumption of more than 200 kilograms per year, for about one million residents.[31]

It is more difficult to gauge the need for oil; annual consumption is thought to have been no less than 320,000 *amphorae*, the equivalent of 22,000 tons.[32] Furthermore, there was a demand for luxury items—a demand which, although more limited, was exacting and quite regular: spices, meats, fish and other expensive foodstuffs, costly fabrics, elegant furniture, writing implements, products for lighting, medicines, perfumes, marble and other materials for high-quality construction, precious gold and silver objects for homes and personal adornment. It has been stated, for good reason, that the most difficult task of the imperial economy was to keep Rome properly supplied and fed; and we have seen how Aristides described the capital as the emporium of the world. Two centuries earlier, Sallust—not with purely apologetic intent—had already observed that "in Rome anything could be bought." Everything there had its price.[33]

To the rhetorician who had come from far-off Mysia, the sea did not seem large enough to contain all the merchant ships unloading their provisions for Rome at Ostia, or sailing up the Tiber to the anchorages of the Portus and the Emporium, at the foot of the Aventine hill. Many centuries later, standing before another river and another sea, a modern voyager would conceive the same idea as he contemplated a new urban miracle. For the young Engels, who had just arrived from Germany and who spent the years 1842–1844 restlessly and inquisitively roaming the streets of London ("a city in which one can wander for hours [. . .] without seeing the slightest sign of the approach of open country"), the sight of the Thames crowded with ships, which left free only "a narrow shipping lane in midstream," was an unforgettable experience: "I know of nothing more imposing than the view one obtains of the river when sailing from the sea up to London Bridge." And London revealed itself to him—just as Rome appeared to Aristides—as "the commercial capital of the world." The impressions of the modern observer are so similar in tone to those of the ancient one that they could almost be mistaken for the other's. For both Engels and Aristides, gazing at cities at the center of two extraordinary "world economies," amazement was the reward for the voyage, the ideal destination of their minds: "All this is so magnificent and impressive that one is lost in admiration. The traveler has good reason to marvel at England's greatness even before he steps on English soil." [34]

But there was an abyss between Defoe's satisfaction—or Engels' astonishment—and Aristides' admiration: what separated them was actually the distance between the ancient empire and the modern one. In all three observers we find the same giddy reaction to the sheer quantities before their eyes. Rome at the height of its expansion and London on the eve of the Industrial Revolution (cities virtually equal in population, among other things), or London a century later, at the peak of its transformation, must have appeared to them to be gigantic aggregations held together by superhuman forces. Yet we suddenly realize that the web of associations and ideas that runs through their observations is different. Defoe—and Engels, even more pointedly—were not voicing isolated expressions of wonder at the great volumes of commerce and consumption: their impressions led straightaway to the notion of the production that underlies and made these large quantities possible, and therefore to the economic process as an integrated cycle of production, distribution, and consumption. "And it is by their expensive, generous, free way of living, that the Home Consumption is rais'd to such a Bulk, as well of our own, as of foreign Production," wrote Defoe (and Mandeville and the classical economists would have agreed). For his part, Engels immediately transformed his amazement into impassioned indignation at the violence of the factory system that he had discovered lay behind the attainment of these gigantic dimensions. In Aristides, on the contrary, the sight of an accumulation of goods (and transport) that he considered equally immense immediately withdrew into itself: he was contemplating an inert quantity, not related to any kind of production but only the consequence of commerce and conquest, in that it was acquired by Rome solely by virtue of her unprecedented success in extending her political dominion. It was indeed an enormous concentration of goods; but its abundance was destined to conclude in a sterile consumption and an opulence that could only end with the profligacy of the privileged classes and the representation of unlimited political force.

In contrast, the moderns considered the production cycle and the expansion of markets—trade and industrial capital—to be connected by a very tight bond; these formed a single circuit that was capable of self-reproduction and continuous growth. As the ancients saw it, nothing united these things—they seemed to constitute two separate worlds; the expansion of trade seemed to be suspended in the void, and explicable only because of the political supremacy of Rome. No, the two empires were not equal.

(3)

The Industrial Revolution in England was triggered, in its ultimate stages, by a series of technological innovations whose effects reinforced one another in an unprecedented virtuous spiral. It succeeded in transferring the focus of production from agriculture to urban factories dominated by machines—an unprecedented shift, and one of incalculable significance. From that point on, no fundamental events in Europe would take place in the countryside. Although this radical change had a certain air of fortuitousness, it could have happened only at that time and in that place[35]—even if history often delights in hiding under the mask of chance the appointments it has prepared with the greatest care.

The new role played by mechanized urban factories resulted in another change of great importance: as the dominant figure in the production cycle, the capitalist entrepreneur-manufacturer replaced the landowner, the recipient of agrarian income—a protagonist who had long been on the scene, in all of his ancient and medieval variants. It is also possible that, in certain contexts, this change did not coincide with the advent of new classes but was induced by a transformation that was entirely internal to the old agrarian nobility—as Immanuel Wallerstein believes,[36] generalizing perhaps a bit too confidently. In any case, the new configuration had consequences of vast significance: in Europe—England, France, the Netherlands, and Germany—it ushered in the capitalist bourgeoisie, which from that point on was to govern the destinies of the Western world with its culture and dynamism. Production was dissociated from agrarian yield, and successfully integrated land, capital (both industrial and commercial), and labor—or, from another point of view, production, circulation, and consumption—in a single network of commodities and a sole chain of self-regulating markets. They became the segments of a self-sustaining series, stably centered on its own internal cycle. Everything that was produced was sold on the market, and all income was derived from sales, including that of the labor force. It was precisely this completeness, this well-ordered fluidity, that Defoe intuited in his description and that Engels saw plainly during his walks in the London suburbs. And the great works of classical economic thought, from Adam Smith to Karl Marx, flowed from an interpretation of these dynamics.

Nothing of the kind ever happened in the Roman economy. Here, the most important aspects of productive activities had always taken place in rural surroundings, within the framework of agrarian revenues. Comercial capital, although it had developed to a notable extent, never succeeded in breaking into the sphere of production—that is to say, it never became "industrial capital" in the strict sense of the term. It remained confined to a separate realm, as the simple mediator between surplus agricultural products (the ones not needed for the sustenance of the laborers) and the consumers of the surplus, who were concentrated in urban areas. And the great merchants never successfully established the financial and logistical foundations that would later be typical of the medieval "companies": they never developed a complete system of entrepreneurship and associations. The mechanisms of cooperation and concentration almost always remained foreign to them, and the promising model of the "publican society"[37]—propagated only during the late republican period—was not adopted outside the lone sector of tax collectors.

The dearth of archeological evidence is physical verification of the relatively limited scope of the Roman manufacturing base: in the entire territory of the empire, from the Rhine to the Euphrates, there is no trace of any cluster of remains that might have been comparable to a modern-day industrial area, or even to an eighteenth-century one.[38] Nor could extant parts of any ancient city be properly designated "industrial zones," although we should not minimize the value of the forms of production that may have taken place there (manufacturing in Pompeii, as Jongman reconstructed it, is a good example),[39] and it would be dangerous to presume that all the cities were parasitic, living on consumption alone. David Hume's old observation from a 1741 essay—"I do not remember a passage in any ancient author, where the growth of a city is ascribed to the establishment of a manufacture"[40]—remains difficult to contest. The growth of cities during the empire—so admired through the ages, from Aristides to Rostovtzeff—never succeeded in becoming a true "urban revolution" for the very reason that this indispensable productive base was lacking.

Despite the impressive amount of available goods, during the entire history of Rome a coherent industrial system never formed. It is easy to exaggerate the role of standardization in the fabrication of products—as evidenced, for example, in archeological discoveries such as ceramics. But these were the exceptions, not the rule. Industrial archeology is not a discipline that can be transferred from modern England to Roman Italy or Gaul.

The social consequences of the uninterrupted hegemony of the countryside, albeit in the presence of a significant mercantile economy, marked the course of the entire history of the empire. True bourgeois entrepreneurship in production never materialized in the Roman world. And the word "bourgeoisie" itself—so resonant with meaning in modern Europe—cannot properly be used in connection with any Roman class.[41] The concept may be useful to us in understanding the transformations of the late Middle Ages—in Florence, for example, or in Bruges or Antwerp—but it does not help us grasp the uniqueness of the ancients.

We can state that, from the second century B.C. to the era of the

Antonines and the "military principate" of the third century, the social history of the Roman Empire was marked by this absence: in the capital, the Italian municipalities, and the cities of the wealthy ring of provinces, the more (at certain times) the basis for a possible emergence of a bourgeoisie solidified, the more unfailingly its realization went astray. (In some ways, this state of affairs is reminiscent of czarist Russia in the eighteenth and nineteenth centuries, before the liberation of the serfs.) On at least one occasion, the score was quite close; we will return to the subject below.

The problem was not only economic in nature; it was also one of cultural evolution. Even in the most mature municipalities and provinces, the classes which began to emerge in the middle of the third century B.C. and whose activities were connected with mediation and commercial speculation, the administration of the exploitation of the provinces, and even elementary forms of financial activities—contractors, merchants, and "bankers" (some of whom are enthrallingly depicted in Cicero's letters and Sallust's history)[42]—were unable to dissociate the ultimate goal of their economic behavior from the model of wealth represented by agricultural revenues, or to distance themselves sociologically and intellectually from the magnetic field emanating from the agrarian aristocracy. In other words, they never managed to create for themselves an organizational and behavioral paradigm that was centered on productivity and reinvestment instead of on revenue. Acting quite often themselves as figureheads or confederates of noble families, they were never capable of constructing a set of strategies and choices, or establishing a system of values, that were independent from the aristocratic ones. People like the Buddenbrooks could never have lived in Rome; only parvenus ("new men") could, engaged in the struggle to attain minor nobility. People, that is, who had been freed from all routines of an economic nature, thanks to the stability of agricultural revenues.

Some modern historians have been so dazzled by the strongly individualistic features of the Roman society and mentality—in many juridical concepts and doctrines, for example—that they considered them to be at the very least forerunners of their bourgeois counterparts. But their perspective was misguided. Individualism was certainly an indisputable element in the self-representation of the dominant classes in Rome, but its origins had nothing to do with the genealogy of the bourgeoisie. It was derived instead from self-sufficient atavism—of which it constituted the fully developed cultural and moral heritage—together with the warlike and "heroic" attitudes of the early civic patricians. It was the reelaboration of an archaic character trait, not an anticipatory sign of either modernity or capitalist economic anthropology. As Paul Veyne correctly perceived, it was only a strategy on the part of the aristocracy to bring about the economic security and independence of landowners.[43]

The inevitable recycling of any accumulations of wealth back into the land was a result of the one-dimensionally aristocratic nature of all social ascent. The focus of upward social mobility and emulation of the modes of behavior of the elites was on achieving or imitating the standard of living of the Italian agrarian nobility—a constant that was diffused throughout the imperial world. A single figure thus firmly occupied the center of the economic stage: the aristocratic *rentier*. Large-scale commercial activity—when it was not a secondary function exercised for the benefit of the same landed nobility—occupied merely a transitional role in society, as a steppingstone toward the accumulation of agricultural assets. The history of Roman commerce—unlike that of medieval Florence or the Hanseatic cities or, later, Holland and England—was not a history of great mercantile dynasties. And in contrast to Italy in the late Middle Ages and the Renaissance, Rome produced no treatises on commerce, whereas it did produce some on agriculture (as we have already mentioned). The techniques of merchants were merely rough rules of thumb, unworthy of more dignified systematization. In Pliny's view, the expertise of both merchants (he uses the example of drapers) and farmers consists in circumstantial knowledge: they decipher signs in order to take best advantage of the proper moments (when to plant or when to sell).[44] But the peasant observes "his" land and "his" bushes to determine the temperature of the area from the falling leaves and thus calculate the right moment for sowing. His familiarity with the property—the intimacy between man and earth—enables him to venture his predictions. In contrast, the merchant—by definition a rootless person, a "migratory bird" (in the words of Columella),[45] a man who lives "between the waves and the seas"[46]—in order to make his forecast has no alternative but to consult the far-off and "insidious" stars (through a subtle play of semantic resonances, the word Pliny uses associates the state of mind of the observer with the quality of the object upon which he is rapaciously spying). In this way, the merchant scrutinizes the stars as if lying in wait, with the "avidity" proper to his profession, while the peasant, completely "unlearned in astronomy," pays them no heed at all.

Actually, only small-time traders, those who bought merchandise to resell it at retail, were generally viewed with such strong disapproval. Deceit and fraud seemed to be their only route to profit; as Cicero wrote, "they would get no profit without a great deal of downright lying."[47] But he himself (and Cato before him)[48] seemed to value "trade, [. . .] if wholesale and on a large scale, importing large quantities from all parts of the world and distributing to many."[49] This distinction was to survive throughout the Middle Ages and reach the threshold of modern Europe; it remained alive in seventeenth-century France in the difference between the great *négociants* and the small *marchands*.[50] The great merchants fed entire cities; after all, in Rome as in *ancien régime* Paris, they performed an essential civic function.[51] But in order to be truly valued, they eventually had to become *rentiers,* as Cicero affirmed without hesitation: "Nay, it even seems to deserve the highest respect, if those who are engaged in it [trade], satiated, or rather, I should say, satisfied with the fortunes they have made, make their way from the port to a country estate, as they have often made it from the sea into port. But of all the occupations by which gain is secured, none is better than agriculture, none more profitable, none more delightful, none more becoming to a freeman."[52] An honored position necessarily had to be connected with landholding.

The original scission between the market and the natural economy thus brought about a second division, between revenue and commercial capital—between production (both for direct consumption and for sale) and mercantile circulation. Even when these functions tended to find social expression through the same social classes, they remained intrinsically separate, not integrated into the same economic cycle. Where production was oriented toward exchange, and where distinct elements of "mercantile calculation" made their way into the management of slaveholding agricultural concerns, there was no sign of the transformation of commercial capital into industrial capital, through the reinvestment of profits. And despite the presence of considerable liquidity and accumulated wealth, the forms of production never assumed the appearance of an authentically capitalist agrarian or manufacturing organization.

The owner of land and slaves remained a rentier, never becoming an entrepreneur. In accord with Cicero's guidelines, the highest aspiration of the most important merchants throughout the empire, from Syria to Spain, was to convert their profits into land and take their place among the ranks of the lower nobility engaged in local careers, whose prestige seemed undisputed. Thus was perpetuated an insurmountable disjunction between the perpetuation of the "nonindustrial" characteristics of production and the stimulus of mercantile growth, which despite its strength was unable to impose its own rationality on the entire system of production.

The special significance of this scission was quite clear to both Weber and Karl Polanyi (to the latter, even to an excessive degree). But it was Marx once again who, in a draft written in the 1860s, gave it its first and perhaps most thorough expression.[53] He successfully linked the conditions of existence of capital in the ancient world with the fact that it had been restricted solely to the sphere of the circulation of commodities: between this sphere and the apparatus of production he found the same alienation and reciprocal indifference that, as we have seen, marked the entire "dual" system. ("Because commercial capital is confined to the sphere of circulation, and because its sole function is to mediate the exchange of commodities, no further conditions are needed for its existence [. . .] than are necessary for the simple circulation of commodities and money.")[54] The dualism of the Roman economy was now clarified through the mirror of a reconstruction in which theory and history illuminated each other. The inability—in social, cultural, and economic terms—of commercial capital to embrace the world of production completely, and to transform itself into industrial capital, was the insurmountable obstacle that prevented landed proprietors and merchants from becoming true capitalist entrepreneurs, and opened a qualitative chasm between the Roman forms and the modern developments of the European economy.

Although this intrinsic weakness made a true leap forward impossible, it did not immediately cause stagnation. Instead, it brought about a phenomenon that could be defined as "closed development" or "growth without modernization." During the long period of imperial peace, the Romanized aspect of the Italian landscape—with cities, *villae*, large estates, vineyards, olive groves, orchards, and cultivated fields of grain and cereals—proliferated throughout the territory of the empire. And the profits accruing to agricultural concerns from the commercialization of their products reached considerable dimensions: an annual return-on-investment of approximately 6 percent, even 10 percent in some years, according to the calculations of Duncan-Jones, which were based on reports from Columella and Pliny.[55] If we also keep in mind the amount of resources concentrated in Rome through the exploitation of the provinces, it would seem that in purely quantitative terms there was enough wealth, over a long enough time, to have given rise to modes of accumulation that could have been transformed into a first wave of capitalism. Evidently, the problem lay elsewhere.

But far from multiplying the number of investments and technological improvements, the availability of wealth triggered considerable unproductiveness and waste. The disintegration of ideals and ethics that might accompany affluence had long been the nightmare of part of the ruling class, who were always aware of this danger—the dark side of opulence and imperial power. From Cato to Sallust, and from the late-republican legislation against extravagance to the moralist poets of the first century A.D., many believed that behind the accumulation of wealth—which was, however, never forsworn for its own sake—constantly lay the risk of secret evil that corrupted the soul. There was never the least hint of what was to become the proto-capitalist ethic of reinvestment, productivity, and business.

The labor forces at the very heart of the empire were the first to be dispersed. The transformations in agriculture, with the regular and increasingly intensive use of masses of slaves, had removed an ever-growing number of citizens from the countryside of Italy. As we have seen, part of this now-surplus labor served as fodder for the war machine. Beginning with the first century B.C., long-term or very long-term professional soldiers occupied the same position in the sociology of power as the peasant farmers in the old republican orders; they formed the base of the entire military apparatus, and were at the same time a decisive component in the formation of political consensus. And from the

Severan age on, the entire constitutional aspect of the principate was to assume the features of a complex "military monarchy."

But for the most part what the new economic reality meant was the pure and simple disbanding of the labor force; pushed out of the system of *villae* and large estates, laborers were unable to find other regular and stable roles. According to the calculations of that slave-dependent society, it cost less to feed those men (and their families) in Rome, as utter parasites, than to make use of their labor in some productive way. Thus was created an extensive band of primarily urban structural unemployment and marginalization, right in the center of the empire, to which the political authorities were forced to designate a considerable share of resources, in the form of both foodstuffs and services (games, spectacles, housing)—the "bread and circus" described in a deservedly famous book.[56] The survival of those masses, composed of citizens of the dominant world power, depended on nothing more than their ability to sell their political endorsement. And they did this with great success during the entire late republican period—after the Social War—and later, in other ways, throughout the whole imperial era. They constituted an amorphous and unstable throng, ready to take maximum advantage of the precious revenue of its political position, moved by elemental psychological mechanisms: a knife always pointed at the throat of established power—but a force that, in the beginning, the principate knew how to exploit with consummate skill and rationality.

Marx's paradigm explains another peculiarity of the Roman economy. In modern industrial production, due to the continuous movement among production, circulation, and consumption, the capitalist dynamic always has a cyclical configuration in which "presuppositions which originally appeared as conditions of its becoming" are transformed into the "results of its presence,"[57] and the entire circuit, thanks to this circularity, seems perfectly capable of self-sufficiency (in keeping with the kinds of reciprocities sensed by Defoe and analyzed by the classical economists). In the ancient system, on the contrary, the circulation of commercial capital was unable to sustain itself or to control the conditions of its own existence. In order to reproduce itself, it constantly needed new inputs from external sources. In this world "the extremes between which commercial capital mediates are given, so far as it is concerned, just as they are given for money and its movement. The only thing necessary is that these extremes should be present as commodities, whether production is over its whole range commodity production or whether it is merely the surplus from producers who work to satisfy their own direct needs that is put on the market. Commercial capital simply mediates the movement of these extremes, the commodities, as preconditions already given to it."[58] And again, in a text from a few years before: "At no point did the process ignite from within; rather, the presuppositions of money circulation lay outside it, and it constantly required a new push from the outside. [. . .] Value as such did not sustain itself in and through circulation as predominant over the process of its transformation [. . .]; nor was the *use value* itself (as is the case in the capital production process) produced by the *exchange value*. With capital, the consumption of the commodity is itself not final; it falls within the production process; it itself appears as a moment of production— i.e., of *value-positing*."[59]

One of the external elements that commercial capital did not succeed in transforming into the form of commodities (one of the "preconditions" of its formation, which were not successfully transformed into "results" of its existence) was slave labor, which was indispensable for the creation of the majority of goods put on the market. In this case, the slaves themselves, both as persons and as producers, were a "commodity"—the commodity was not just their labor, which, being inseparable from the men and women who provided it, in fact had no value of its own (as we shall see).

Yet slaves were a special kind of commodity: they could be bought and sold, but (as we have already said) they could not be "produced," as slaves, by the economic system. If the availability of a labor force does not depend on a contract, a market-based exchange, but rather is regulated by extramercantile constraints, it is no longer an element intrinsic to the economic cycle. It serves as an external and independent variable—an uncontrollable precondition, but one on which both the organization of production and the circulation of other commodities indissolubly depend. And it is to the heart of this connection that our account now takes us.

Chapter Nine

Slaves, Nature, Machines

I. Ancient and Modern Slavery

(1)

In the year A.D. 61, during Nero's principate, Rome was rocked by a sensational crime, an *insigne scelus*, as Tacitus wrote in his account of the episode.[1] L. Pedanius Secundus, a prefect of the city (probably since A.D. 56), a consul in A.D. 43, and one of the best-known politicians in the capital, was murdered by a slave in his house in the middle of the night. Pliny mentions that during his magistracy an owl had entered the *cella* of the Campidoglio—a bad omen.[2]

The Pedanii were Romans from Spain (their name perhaps indicates Etruscan origin) who lived in Barcelona, in Tarraconensis. A family of high position and power in the heart of the empire, it was among those that were closest to the court. One of its members, Cn. Pedanius Fuscus Salinator, a consul in A.D. 118 together with Hadrian, was to marry Hadrian's niece Julia before mysteriously disappearing from the scene.[3]

Like many other members of western provincial elites who came to Rome during the first century, L. Pedanius Secundus lived lavishly, emulating and exceeding the ostentation of the old Italian aristocracy—nobles like Licinius Sura, who resided in a very elegant house on the Aventine next to the Temple of Diana, or Valerius Asiaticus, who had bought the gardens of Lucullus, or Julius Vestinus, whose palace overlooked the Forum. In his apartments, Pedanius had had four hundred slaves at his service[4]—an enormous number, even in those days. And it was within his home that the motives for the crime had crystallized. Opaque and scandalous, they are hinted at circumspectly in the

Annales.[5] Perhaps they arose from a broken promise—a freedom capriciously revoked—after a price had been agreed upon by slave and master; or, even worse, from a secret love triangle involving the killer and the victim, who were competing for a certain boy's favors.

Almost certainly on the initiative of the prince himself, the senate arrogated the trial to itself by exercising its jurisdictional competence.[6] Tacitus was in a position to report on its progress and results by consulting the proceedings of the sessions, as he had permission to do.

According to the Senatus Consultum Silanianum of A.D. 10, an ancient ordinance that was upheld during the Augustan era,[7] when a master was the victim of a homicide all of the slaves who lived with him were to be tortured and then put to death. The terrible "reasonableness" of the regulation—"slaves are a very difficult possession," wrote Plato in the sixth book of *Laws*[8]—is reflected again in Ulpian's detached prose, as he comments on it two centuries later: "Since no house could otherwise have been made secure, if not by forcing the slaves under the threat of death to defend their master both from dangers within the dwelling place and from those outside it."[9] An implacable objective responsibility rested on the shoulders of the slaves, compelling them to become utterly ferocious guardians of their lords; they vouched with their lives for the success of their vigilance.

But following the letter of the law would lead to fearful consequences in the case of the death of Pedanius. Hundreds of slaves lived in the same apartments as the murder victim ("under the same roof,"[10] in the words of the decree). It would be necessary to resort to mass torture and executions, and the certain sacrifice of a large number of innocent people ("without guilt," as Tacitus wrote).[11] Even if it was suspected that the killer had not acted alone and the accomplices had organized a true slave conspiracy, this indiscriminate punishment would still strike a large number of slaves who, even if they had been extremely zealous, could not possibly have known about or prevented the criminal plan. Among them were certainly women and children.

In order to save these unlucky people and exert pressure on the senate, even the urban plebs was mobilized to action, and almost to revolt. This kind of behavior was absolutely unprecedented, because as a rule no one fraternized with slaves—especially the lowest social strata, who thronged the arenas where gladiators were periodically massacred. But in the course of their work, many of Pedanius' imperiled slaves must have had opportunities to establish relationships, to strengthen ties of friendship and everyday business dealings, to make themselves known and appreciated. These were connections that meant something in the social fabric and the daily routines of the common people who crowded the imperial metropolis, the swollen body of Rome. To execute these slaves would unsettle and ravage the district, the lives of hundreds (perhaps thousands) of families, the entire area. It would deal an intolerable blow to the rhythms and equilibria of the city.

Even among the senators, a faction supported leniency. According to a likely hypothesis, the presence of Sempronius Proculus—a prominent jurist with close ties to the court, a friend of Seneca's, and the author of very important works—helped to buttress its ranks. A less violent solution would probably not have displeased the emperor himself, perhaps also because it would have propitiated the plebs, the precious ally of the ruler. Furthermore, these were the final months during which Nero had Seneca at his side, who, in the forty-seventh letter to Lucilius, would later propose—though in a purely literary, hypothetical manner—a less intransigent model for master-slave relations.

On the day the case was decided, Gaius Cassius Longinus, the other great jurist of the era, rose to speak in the senate. A descendant of Q. Aelius Tubero and Servius Sulpicius Rufus, he had been born into an ancient aristocratic family and raised on prorepublican values. After the upheaval of A.D. 62, he would be banished to Sardinia (then recalled to Rome by Vespasian). His would be an epoch-marking oration.[12] Tacitus reported its essential points reliably, in direct speech.[13] Here, roughly, is what he said:

A consular officer, a prefect of the city, has been murdered in his own house, through a conspiracy of his slaves. If you decide to grant impunity for a similar crime, who will ever be able to feel safe, if neither holding very high office nor owning a large number of slaves was enough for Pedanius Secundus? Our fathers—to whom we owe the regulation whose application is now being discussed—always distrusted the nature of slaves, even those who had been born in their own fields and in their houses, and who from infancy had been raised in the affection of their masters. And now can we, whose slaves hail from a great diversity of peoples, practicing religions and following customs very far from our own (when they are not totally atheistic)—can we keep them in check through any other means than by resorting to terror? "It is true that, because of this, innocent people will be sacrificed; but every exemplary punishment always contains an element of injustice, which is carried out on individuals in the name of the utility of the entire people." No one dared to offer a rebuttal to the words of the jurist—not Seneca (so far as we know), and even less the prudent Proculus (whose entire life failed to earn him a single line in Tacitus), although—as a proponent of the theory that the use of law should be characterized by equity—he was probably the target of Cassius' lapidary remark on the harsh relationship between individual injustice and the collective good. The death sentence was therefore pronounced and executed. The rioting plebs was kept at bay by the army, then silenced by a threatening edict issued by the prince.

Despite the prominence of the persons involved, this episode was not a major historical event. It was little more than an unremarkable news item in the difficult years of Nero's principate, just before Burrus' death and Seneca's disgrace. It is likely that the only reason for Tacitus' report is that it offered him an opportunity to relate the speech of Cassius, whose Sallustian accents must have pleased him.

Nevertheless, without wishing to exaggerate the importance and meaning of this episode, we must note that it is difficult to find any ancient source that more vividly brings to life—in all of its social, institutional, and mental particulars—what Roman slavery was, and how its most deep-rooted aspects were manifested. Even in a situation rendered extreme by the number of clearly innocent victims, and where no great economic or political interests were directly affected and no problem of public order loomed, it was enough simply to raise the specter of a possible relaxation of the bond of terror supposedly linking slaves to their masters for an irresistible conditioned reflex of total coercion and domination to be triggered in the majority of the 900 senators. These men were certainly not bloodthirsty; rather, they were realistic and prudent. But in a world—a civilization—which was based on the daily unconditional dependence of millions of slaves, and which still remembered the nightmare of the terrible spread of revolts at the end of the republican era, they firmly believed that the exercise of the ancient aristocratic virtues—the very same prudence and realism—could also require them, in certain cases, to ordain a cold-blooded massacre.

(2)

It is difficult to doubt that Roman society between the Punic Wars and the century of the Antonini was a slave-based society. Often, for various reasons, the "ideologies of the moderns" (to use one of Finley's expressions) have tried to mask this incontestable evidence. And many have done their best to temper the historical record, and to prevent the pure image of the "classical" world, which was to a large extent their own literary invention, from being sullied by a stain of this kind.

But even if we consider only the quantitative evidence, the least hesitation would be unthinkable. It is believed that in the Augustan years, at the end of the first century B.C., at least 35 percent of the entire population of Italy consisted of slaves—about 2 million (3 million, according to a possibly more accurate conjecture). And this impressive number and very high proportion was maintained for more than a century.[14] Moreover, slave labor had a major effect on the quality and performance of the system of production: without the presence of slaves in agriculture, manufacturing, and the service functions, the economic and administrative spheres of the empire would never have reached the levels described in the foregoing chapters.

To be sure, outside Italy the situation was different, and we cannot expect the proportion of slaves to have been equally high at the distant borders of the empire. Nevertheless, numbers aside, the presence of a considerable slave population can be clearly traced in Sicily (we will discuss this shortly), Cisalpina, Africa, the mineral-rich regions of Spain and Greece (in strong concentrations), Gaul, especially in the southern areas, and almost all of the eastern provinces. The large coastal cities had especially high numbers. In Roman-era Alexandria, there were more than 100,000 slaves (about 25 percent of the total population, according to Malowist's careful calculations).[15] And as late as the fourth century A.D., rich citizens in Antioch owned 1,000–2,000 slaves each. There is no reason to believe that the situation was very different in Carthage or Marseilles.

Other societies at various times have made regular use of slavery. Slaves were present almost everywhere along the coasts of the Mediterranean during the first millennium B.C., but it was only in Athens in the fifth and fourth centuries B.C. that slavery reached levels comparable to those in imperial Italy—yet in a much smaller area, and therefore with smaller actual numbers (not to mention other differences).

We can also look outside the ancient world. If we disregard the Western Middle Ages for the moment, the case of the Americas immediately comes to mind. After their conquests, the Europeans built several societies on the basis of forced labor, importing slaves from western Africa in order to make up for the lack of manpower—the Portuguese and Spaniards in Brazil and the Caribbean, and the English in North America, where the system survived the formation of the United States and the constitutional principles of the "Founding Fathers." It would take another eighty years to abolish it, and a harsh civil war.

Of all the instances of modern-day slavery, those in North America have been the ones most passionately investigated in contemporary research, especially by historians in the United States. Thanks to a rich collection of available documentation, ranging from statistics to folklore and oral tradition (evidence that unfortunately is lacking in the case of slavery in antiquity), one can safely say today that the North American case offers the best known and most fully analyzed system of slavery in all of human history.

The flood of research, which in recent decades has produced an immense bibliography, has become a symbol of the new civil conscience in America. The attention given to this subject stems from various causes: the need for information about a great national question, which Tocqueville had already identified as the most important problem the United States would face in the future, and which resurfaced dramatically in the second half of the twentieth century thanks to the struggle for civil rights; the cultural and political necessity of closely examining the historical identity of Africans in America; and, not least, the twists and turns of an intense methodological debate. Indeed, since the end of the 1960s, slavery has been the preferred research topic for the controversial studies in "quantitative" history (the field of "cliometrics," of which Robert Fogel's work represents perhaps the best known and most thought-provoking example).[16]

The broadening of the knowledge base has had significant consequences, enabling researchers to modify stereotypes that had been fossilized since the years of the abolitionists, with the writings of Frederick Law Olmsted[17] and John Elliot Cairnes.[18] Many commonplaces, originally born from the need to denounce uncompromisingly, on the basis of the data then available, the ethical and social degradation caused by an appalling practice, had later turned into obstacles to the proper understanding of the slaves' true output and of the way in which their cultural autonomy resisted the homologizing pressure of their masters.

The new scholarship has revived an old historiographic problem. To what extent can the observation of modern conditions aid in understanding ancient phenomena? In other words, can American slavery shed light on Roman slavery? Henri Wallon, the first great scholar of Greek and Roman slavery, had no doubts: his *Histoire de l'esclavage dans l'antiquité* (History of Slavery in Antiquity), published in Paris in 1847,[19] opens with a long introduction on "slavery in the colonies," and is filled with references to official reports by the colonial councils of Martinique and Guadeloupe. More recently, even Moses Finley has taken the same tack, though somewhat cautiously. But is this position still valid, given the new information that has been uncovered (which Finley himself, to the extent that he could have known and used these findings, seems to have overlooked completely)?[20] Can we confidently make use of the new perspectives on North American slavery to modify the way we interpret Roman or Athenian slavery?

In broad terms, the answer cannot but continue to be positive: the nature of historical thought is intrinsically analogical and depends upon confrontation and comparison. On certain important questions dealing with the productivity of slave labor, we will see that recent American research can prove valuable for historians of antiquity. But the seductiveness of some comparisons cannot hide an essential difference that must not be overlooked: the contrasting role of the two systems in the economies of their eras.

Modern slavery, which was entirely colonial in origin—in Brazil, the Caribbean, and the American South—took hold and became established for particular reasons (the scarcity of manpower in the New World and the contemporaneous settlement of Europeans along the coast of West Africa) in rural areas that were relatively peripheral, if not actually marginal, to the more industrial heart of the new European and American economies. In these areas the slave system faced problems of compatibility with the much more expansive and dominant mode of production that was based exclusively on wage labor.

In contrast, the Roman system of slavery, insofar as its achievements and organization were concerned, represented by far the most advanced and unifying economic form found in any ancient civilization. From the standpoint of production, no real alternative to it ever existed, either in theory or in practice. It was truly the force that propelled the entire Mediterranean economy. The great theoretical minds of the Greek and Roman world, from Plato and Aristotle to the jurists of the age of the Severi, considered it a social necessity, consistently referring to it as conforming to a "rule of nature" or, in any case, as a universally accepted principle, as did the Roman philosophers and jurists who distanced themselves from the more ancient model. Here, as is often the case in history, the tendency to assume that the basic mechanisms of the dominant economic system of one's own time are inviolate laws acts as an invincible cultural force. And this explains in part why almost all the schools of ancient ethics—including Christian ethics, ranging from the precepts of Paul to those of Augustine and the bishops of the fourth and fifth centuries[21]—could accept this institution without too much discomfort, taking it for granted that human beings should be divided into masters and slaves, and that those in bondage could be constrained to the point where they were completely denied the right not only to determine their own actions and destiny, but even to control their own bodies.

Recognizing the diversity of positions helps us to place the comparison in its proper perspective, and to avoid new distortions that an updating of it would in turn provoke. The most important advantage that scholars of ancient history gain from this comparative approach is that it dissolves the aura of irrationality, inefficiency, and primitivism in which many modern interpretations have enveloped classical forms of slavery. Instead, we have learned that, moral judgments aside, a system of slavery can under certain conditions (thanks mostly to the abilities of the slaves themselves) be the expression of a functional arrangement and an internal logic which, from the point of view of production, make it very different from a mechanism in a state of permanent crisis. To be sure—and we have already said this—slavery is always "a total social fact"[22] and cannot be reduced to its purely economic consequences. It has a long-term social, cultural, and institutional impact on the entire environment in which it develops. But we must measure and evaluate its economic aspects for what they are, without introducing extraneous elements into the analysis that can distort its meaning.

The traditional view of American slavery was based on five foundation stones of historiography which remained virtually fixed from the end of the nineteenth century to the 1940s, from James Ford Rhodes[23] to Richard Hofstadter:[24] investing in slaves was, if not doomed to failure, at least highly risky; slave labor was economically inefficient; slavery had caused the stagnation (or at least the slower growth) of the Southern economy before the Civil War; the living conditions of the slaves were generally extremely harsh; the system was headed for rapid demise in any case, war or no war. Even Ulrich Bonnel Phillips' famous book *American Negro Slavery* (1918),[25] which was long given excessive importance, contested only one of these points, substantially accepting all of the others. (The one with which Phillips disagreed was that the living conditions of the slaves were oppressive. He substituted an almost idyllic image of the treatment of slaves on Southern plantations—an image which was subsequently repeated even in the works of Eugene Genovese.)[26]

But a wave of new research led to the overthrow of the old interpretation. Kenneth M. Stampp's well-received 1956 book[27] can be considered the first of the new line, which continued with studies by Alfred Conrad and John Meyer, and later with Robert Fogel and Stanley Engerman's *Time on the* Cross (1974) and Robert Fogel's monumental four-volume *Without Consent or Contract* (1989–1992), though these works took different approaches.[28] According to the new thesis, investing in slaves was in no way a bad business decision; indeed, it was often a profitable activity.[29] Slave labor was far from inefficient: in 1860, agriculture in the Confederacy was about 35 percent more productive than agriculture in the Union states, and manufacturing in the South, which used slave labor, was 40 percent more efficient than that in the North, which used wage labor. The slaves were not at all lazy, indolent, and unfit, as the traditional racist stereotype alleged; on the contrary, their work was reliable, diligent, and intelligent. And they proved to be successful in more than just the usual agricultural activities, for those who worked in the urban factory system compared favorably to wage laborers; and the demand for slave labor in Southern cities was growing, not declining.

As for the stagnation alleged by earlier historians, from 1840 to 1860 per-capita income increased more rapidly in the Southern states than in the rest of the country. Their growth rate was equal to that of Italy just before the Second World War. And the living conditions of the slaves in the first half of the eighteenth century were, on average, no worse than those of wage-earning industrial workers in the United States or England. In sum, according to the new argument, slavery was not on its deathbed at the beginning of the Civil War. Indeed, all indications seemed to point in the opposite direction: Southern property owners believed they were on the eve of an unprecedented age of well-being and prosperity.

The components of this reconstruction are not all equally persuasive. For example, its conclusions about the long-run functioning of slavery perhaps do not sufficiently filter out the short-term effects of the extremely positive trends of the cotton market in the middle years of the nineteenth century. But to go into particulars on each point would take us too far from our primary subject. In any case, the overall assessment is difficult to contest: when American slavery was eliminated by Lincoln and the aftermath of the Civil War, it did not lack competitive capacity, vitality, or a promising future. In their desire to denounce the horrors of slavery, old-style abolitionist historians ended up unwittingly reproducing a racist mode of thinking. They preserved a portrait of inefficiency and maladjustment that inevitably slipped from criticizing the unfairness of the relationships of dependence to underrating the true attitudes and the concrete work of the men and women constrained by this bondage. Rejection of the system of slavery became underestimation of the virtues and talents of the slaves.

To be sure, the opposite risk is also present: a frankly positive appraisal of the performance of slave labor can, if considered superficially or maliciously, appear to some extent as an ambiguous justification of this system—an "apology for centuries of exploitation," as Fogel says.[30]

And it is no coincidence that he feels it necessary to end his work by updating the reasons for denouncing slavery. Condemnation remains imperative, obviously, but it must take into account the conclusions to which the revisionists have arrived. In Fogel's words, what is called for is "a modern indictment."[31]

But a different question is of more interest to us: To what extent does the discovery of a case of clear compatibility between slavery and modern capitalist development (which is the underlying conclusion here) force us to take another look at the idea that production by means of slaves can lead only to a negative appraisal of the quantitative potential of all ancient economic systems, in particular the Roman one? Or, from a different perspective, can the reappraisal of the economy of the American South be expanded to the point of calling into question the equation between the increased use of free labor and the strengthening of capitalism, which thanks to long tradition we are accustomed to considering the economic foundation of modernity?

(3)

The cost of a slave in imperial Rome was not high. Between the late republic and the early principate, prices remained relatively stable, fluctuating between 1,000 and 2,000 sesterces (1,000 sesterces was also the sum necessary to buy one *iugerum* of land suitable for a vineyard in Italy, according to Columella).[32] But it was not unheard of to find much higher prices, even as high as the 700,000 sesterces it cost to purchase a "slave grammarian,"[33] as Pliny relates. But that must have been an exceptional case.

When we consider the size of many estates in Italy and the provinces, which in that same period might easily be worth tens of millions of sesterces,[34] we can imagine how common it must have been for the ruling classes to assemble organizations consisting of several hundred subordinates. Clearly, the example of Pedanius Secundus was anything but an isolated one.

The slave trade was one of the most successful commercial activities of the Roman Mediterranean. In the second and first centuries B.C., the golden age of imperial slavery, an unprecedentedly high level of supply was maintained by the virtually uninterrupted sequence of victorious wars of conquest (thousands upon thousands of prisoners were sold to merchants following in the wake of the troops, then resold at higher prices) and the indefatigable activities of full-scale bands of pirate slave-traders—the same ones who, having become too powerful and a danger to navigation, were eradicated by Pompey. The port of Delos (on the island sacred to Apollo) was perhaps the largest marketplace; according to Strabo, up to 10,000 prisoners could be sold there in a single day.[35]

Ships and the sea appear often in the history of slavery. An instruction manual for captains employed in the slave trade, written in Great Britain at the end of the eighteenth century (at the height of the English support of slavery), prescribed in microscopic detail—with the obvious aim of defining the limits of the contractual responsibility of the transporter—the space which every prisoner had to be given during the ocean crossing: for men, an area measuring six feet by one foot four inches; and for women, an area five feet ten inches by one foot four inches. In the two drawings that accompany the instructions (to make things clearer), the slaves are shown lying on their backs in the hold, in positions they must have had to maintain during weeks and weeks of sailing. In these chilling stylizations, they look like tin soldiers in a box: bodies are tightly packed, herring-bone style, between the two lateral rows (in which the slaves lie perpendicular to the sides of the ship) and the central row (in which the men and women are parallel to the walls). Not a single millimeter of space is wasted. Clear strokes of the pen, rational use of layout and image, premeditated and relentless annihilation of the victims' humanity: in short, the archeology of the concentration camp.[36]

It would be hard to imagine that Roman slaves fared any better—though the distances they traveled were shorter, the ships were smaller, and keeping transport costs to a minimum was likewise necessary. Evidence of a few solitary cases has survived in Labeo and Ulpian—a mother, a daughter, a death. Obviously, they were mentioned only for juridical reasons.[37]

There were other modes of servile subjugation in the Mediterranean world, in addition to chattel slavery (that is, slaves who were subject to unlimited sale and resale, like any other goods or domestic animals). At the same time—and in certain respects before that time—Greek society engaged in a different form of dependence, which is known as "Helot." (Its name connects it with Sparta, but it existed throughout the Doric area.) Here, the bondage originated with the voluntary submission of a group or an entire population, who entrusted themselves to their victors in return for sustenance and protection. In this type of subordination—which was described by Theopompus in the fourth century B.C.[38] and later by Posidonius (as we shall see)—the captives could not be sold. The very term "slave" was not really applicable to them, as we read in the sixth book of Athenaeus' *Deipnosophistai*,[39] which presents an entire list of known forms of bondage, none of which are comparable to the model of chattel slavery.[40]

The latter type, which according to an ancient tradition was first practiced on the island of Chios,[41] and which according to Timaeus[42] (with whom Polybius disagreed)[43] did not originate in Greece, established itself in Corinth and Attica. But only in fifth-century Athens, as the city grew into a mercantile and imperial power, did it become the dominant form—and already Herodotus recalled the time when the Greeks did not own slaves as being far in the past.[44]

In Roman society as well, the practice of using chattel slaves spread at a relatively late date—not before the third century B.C., as we have seen. But it met with instant success, eclipsing the level of slavery in classical Athens. The reasons for its overwhelming appeal can be identified if we recall a coincidence that we have already discussed from a different angle. The conquests had opened up vast rural territories to the Romans, extending from Cisalpina to Sicily and into Africa and Spain. But at the same time, the constant wars and their consequences for the accumulation and distribution of wealth had socially ruined (and politically weakened) the class of farmer-landowner-soldier, the sort of men whose solidarity had made possible such great success for the republic. Paradoxically, they were prevented from enjoying the fruits of their own victories. It is likely that the crisis also had significant demographic effects, besides the well-known mass uprooting and flight to the cities. Indeed, the rural areas conquered by the Romans proved to be dramatically empty, facing a structural need for low-cost manpower, which the progressive concentration of landholdings into *villae* and large estates made even more acute in regions ranging from Campania to Etruria to Sicily.

But during the same decades, wars (and pirates) had also produced an unprecedented number of slaves: hundreds of thousands, and millions certainly in the second and first centuries, if we consider the 150,000 Epirotes brought to Rome in 167 B.C.,[45] or the one million Gauls captured by Caesar in his expeditions, according to Appian and Plutarch.[46] These slaves constituted an almost unlimited reserve of labor, which could be transported easily from one end of the Mediterranean to the other as required. Thus, circumstances combined to form an invincible force, against which the efforts of the Gracchi were futile.

In Plutarch's account—which relates the content of a letter written by the younger of the two brothers—while crossing Etruria on a trip to Numantia, Tiberius Gracchus was horrified to see "the desolation of this countryside" and to realize "how the farm work and the pasturing of the flocks was entrusted to barbarian slaves." These sentiments gave rise to his reform project. "The wild beasts who inhabit Italy all have dens or holes in which to rest," he wrote, "but those who fight and die for Italy have nothing but the air and the daylight. [. . .] They fight and die to defend the wealth and luxuries of others, and they are called the rulers of the world, while they do not have even a clod of earth to call their own."[47]

The slavetraders, pirates, and victorious generals were not the ones who invented the new agrarian order. The arrangement was a result, originally quite independent, of a different sequence of events which were primarily political and military. The demand had preceded the supply, so to speak. But from at least the latter half of the second century, it was slavery that supported the economy of the countryside and made production profitable for the marketplace; and this led to the vertiginous demand for ever new supplies of servile labor. Slaves, as Diodorus wrote, were now bought by whole gangs.[48]

The growth of Roman commerce thus weighed almost entirely on the new organization of labor. The more this system took hold, the more the slaves ended up paying the price. They were commodities—often branded with fire, as if they were ceramics—producing other commodities in an endless circle.

The reification of bodies was accompanied by violent coercion exercised with cold technical precision. In Italy there existed commercial enterprises which, on behalf of the masters (or local magistrates), undertook the preparation and execution of torture inflicted on unruly slaves. Others dedicated their professional efforts to capturing fugitives. A municipal regulation found on an epigraph in Pozzuoli, near Naples, and dating from the final years of the republic or the early years of the principate, provides a detailed description of the obligations of the contractor in arranging for hangings and crucifixions, and the amount to be paid to the executioner: four sesterces, hardly more than the wages of a store clerk.[49]

Although Rome never practiced any type of servitude that could properly be termed Helotry, in the course of its history there were a number of intermediary forms between chattel slavery and complete liberty: the debtor's bondage of the archaic period, the patriarchal slavery of the early centuries, the parental subordination imposed by authoritarian relationships in families (a type of authority which lasted into the republican era), and the colonate of late antiquity. It would also be untrue to claim that there was no wage labor in the cities or in rural areas. We already know—and recent research continues to confirm—that slave and wage labor coexisted in Italian agriculture during the first century B.C., at the high point of imperial slavery. Their permanent juxtaposition was necessary to the productive functioning of *villae* and large agricultural landholdings. (We also know that in the agrarian regimes of the peninsula, small farms never disappeared either.)

Apart from the proportions of slave and wage labor, in the social and mental constructs of the ruling classes slavery was the dominant paradigm for all representations of manual labor. In contrast to prevailing practice in medieval societies, the work of wage-earning laborers in urban workshops and of agrarian plebs on farms was not taken into account—above all culturally, but not economically or politically either—in any successful model of production and organization. All wage labor was drawn into the obscure orbit of an almost totally analogical assimilation with the condition of slavery; at the beginning of our story we looked at Cicero's unequivocal position, which reflected opinions that were prevalent throughout the entire history of imperial society (a topic we will return to shortly). As for small landholders, with the defeat of the Gracchi's efforts and, later, the advent of the principate, they no longer had a role on the great stage of Roman history.

The use of slaves became the ideal functional means of agricultural exploitation, slave labor the basis of all manufacturing, and the owner of land and slaves the ultimate protagonists of every organization of production. Reversing the letter—but not the substance—of one of Finley's statements,[50] we can say that it is impossible to separate the society of Rome—its material foundations, obviously, but also its ideas, convictions, mentality, ethics, and even its anthropology—from the context of slavery, through which it expressed itself for so long.

Such widespread and at the same time highly concentrated slavery—even if with varied ethnic origins, functions, cultures, and standards of living—could not but have a profound effect on the behavior and emotional life of the free population. Let us attempt for a moment to consider what effect it must have had on the formation of character and worldview to be in daily contact with masses of men and women over whom was exercised total and absolute power, with no need to resort to the most extreme of measures (the right to inflict death) to demonstrate its unprecedented coercive force: it was a violence built into the institution itself, entirely apart from the personal inclinations of individual masters. We can now form some idea of the abyss that separates the experiences of a Roman citizen, the microphysics of the powers that enveloped him, the forms of socialization to which he was subjected—including such things as language, law, and the realms of affectivity and sexuality—from those of a man in the contemporary Western world. An American example may help us in our effort to reconstruct the ancient mentality. In a conversation with Tocqueville on December 15, 1831, an anonymous farmer in Sandy Bridge, Louisiana, succinctly explained the effect of slaves on him and his fellows: "We are accustomed to doing nothing for ourselves."[51] For the sake of simplicity, in our little experiment we have chosen the perspective most familiar to us: that of the masters. But one could also attempt to imagine the lot of the slaves, although this would require an even more strenuous leap, because a cultural anthropology of ancient slavery—which would bring us in some ways closer to the thoughts, feelings, and folklore of that world, penetrating beyond the filter constituted by depictions of the masters—is virtually impossible. We must resign ourselves to the fact that the inner makeup of slaves in Rome or Antioch (or, for that matter, a peasant in Etruria or Gaul) is just as inaccessible to us as almost all of the everyday items that filled their daily lives. Despite the miracles of archeology, the process by which objects have been selected has not been any less drastic or less "class-bound" than the one that has determined the survival of ideas. Both have been subject to the irremediable destructiveness that history reserves for the memory of the weak.

(4)

The Roman Mediterranean was thus not only a sea of commodities and merchants, but also one of slaves—and for a period of time a sea of slaves in revolt. So it must have seemed to Posidonius (the philosopher from Apamea and advisor to Marius, Pompey, and Cicero), who traveled it at length, from Asia Minor to Spain, during the last years of the second century and the beginning of the first century B.C. in an attempt to satisfy his inexhaustible curiosity about history and ethnography.[52] His writings, to which Luciano Canfora has called attention,[53] have not survived. But one stratum of them is clearly present in the fragments of Books 34–36 of Diodorus Siculus' *Bibliotheca historica,* and also in the sixth book of Athenaeus' *Deipnosophistai.*

According to Posidonius, Roman slavery was misguided and in crisis.

From 135 to 101 B.C., the empire had been shaken by two major slave rebellions. They had erupted in the Sicilian countryside, where the spread of large monocultural grain-producing plantations after the Roman conquest had concentrated large numbers of slaves—surely on the order of hundreds of thousands. The Italian peninsula had already seen more limited episodes of insubordination, which Livy unfailingly recorded:[54] one near Rome, in Setia and Praeneste, in 198 B.C., which resulted in the execution of 500 rebels; one in Etruria in 196; and one in Apulia in 185, in which 5,000 were condemned. By 140 B.C., Sicily was already overrun with bands of fugitives sacking and destroying at will. But the uprisings of 135 were a much more serious matter. ("A slave revolt of such magnitude had never been seen before. [. . .] The entire island was at risk of falling into the hands of the rebels," Diodorus reported.)[55] They developed while Rome was involved in a difficult war of repression in Spain, which ended in 133 after the long siege of Numantia. The insurgents, Syrians for the most part, conquered cities (Enna, Agrigento, and Taormina), crowned a king for themselves (Eunus), coined money, formed an army (which according to Diodorus was as large as 200,000), and succeeded in attracting to their cause some of the most marginalized members of the free population,[56] in an alliance whose menacing shadow would reemerge in the course of the first century and reach as far as Catiline, creating a constant worry for the ruling classes of Rome. Moreover, it is probable (although this cannot be confirmed) that the revolt in Sicily was somehow connected to other insurrections that broke out at the same time in Asia, Attica, Delos, and even in Rome itself. It would be an exaggeration to think that there was a single purpose behind all of the rebellions on both shores of the Mediterranean, but the news must have been in circulation. And it is unlikely that the synchronism of the events was fortuitous: something was truly threatening to crack in those years.

In 133 B.C. the Sicilian revolt was still in progress. According to Appian's account, Tiberius Gracchus was able to cite it as a topical example of the dangers caused by the concentrations of slaves that the vast size of some agrarian properties made necessary, and as an argument in favor of his proposal to reconstitute small (and medium-sized) rural landholdings, which functioned on the basis of wage labor.[57] It was not until 132 B.C. that the consul Rupilius managed to retake the cities and definitively gain the upper hand. Diodorus relates that when all hope was gone for the rebels trapped in the besieged city of Enna, in order to inflame his men and spur them on to their final struggle, Eunus decided to represent "actions on stage, with which the slaves portrayed the rebellion against the masters and reproached them for the arrogance and violence that in the end had brought them to ruin."[58] This is a rare and valuable piece of information. For a single moment, through the memory of an improvised theater of desperation, the abraded culture and inventions of those with neither voice nor history come to light. Even on the point of death, the slaves indicted the blind despotism of their masters, not the existence of slavery as such—this would have been out of the question even for them, even at that moment.

In 104, about thirty years later, the revolt repeated itself, again while Rome was going through a difficult period. The Jugurthine War had just ended (marking the exacerbation of the internal political conflict— Sallust would pronounce it the first step in the struggle against the arrogance of the aristocracy, the "haughtiness of the nobility"),[59] and only the year before, the Roman legions had suffered a disastrous defeat at the hands of the Cimbri at Arausio, in Gaul. As before, the rebels chose a king for themselves (Salvius, who was followed by Athenion), and engaged in a long struggle, aimed more at the countryside than at the cities, in a reversal of the strategy of the earlier uprising. They resisted until 101, when they were vanquished by the consul Manius Aquilius.

According to Caecilius of Caleacte (an ex-slave who, after being freed, had become a master of rhetoric and the author of the *History of the Servile Wars*, a work quoted by Athenaeus), the insurrections had a fearful human cost: a million dead.[60] The number is exaggerated, even if we suppose that Caecilius was including not only the casualties of the Sicilian wars but of all of the rebellions that broke out virtually simultaneously in the empire. Nevertheless, it gives some idea of the vast extent of the phenomena and the masses of people involved in them (and also, probably, of the ferocity of the repression).

Posidonius attributed the spread of the revolts to the inhuman living conditions of the slaves[61]—not only on the large farms, but especially in the mines.[62] He had traveled extensively, and, like Antisthenes (whose works he had surely read) and Polybius, he could have formed a first-hand impression of the results of imperial conquest in the Mediterranean. In Spain, he had a chance to become personally familiar with one merciless and unremitting form of work: mining. The slaves in the mines constantly sought and begged for death, which they considered preferable to the unbearable torment they were suffering. Conditions in the Greek mines at Laurion could not have been any better. In virtually the same period, Lucretius responded similarly to the plight of slaves.[63] In Strabo's view, however, the harshness of Posidonius' descriptions seemed inappropriate and irritating;[64] he considered them a useless quest for pathetic effects. Different reactions to the reality that was before everyone's eyes.

Posidonius was perfectly aware that slave revolts were nothing new; he was certainly familiar with Thucydides' account of uprisings that dated from as early as the Peloponnesian War,[65] when more than 20,000 slaves escaped from Attica during the Spartan occupation of Decelea. But what he must have found characteristic of his own period was that the expanding need for chattel slaves throughout the world was related to the spread of a mode of production, from landed estates to mines, that was based on the growth of trade and the increasing human exploi-tation of nature. For him, the strengthened connection between servi-tude and the "worldwide" compass of the empire (today we would say, between slavery and the operations of the "world economy") were lead-ing to the inevitable dehumanization of the slaves, and were driving them to rebellion in several different places at the same time, a simulta-neity that could not have escaped his attention. (As Diodorus wrote, "All this took place unexpectedly, for the most part, and contrary to all ex-pectations; but for anyone who is able to assess the events in a politically reliable manner, the sequence of events was actually quite logical.")[66]

Posidonius' analysis is even more meaningful if we consider that the philosopher was not at all a radical enemy of slavery; nor did he give any consideration to the possibility of a world without slaves.[67] His thinking (adopting that of Theopompus) was limited to drawing distinctions be-tween kinds of slavery: good slavery, which was "in conformity with na-ture" (patriarchal or Helot slavery), and "degenerate" slavery,[68] made necessary by the growth of trade (at one time Athenian, but now, on a much larger scale, Roman), which was based on the abuse of chattel slaves. The latter was the kind that led to disaster, to the fatal outbreak of double-edged violence: violence caused by the masters' arrogance and greed, and violence generated by the slaves' fierce hatred.

The philosopher from Apamea was not in the least democratic, even in the ancient sense of the term. Indeed, his conservative conduct resem-bled that of the senatorial nobility. (In his view, Pompey was the man of the hour.)[69] And his polemics against the "degenerate" form of slavery were brought on by his open aversion to the Roman *equites*,[70] his fierce objections to the classes of merchants, speculators, and conquerors, whose insatiable thirst for profits had forced an institution "in confor-mity with nature," which at its origin had occupied its proper place in the cosmic pattern of universal harmony, to be corrupted into a mecha-nism of brutalization and oppression which would eventually attract di-vine punishment. That had already happened to Chios,[71] and could very well happen again to the new masters.

But his ideas were dramatically out of date, reflecting his fond hope for a return to a patriarchal, Hesiodic, substantially autarchic society whose hierarchies would be firmly respected—a far cry from the dam-age caused by wealth and money.

Were these simply the unrealizable dreams of a traditionalist philosopher? He was not alone. As we have seen, Tiberius Gracchus likewise cautioned against large concentrations of purchased slaves, and he was unsympathetic to the needs of the large landed estates. And he was no less concerned by the Sicilian uprising. To be sure, his fears had other origins and other motives: he was not a theorist, and he was a democrat, at least in terms of the forces he relied on and according to the Roman conception of politics. But the solution he envisaged, although it was far better articulated and defined than the utopia of Posidonius (while still remaining a government program), anticipated one of its essential aspects. Like Posidonius, Tiberius proposed impeding the concentration of slaves through a forced return to the past. He urged using legislative means to revive small farms, which, by fostering the rural plebs, would have permitted the restoration of the community of farmer-citizen-soldiers: the very society which was responsible for the greatness of the republic, and which the empire was in the process of destroying.

Both of these perspectives had what we might call a common archaizing feature. For both the worried thinker who was on the side of the nobility and the politician who was close to the agrarian plebs, the only way to combat slavery was to look backward, by searching only in the past for models of social and civic life which could circumvent the mechanisms of production that had transformed their own era. Both solutions were impossible—the tribune's apparently realistic solution no less than the philosopher's obviously illusory and utopian one (as history was rapidly demonstrating). But their shared implausibility also contained an element—albeit hidden and reversed, so to speak—which, as we shall see, is essential for the interpretation of future events: the existence of a very strong connection between slavery and imperial "modernization." Even the harshest critics could not figure out a way to sever this tie without the reinstatement of economic self-sufficiency, which would have necessarily marked an extraordinary reversal, and the outright restoration of a now-distant era.

From Sicily we now go to Capua. The last major slave revolt of antiquity—the most impressive and best known of all—erupted thirty years later, in 73 B.C. (by then, Posidonius had long since retired to Rhodes). It broke out in a school for gladiators, not far from Rome. The cyclical regularity of these rebellions is surprising: during a seventy-year period, every generation of slaves had its own insurrection. And their timing was also noteworthy: they coincided with Rome's political and military difficulties. This time it was Sertorius in Spain, Mithridates in the east, and the pirates in the Mediterranean who had to be dealt with, as Appian could not help observing.[72]

The first hideout Spartacus used was near Naples. From there he traveled more than 3,000 kilometers in the course of two years, holding the Roman armies in check and single-handedly leading an armed force that at times reached 120,000 strong (according to Appian).[73] Sallust described him as a person "endowed with strength and courage to an extraordinary degree."[74] These virtues contributed to the legend of the great commander which so much modern literature has constructed by embracing and reshaping an interpretation that the Romans had already conceived.[75] And he was depicted as a "revolutionary hero," corresponding to a romantic ideal,[76] or his adventures were analyzed according to an automatically class-conscious model.

In reality, Spartacus made a sincere attempt to introduce certain forms of egalitarianism among his followers.[77] Since he was Thracian by birth (like many of his followers, but some also came from Gaul and Germany), we can assume that he was influenced by Hellenism. Moreover, he probably realized that he needed to seek solidarity and alliances. Italy had recently emerged from the serious conflicts of the Social War, and although it is hard to believe that Spartacus truly succeeded in reopening the wounds caused by this bloody clash and in winning over the populations of entire cities, we know for sure that groups of free *Italici* who belonged to the lowest levels of society, men of the rural plebs who were now disinherited and driven to the wall, followed him, attracted by his victories, and shared his fate. His death in battle, surrounded by the armies of Crassus and Pompey, was followed by pitiless repression: 6,000 slaves were tortured and crucified on the road from Capua to Rome.[78]

The lesson was definitively learned: thereafter, the only revolts in the empire were localized episodes and forays by isolated bands. But in the decades bridging the second and first centuries B.C., not only did the nightmare of a large-scale liberation of the slaves and their organic alliance with the multitudes of those who had nothing more to lose take

shape as a fear of a generalized insurrection, spontaneously conceived
and executed by the masses of prisoners—as in Sicily, the Orient, and Italy. A different phantom began to haunt the souls of the ruling classes:
the fear that freeing the slaves and involving them in political campaigns
might become one of the objectives of anti-aristocratic "popular" extremists. In the final phase of his battle, Gaius Gracchus seems to have
contemplated the conclusive and symbolic gesture of a general emanci-
pation.[79] And after Spartacus, both Catiline's followers (if not the leader
of the plot himself)[80] and Clodius, still later, were thought to have attempted at various times to include groups, and even masses, of slaves in
their strategies of insubordination and open conflict.[81]

We do not know how realistic these plans actually were, or whether
we should consider them, at least in part, simply the product of widespread falsifications circulated by their adversaries, and reported by ancient historians, in order to deter moderates from possibly sympathizing
with the democratic extremists. But it is undeniable that for more than
eighty years, from about 140 to about 50 B.C.—with the republic's institutions racked by crises, and the slave economy experiencing turbulent
growth—the danger of revolt, and of a possible alliance between the
slaves and the desperate dispossessed in the countryside, was something
more than a groundless and irrational fear. The risk was to some degree
plausible, a cloud on the future of the aristocratic republic. At the same
time, it was an idea that—among the members of the circles of Catiline
and Clodius—must have taken hold in the mind of more than one popular extremist. Slavery raised new problems of organization, discipline,
and control, and possible links with the aggravation of political conflicts
that had never before been experienced in ancient societies. This was
a sign that a critical threshold, even in terms of numbers, had been
reached in the relationship between free men and slaves, and that the entire social structure could have been at risk, during that dramatic season
when it seemed that anything could happen.

We shall return below to the new prospects that arose in those years.
The end result, one out of many possible outcomes, was a definitely consolidated slavery and the birth of a new ruling class. An original equilibrium was formed that was no longer based on the lone primacy of the
old republican nobility but was founded on the interrelation of more
complex forces: the elites of Italy and of the provinces, the urban plebs,

and the army. The strength of the repression and the end of the civil wars—no less than the wisdom of the Roman juridical system in instituting, from the second half of the first century B.C., a "law of slavery" capable of absorbing and integrating some of the impulses that might have again caused uprisings among the slaves (and that we will also soon discuss)—eliminated the faintest shadow of rebellion in the space of a few decades. But the lingering memories were destined to leave a permanent mark on the ideas and behavior of later eras.

II. Cultures of Slavery

(1)

According to Cato[82] and, later, Pliny,[83] the proper care of a vineyard in central Italy required the labor of the equivalent of one specialized slave for every ten *iugera* of land (2.5 hectares); according to Columella,[84] a champion of intensive farming intended for the general market and entailing large investments of capital, the optimal ratio was one to seven. The production of grains and vegetables on monocultural farms and large landed estates required fewer farmhands and less skilled labor: eight slaves were sufficient for a property of 200 *iugera* (fifty hectares), according to the Sasernae, as quoted by Varro.[85] Thirteen slaves worked in the 240-*iugera* olive grove described by Cato;[86] but this must have been a mixed-crop farm, with cereals and livestock in addition to the olive trees. The Sasernae, Columella, and Pliny also calculated fairly precisely the rhythms and productivity of the slaves' activities in the countryside,[87] including the number of lost workdays to be expected per year, and the quantity of work that each slave could perform per day in various agricultural activities.

Some of these statistics have been the subject of debates among modern historians. Richard Duncan-Jones[88] and Andrea Carandini[89] have scrutinized virtually every number in great detail, without always arriving at the same conclusions. But if we look beyond the details, what is compelling is the basic impression that these accounts make, which is completed and reinforced by legal cases—from the late republican period, in texts by Servius, Tubero, and Alfenus, to the time of the Severan emperors, as shown in Paulus and Ulpian.[90] Even if there is no sure way to compare the calculations, estimates, and models offered by classical commentators with those produced by modern agricultural or industrial enterprises, these data demonstrate a refined and subtle knowledge of slavery. They are a storehouse of empirical observations and of long, wide-ranging, painstaking experience.

The forced participation of slaves in Italian agriculture and production (Crassus owned a construction business which employed 500 bricklayers,[91] and gangs of slaves were commonly engaged in the mass production of ceramics) had led to the elaboration of carefully determined hierarchies of tasks and functions, and various means of apportioning workloads. The system developed procedures for use and supervision which ensured a level of productivity bearing no resemblance to the uncouth inefficiency that many historians have attributed to it.[92] The Roman system showed a talent for exploitation not found even in classical Athens (at least, it was not as well documented there). As with slavery in the United States (where, to be sure, industrial factories already served as examples), the Romans were able to exploit with endless shrewdness the wealth constituted by the human resources of the slaves, and to take advantage of their numerous distinctive cultural and ethnic characteristics. Available for use was a wealth of different types of physical and mental energy and of noteworthy abilities and talents, which the violence of war and plunder had uprooted from their places of origin and transplanted to the center of the empire.

Further on, we will discuss in greater detail the diversification of jobs and the hierarchies of status that existed within the world of the slaves. But the distinctions should not be exaggerated, in terms of either their quantitative or their social significance: the majority of slaves remained associated with manual labor, in both the city and the countryside. To the ancient mind, from classical Athens to imperial Rome, the humanity of these masses seemed crushed and absorbed by the mechanical nature of their compulsory work, which tended to be unchanging and repetitive. From their masters' perspective, their lives were immured in the forced monotony of tasks dictated by others. They were, in short, human machines: automata. And it was precisely in this way—as an "animate instrument"—that Aristotle defined the slave, in a well-known passage in the first book of the *Politics*.[93] And in the eighth book of the *Nicomachean Ethics*, the identification was pushed even further: "The slave is an instrument endowed with a soul, and the instrument is an inanimate slave."[94] The Romans adopted the same way of thinking in their social and mental models. As if it were a matter of course, Varro spoke of a method of classification that divided "instruments" into three categories: "vocal" (slaves), "semivocal" (cattle), and "mute" (carts)[95]—though in reality the greater adaptability of the structure of Roman slavery, and the presence of juridical doctrine that had introduced many distinctions, made this definition in some ways less material, and gave it a particularly doctrinaire and scholastic significance, as the expression of an ancient commonplace.

But the original contours of Aristotle's schema were more subtle and intricate, in the context of the difficult passage in which it appeared. In addition to the division of the "instruments" into animate and inanimate, he also proposed the criterion of whether they were intended for "production" or "action."[96] An instrument of production was one whose use generated something new—for example, a shuttle, by means of which cloth was produced. In contrast, from an instrument of action nothing was gained but its own use; this was true of a bed or a piece of clothing. "But life is action, not production,"[97] added Aristotle; and the Greek man "acts" when he uses things, not when he makes them, as Jean-Pierre Vernant has demonstrated with his usual shrewdness.[98] With respect to his master, the slave—simultaneously a living being and a piece of property—was an instrument of action, not production: nothing could be directly obtained from his use; nor, on the other hand, was he capable of "acting." He was not a free man—he was only "an instrument for living."[99] But in contrast to the other soulless instruments, he, as a living automaton, had energy that enabled production (by inanimate instruments) to be put into action and to realize its aim. Aristotle also wrote: "If every tool could perform its own work when ordered, or by seeing what to do in advance, like the statues of Daedalus in the story, or the tripods of Hephaestus which the poet says 'enter self-moved the company divine' [this is a quotation from the *Iliad*][100]—if thus shuttles wove and quills played harps of themselves, master-craftsmen would have no need of assistants and masters no need of slaves."[101] "If the shuttles wove by themselves": no modern reader can contemplate this phrase without a shiver. Time has cast upon it the shadow of a dizzying coincidence. How can we not think of the mechanical looms attached to the first steam engines, at the dawn of the Industrial Revolution, which, by finally making the shuttles move "by themselves," were the first steps in the transformation of factory work, filling the markets with goods? It is as if history were trying to confirm—by overturning the factual premises of the example but conserving its validity—the truth of Aristotle's reasoning, by making it seem an enigmatic premonition, somewhere between a vague foreshadowing of machines and an unconscious display of his own desire. To be sure, in the short run, modern mechanization did nothing to liberate human beings; on the contrary, it imposed on their exertions the additional constriction of a purely artificial and indefinitely repeatable rhythm—to the point where Samuel Butler could even imagine an Industrial Revolution in reverse.[102] And when all of this began, slavery had already been virtually eliminated in the West, except in America. But how could one deny that automation (Butler also has passages of extraordinary foresight on the "intelligence" of machines) was about to change the world's future?

The first book of the *Politics*—probably the last to be written, out of the eight that compose the work we know today—was drafted during Aristotle's second Athenian period: that is, sometime after 334 B.C., when Alexander had already undertaken his conquests. As Finley noted, it contains the only attempt at a theoretical discussion of slavery to be found in any ancient culture. Aristotle's analysis took the whole classical Greek experience of slavery as its field of observation[103]—a system which, although certainly less mature than that of Rome, was nevertheless elaborate enough to allow its self-portrayals (like those of Aristotle) to describe later, more complex realities that developed along the same lines. (This is precisely what we do when we use the ideas of Adam Smith and David Ricardo to explain situations that have evolved beyond the ones that originally inspired their thinking.) Moreover, by around 400 B.C. slaves constituted about 30 percent of the population of Athens[104]—a proportion very close to that of Augustan Italy.

With a clarity that leaves little room for interpretation, Aristotle demonstrated the indispensability of slavery by means of a *reductio ad absur-*

dum in which the absolute need for slaves was linked to the lack of self-activating instruments of production (Alexandre Koyré speaks of "resignation" in the face of a lack of machines).[105] Only in a fantastic world where shuttles were capable of weaving by themselves could the institution of slavery be dispensed with. This argument was not even totally original. We find the same idea—though presented in an ingenious and grotesque key[106]—in a fragment by Crates dating from about one century before Aristotle's writings. Here, as well, the lack of slaves is offset by the miraculous actions of household objects: tables, kneading troughs, and cups move by themselves, in response to human commands.

Slaves in the place of machines: the ancients had an intuitive understanding, albeit intermittent and nebulous, of the relation between slavery and what we might in retrospect call the limits of classical mechanization—the idea that slavery was located at the intersection between the needs of society and their fulfillment between plans for production and the tools for realizing them, where the state of technological advancement determined a chronic and irremediable shortage of mechanical energy. The muscles and sinews of the slaves compensated for this lack with an intelligence and flexibility of execution that were otherwise unattainable. "For poor people, oxen take the place of slaves," wrote Aristotle,[107] outlining a precise hierarchy of the sources of energy. Centuries later, not even Cicero, who modified the schema of the *Politics* in fairly important ways, was to deviate from this position.[108]

In fact, a traditional explanation, familiar to modern historians, which conformed—perhaps unconsciously—to ancient thought and translated it into a somewhat deterministic interpretation, has for some time directly linked the demand for and massive use of slaves to the fact that the means of production were almost completely unmechanized. To replace machines, Greece and Rome invented production by means of slavery.[109] But in a short essay written in 1959, radiant with lucidity and talent, André Aymard reversed the terms of the problem: it was not the lack of mechanization that made the use of slaves indispensable, but rather the contrary. The massive presence of slavery determined the "technological stagnation" of Greece and Rome.[110]

This hypothesis (aside from the generic reference to "stagnation," which we pass over for now) brings us much closer to the heart of the problem, despite the fact that it follows an excessively linear schema of cause and effect—proceeding from the absence of machines to slavery—which manifestly oversimplifies the true course of events.

Actually, it is impossible to determine a causal relationship in either direction. We cannot deduce that slavery directly resulted from the absence of machines, nor can we simply say that slavery was responsible for the lack of machines. But the latter point of view has the advantage of calling attention to the crux of the matter, which is not the history of technology but the entire social and mental configuration of the ancient civilizations. Moreover, we must not forget that the most notable period of technological progress in antiquity—for the Hellenistic world, between the third and the first centuries B.C.—coincided almost completely with the apogee of slavery in the Mediterranean.

There is a necessary conclusion. In the historical development of classical Greek and Roman society two elements have always tended to point to an inextricable link: the presence of slavery and the lack of machines in the production process. Careful examination reveals that this was already apparent to the ancients, from Aristotle to Varro to the Roman jurists. In the image whose persistence we just discussed, which depicted the slave as a simple instrument subject to the designs of another person's volition—the slave as automaton—this same intrinsic simultaneity was precisely reflected: the man forced by his position as slave to take the role of a machine—an "instrument"—that was otherwise lacking; the machine, unrealizable by artificial means, assuming the living form of a human reduced to being an object ("a commodity," in Aristotle's terminology;[111] a person "under the dominion" of another, in the taxonomy of the jurists[112]).

In order to go beyond this relationship, a third element—also proposed by Aymard, but without a complete investigation of its implications—must be introduced into the description: the refusal of the ancients to perform manual labor; or, more precisely, the refusal of the Greek and Roman ruling classes, and of their culture, to have anything to do with the material basis of individual or social existence (as was mentioned at the beginning of this account). We must deal not with a diptych but with a triptych: the spread of chattel slavery, the devaluation of labor and handwork, and the perennial shortage of mechanical elements in productive processes. Hidden in the combination of these three characteristics lies the path on which our inquiry continues.

(2)

The configuration is not perfectly symmetrical, however. From a historical and interpretative perspective—in the context of a history that lasted so long as to become an anthropological constant—the depreciation of work in the Greek and Roman world occupies a primordial and privileged position. And we must begin by explaining it.

Where did this obscure refusal come from? Remote clues emerge from its tenacity. Here is Herodotus on the subject: "Whether the Greeks borrowed from the Egyptians their notions about this [the avoidance of menial trade in favor of warfare], I cannot say for certain. I have remarked that the Thracians, the Scythians, the Persians, the Lydians, and almost all other barbarians hold the citizens who practice trades, and their children, in less repute than the rest, while they esteem as noble those who keep aloof from handicrafts, and especially honor such as are given wholly to war."[113] His uncertainty would remain unresolved. His curiosity about every possible connection linking Greece to Asia and Africa caused him to ask subtle questions which were difficult to answer, and remain so even for us, as we increasingly appreciate the number and importance of the archaic links "between the Orient and the Occident," to borrow a phrase from a memorable book by Santo Mazzarino.[114]

The Xenophontic Socrates did not have similar reservations. He firmly supported an opinion that was considered indisputable.

You said it quite well, Critobulos. The manual trades are discredited, and rightly enjoy no respect in the city. They wear out the bodies of both the workers and those who supervise them. Some are forced to remain seated in the shade, and some even to spend their days next to the fire; and as the bodies grow weaker, the minds become more feeble as well. Furthermore, the trades called manual do not leave a single free moment for the benefit of friends or the city, and for that reason those who practice them show themselves to be men of no worth, both to their friends and to their country. And in certain cities, especially those which have the reputation of being dedicated to war, no citizen is allowed to exercise the manual arts.[115]

Age-old common sense and the new philosophy were in full agreement: Herodotus reported an opinion that was widespread and generally accepted, and the Socrates of Xenophon showed himself to be in agreement with this traditional way of thinking.[116] Despite its appeal, the recently propounded idea that a tradition of democratic thought in Athens had proposed a different orientation, less averse to manual labor, does not seem to have much factual confirmation.

Plato's thought, later repeated by Aristotle, was a further elaboration of what must already have been a firmly held prejudice. In the *Republic*, Plato portrayed work as absolutely antithetical to the essential qualities most intrinsic to citizenship. But he cannot be reduced solely to such a drastic contraposition: we must avoid superimposing the rigidity of his social (and ethical) judgments on the delicate theoretical problems he faced in his metaphysical and not simply "civic" appraisal of the "demiurgic" activity of the creation and transformation of perceptible reality. We need only consider the artisan-god of the *Timaeus*, or this passage in the *Gorgias*, among others: "Surely the virtue of each thing, whether of an implement or of a body, or again of a soul or any living creation, arrives most properly not by accident but by an order or rightness or art that is apportioned to each."[117]

The ambiguities of Plato's teachings can probably be considered an indication of trauma and changes that affected the Greek mentality even before the classical period.[118] In fact, we have reason to believe that such a resolute devaluation of material production and the knowledge associated with it was an attitude that could not have dated back to archaic Greece.[119] This could also explain Herodotus' "genetic" doubt, and his care to note that not everyone in his day shared the same negative opinion of handwork[120] and that the Corinthians—the "inventors" of chattel slavery—refrained from sharing it, too. And this is not all. A more remote stratum of thought, one less hostile toward the technology of manufacturing, especially where the "arts of fire"—metallurgy and ceramics—were concerned, is almost certainly reflected in the myths of Athena, Hephaestus, and most notably Prometheus,[121] which were later reworked by Hesiod[122] and Aeschylus[123] (the progression from the "cooking fire" to the "civilizing fire," according to the interpretations of Dumézil[124] and Vernant).[125]

But it would be unwise to read too much into these faint vestiges. If indeed there existed a more favorable attitude, it was not expressed in an unambiguous and straightforward manner, at least in the historical era. Homer and Hesiod already classified craftsmen in the lowest levels of society; and in *Works and Days,* work is simply an irremediable evil.

These are shiftings that help our understanding. Together with a basic and deep-rooted repugnance for a life totally dedicated to material production, an invincible feeling of contempt for the idea of "working for the sake of others" must have played an important role, among the Greeks and Romans, in the genesis and subsequent consolidation of their resistance toward manual activities. This was coupled with an insurmountable prejudice against the lack of autonomy inherent in participating in the productive process, suffered by those who had assumed this function in the city. So long as manual activities took place within the family, in order to meet the direct needs of the producers, it still seemed acceptable. It was a means of protecting independence, rather than of destroying it. Ulysses was an excellent carpenter;[126] Hephaestus made tripods, not just the arms of Achilles;[127] Hesiod's countryfolk did not hold weaving and cooking in contempt.[128] But professional artisans did not manufacture items for their own use; their products were meant to be sold. They worked for customers and for the new businesses, thus submitting to the choices and wishes of others, beyond their own control. They lost their free will, and, as Aristotle would say, became the equivalent of slaves.

The interpretation we are trying out here is far-reaching. It establishes a connection (at least partially) between the resistance toward work and the individualistic mentality which, as we have already mentioned, was emerging in the aristocracies and, later, in the city-states of Greece, the Tyrrhenian region, and Italy.[129] This "Mediterranean" backdrop, shared by a variety of local settings, would help to account for the existence of the same attitude in Rome (in addition to the explanation offered by the assimilation of Greek ways of thinking, which would be impossible to prove).

According to Plutarch (perhaps relying on Varro)[130] and Dionysius of Halicarnassus,[131] from its origins Rome was a city rich in artisans: flutists, goldsmiths, carpenters, dyers, shoemakers, tanners, foundrymen, potters. Both give credible descriptions, which mesh well with a non-primitivized depiction of the city in its archaic period; after all, it is the inscription of a potter, Duenos, that is one of the oldest specimens of Latin writing ever found.[132] And we may reasonably assume that both during the Etruscan era and later, in the fourth and third centuries B.C., before slave labor transformed the quality and procedures of production, these techniques enjoyed a period of particular currency. But the judgment of society was not influenced by this expansion. Artisans were unanimously considered to be on the margins of citizenship, even though, as in Greece, collective disapprobation was focused at first on the work of wage labor. Pacuvius, already employing the usual model, compared it to slavery;[133] and Plautus, in the same breath as he referred to small shopkeepers and tradesmen, spoke scornfully of men "who sold themselves."[134] We can also add Varro, who considered wages "sordid and miserable gain," an "abomination of the body";[135] and Seneca[136] (we have already discussed Cicero).

Moreover, the link between the rejection of artisans' use of their hands, scorn for the notion of "working for the sake of others," and individualism as a social and mental characteristic of the civic bodies and the Greek and Roman aristocracies would also account for another constant of these cultures, which appears to be the single but very important exception to the general discredit encompassing the world of production: the esteem and respect lavished on the rhythms and exertions of agricultural labor—from Hesiod to Plato, Cato, Virgil, and Pliny, not to mention the popular opinion they all reflected—so long as the farmer who owned the land was working it himself.

Here, what mattered was not the materiality of the work and production, but rather, on the one hand, the support of nature, and, on the other hand and most important, the civic and political liberty—the defense of individuality—that daily labor was able to guarantee, by ensuring the economic autonomy of the citizens and their families. While even as early as in archaic Rome the manual crafts appeared more and more to be an urban phenomenon controlled by market forces, in classical Greece or at the height of the Roman republic small plots of farmland and their direct exploitation still continued to support the sovereignty and inalienable individuality of every member of the community. They determined each person's political status, and represented a pillar in the relationship (which at first was purely aristocratic but was later inherited by the nascent democracies) between politics and moral life. Aside from political ties, no other kind of social cooperation except military, or "hoplite," was able to develop successfully in a similar environment. (And in Greece and Rome, although not in the Orient, it was destined to become one of the foundations of *isonomia*, and later of democratic equality.)

This world of small self-sufficient cells constituted the very basis of the city-state, to which a particular original agricultural civilization was linked. An economic form had now become a political institution, and both became a cultural and mental fabric. This was true not only of Rome, as we have already seen, but also of Athens, where by the end of the fifth century B.C. only a minority, albeit a conspicuous one, of the citizens—no more than 5,000—seem not to have been landowners.[137]

The outcome was inevitable. No matter how strongly it was felt, the condemnation of labor and its social interdiction could not but end when it reached those self-sufficient units. Here another set of values prevailed. And by the time the whole economic and political structure of the city-state collapsed—in Athens as well as in late republican Rome—the form of productive labor which had originally made its development possible had already established itself as an ideal model, destined to survive as an exemplar long after its material foundations had crumbled into dust.

But in this new ideological elaboration, it was not so much agricultural labor for its own sake that was esteemed and nostalgically lamented as its ancient civic and political projection, so to speak, and the halo of morality created around it from at least the time of the Ionian aristocracy, and later by Hesiod and the early democracies. Once it was up to slaves to perform these same activities, they lost all their charm: in the eyes of the ruling classes, even tilling the soil now seemed degraded, incapable of demonstrating any redeeming features. As Pliny wrote:

> The fields were tilled in those days [the early republic] by the hands of generals themselves, and we may well believe that the earth rejoiced in a

laurel-decked ploughshare and a ploughman who had celebrated a triumph, whether it was that those farmers treated the seed with the same
care as they managed their wars and marked out their fields with the
same diligence as they arranged a camp, or whether everything pros-
pers better under honorable hands because the work is done with greater
attention. [. . .] But nowadays those agricultural operations are performed by slaves with fettered ankles and by the hands of malefactors
with branded faces! Although the Earth, who is addressed as our mother
and whose cultivation is spoken of as worship, is not so dull that when we
obtain even our farmwork from these persons one can believe that this is
not done against her will and to her indignation.[138]

It would be a very long time before emphasis was placed on the mer-
its of work and technology rather than on the virtues of those performing it (whether slaves or freemen). It was not until the entire ancient
civilization had disappeared that we find the liberating sarcasm of this
brilliant sixteenth-century text: "Certainly, if metalworking [. . .] is
shameful and unseemly for a nobleman, because servants once extracted
metals, farming also would not be seemly because slaves used to engage
in it, and still do among the Turks, nor would architecture, because
some servants have practiced it, nor would medicine, because many
physicians have been servants. And what I say about these trades can
also apply to many others which are exercised by people who were once
prisoners."[139]

(3)

Let us proceed to the third panel of our triptych: the lack of machinery.
In this case as well, we are faced with a complex situation, containing
heterogeneous elements that have fused together. As we have seen, the
flight from work was not accomplished solely by calling on the slaves to
supply the physical energy and skill necessary for production; it also entailed the withdrawal of the ruling classes, in both Greece and Rome,
from everything concerned with the technological and social conditions
under which the processes of production were carried out. A vast world
of relationships, objects, and knowledge was abandoned, leaving a large
dormant field.

But "abandoned" does not mean nonexistent. Instead, it signifies that this world was wholly controlled by a group of "base" intellectual and social practices, in which the accumulation of experiences, observations, and trials, the discovery of ways to create tools and improve their effectiveness, the disciplining and training of men, both slave and free, the conservation and transmission of techniques of production, transportation, and construction, experience with using resources and natural forms of energy—derived from the earth, wind, water, and even the physical strength of animals and people—were all deposited in a series of parallel traditions that were almost entirely oral (writing was found only in short handbooks used as memory aids),[140] and in practical know-how.

This knowledge was limited, undervalued, distant from any great intellectual movements, often indistinguishable from the selfsame material operations or machinery that they directed and guided and that were the only sign of its existence. At a higher level, only a small and isolated group of texts managed to survive: *Problems of Mechanics,* by an anonymous follower of Aristotle;[141] the treatise of Philon of Byzantium, one of Ctesibius' students;[142] Archimedes' *Construction of the Sphere,* which is now lost; Vitruvius' books on architecture (the tenth book was concerned with machines);[143] *On Siege Engines,* by Athenaeus Mechanicus, which was dedicated to the nephew of Augustus; Hero's *Mechanics* (which has survived in an Arabic translation);[144] *De rebus bellicis,* a brief tract that dates from late antiquity and that was written by an unknown and imaginative dilettante.

While modern historians almost never properly comprehended the unique features of this partly hidden universe, they have offered a variety of opinions on it. The positivist approach, which thoroughly disparaged its depth and success, was succeeded by a much more optimistic revisionist one—in part guided by archeology. Although occasionally ingenuous in their belated enthusiasm, these scholars have drastically reassessed, and even overturned, the old scientistic prejudices.[145]

If our reconstruction is to be balanced, it must make distinctions among the various levels. To speak of Greco-Roman "technological stagnation" is imprecise if the reference points used to measure the different rhythms and velocities are not defined.

Comparisons with the contemporary world are impossible to make.

Today the links among science, technology, production, and community life are so strong and so complete, and the pace of transformation is so rapid, that we find it hard even to imagine that social systems could have existed in which any changes in these fields were virtually imperceptible. But we must make this additional effort of empathy if we wish to understand conditions in the ancient world. The societies of that time were not completely lacking in science and mechanical skills, but they were certainly "atechnological," in that they were not specifically oriented toward the accumulation of experience and progress in these areas. Moreover, our present-day horizons, which seem so substantial to us, are rather recent in origin. They date back only a few centuries. For example, to the years when the sixteen-year-old Francis Bacon, living in Paris with his father, probably attended the public lectures on agriculture, mineralogy, and geology given by Bernard Palissy, who had at one time been an apprentice glassmaker.[146] In his unusual curiosity, Bacon anticipated the reassessment of the "mechanical arts" which was to remain one of the foundations of the new European culture, now finally in a position to break with the very long tradition whose origins we have just discussed. As he would later write, the duty of philosophy is to transform, not to contemplate.[147] Leonado da Vinci, too, would share this view. Work, thought, and machines were entering into a relationship that was shortly to change our destiny. A few decades before, Rabelais had not hesitated to include regular visits to technicians and artisans in the educational program of the adolescent Gargantua.[148] It was the middle of the sixteenth century, and the revolution was in full swing.

Can we go even further back in time? Probably so, but not by much. The earliest signs of the new thinking can be found in the work of the intellectuals in the late Middle Ages and the early Renaissance (Giorgione's *Three Philosophers* is a wonderful visual synthesis of the change in their attitudes),[149] in the feverish conjunction of mathematically leaning naturalism and anti-Aristotelian (and antidogmatic) neo-Platonism that marked their studies. In a different context, signs of the same trend are also clear in the statues of the Florentine craft guilds in the thirteenth and fourteenth centuries.[150] The path to Cartesian mechanization philosophy and then to the launch of the industrial era did not begin any earlier.

Yet we can compare the Greco-Roman world with what preceded it, rather than with what was to follow it in Europe. In truth, here again the result is not flattering. If the progress of Greco-Roman society is measured against the tremendous leap forward between the Neolithic Age and the Iron Age, when the basic procedures of agriculture, metallurgy, ceramics, and weaving were mastered, there can be no doubt that a slowdown had occurred. Nothing comparable to the agricultural revolution of the Neolithic Age took place in the era of the great Mediterranean civilizations; indeed, some historians claim that the entire history of Western material culture is contained in the two great transitions of the Neolithic and the Industrial Revolutions.[151] The list of inventions Finley managed to compile makes the total number of achievements of the Greeks and Romans actually seem quite meager:[152] gears and screws, rotary grindstones and water mills, direct screw presses, fore-and-aft sails, glass, concrete, dioptra for surveying (theodolite), torsion catapults, water clocks and hydraulic organs, mechanical toys driven by water or steam, and only a few others.

But it is time for a change of perspective. Let us take a close look at a brief sequence of events.

Hero, a scientist working at the Museum of Alexandria in the middle of the first century A.D. (if we accept the most plausible dating), invented an odd mechanism,[153] later described by Giovanni Branca in his 1629 work on amazing machines.[154] Rousseau still found the device entertaining and astonishing, as he relates in Book 3 of the *Confessions*.[155] It consisted of a heat source, above which there was a container of water; two tubes led from the container's cover to a small movable sphere with two valves. When the water boiled, steam made the sphere rotate and produce long whistling sounds. A variation of the same mechanism was used in Alexandria, up to the time of Ctesibius in the third century B.C., to open the doors of a building when a flame was lit on an altar.[156]

In Hero we also find a description of the odometer,[157] another machine also known to Vitruvius,[158] which must have been used to measure the distance traveled by carts or ships. Placed on the side of a ship (in its marine version) and partly immersed in the water, it was essentially a paddle wheel whose revolutions were recorded. Evidently taking his inspiration from this instrument, the anonymous author of *De rebus bellicis,* which dates from the mid-fourth century A.D., came up with an

idea in harmony with his lively fantasy on machines: he imagined transforming the odometer from a tool of measurement into a means of pro-
pulsion, and building a battleship powered by wheels instead of oars (or
sails). As he wrote, "This *liburna*, because of its impressiveness and the
machines at work within it, faces combat with such a throbbing of energy that through simple friction it breaks to pieces all of the enemy
liburnae that might draw near."[159]

What could make the wheels of the invincible ship turn? The text
gives the answer immediately: teams of oxen—properly stowed, and
yoked to the wheels.[160] But why not Hero's device, which was simply a
sort of turbine and steam boiler, and which by then must surely have
been familiar to the experts? Obstacles of a metallurgical nature, not to
mention difficulties (even conceptual ones) of scale, would probably
have arisen if such a powerful steam engine had been built in the fourth
century. But the author paid no attention to such details; besides, metalworking was more advanced than is commonly believed, at least in some
workshops.[161] If a link had been made between the two inventions, at
least in theory we would have had—far ahead of its time—the design for
a paddle-wheel steamer used later for Atlantic navigation.

Are we engaging in a mere parlor game? Perhaps. But the fact remains
that the contact was not made; and this nonevent, which is almost ir-
relevant for its own sake, has symbolic value for our purposes. It is em-
blematic of a great many other cases of possibilities that went unrecog-
nized and connections that went unmade—examples which are strewn
throughout the history of Greek and Roman technology and experimentation.

Why did this happen? It is unlikely to have been the result of a long
chain of unlucky coincidences. In this series of failed connections and
solutions missed by a hair's breadth, we can perceive a problem that was
related not to technical content but rather to cognitive style and social
organization. It had nothing to do with local obstacles which influenced
individual inventions and isolated skills. The issue was more general:
it concerned the forms and methods by which a society conceives of
the transformational power of artificially created instruments—in other
words, the attitude of an entire civilization toward nature and its phenomena.

(4)

In the two hundred years extending from the middle of the second century B.C. to the middle of the first century A.D., a period marked by the uninterrupted expansion of the imperial economy, Rome mastered and adopted the best of Hellenistic science: the tradition of ideas and experiences centered on the activities of the Museum of Alexandria. It was a conspicuous heritage. Without it, we would not be able to explain Varro, Vitruvius, Frontinus, and in many aspects Pliny himself. Most important, it was the cultural context that, for various reasons, was responsible for bridging the separation, characteristic of the Greeks, between pure speculation and technological applications.

The Romans chose to orient this patrimony of knowledge in many directions, in fields ranging from architecture to mechanics and medicine. But we need not trace each development in detail, because one overarching conclusion is perfectly clear. Even though Roman assimilation of individual disciplines tended to place far more emphasis on operational aspects than on theoretical elements, and even though during those centuries of great expansion the question of how to augment and accumulate wealth was very much on the minds of the leading classes, the idea of making orderly use of the body of acquired knowledge and techniques in order to improve the quality of production cycles systematically—that is, the intuition that the transformational potential of Hellenistic knowledge was particularly applicable to the production of material goods—never became a project that was pursued in an organized manner, or a cultural phenomenon that was in any way widespread. In other words, there was no point at which the availability of capital (both public and private) intersected with the technological potential for economic purposes. None of the great engineers and architects, none of the incomparable builders of bridges, roads, and aqueducts, none of the experts in the employment of the apparatus of war, and none of their customers, either in the public administration or in the large landowning families, understood that the most advantageous arena for the use and improvement of machines—devices that were either already in use or easily created by association, or those that could be designed to meet existing needs—would have been farms and workshops.[162] A number of archeological discoveries have demonstrated that, from the outset, the use of water mills (an invention dating from the first century B.C., which grew out of an earlier mechanism, the hydraulic lifting wheel) was more widespread than was formerly thought, and that quite a few installations were in existence even before late antiquity.[163] But no optimistic interpretations of the data can counter the fact that, with the exception of milling, all of the potential for productive use of the water wheel—its capacity for accumulating and making available large and regular quantities of nonhuman and nonanimal energy—were almost entirely overlooked. Moreover, even the use of mills seems to have been rather casual, never a result of an organic program of technological innovation.

The evidence cannot be denied. The conundrum we have brought to light cannot be resolved if we remain within the realm of the history of technology. The cognitive surrender of the world of production to lesser forms of learning, fragmented by the particularities of obscure traditions and local expedients—a reality in which everything seemed already consummated and nothing remained to be discovered—alludes to a more remote disconnection that dominated the history of the Roman people; or even the history of humankind in the ancient Western world, we might assert, albeit with caution. That rupture had destroyed the link, which for modern people is quite strong, between the urge for knowledge and the transformation of the individual's external surroundings. It had rendered the speculation of the ancients almost a prisoner of itself and of its metaphysical reveries. Nothing was considered worth investigating that did not lead to a direct self-examination of the individual's consciousness of the methods and nature of his own activity, or to a contemplation of the forms, equilibria, and principles which were thought to be buried beneath material phenomena and believed to be secretly and harmoniously aligned with the rhythms and power of the mind capable of discovering them.

It would certainly be oversimplifying to attempt to embrace an entire civilization within the features of a single epistemology. To be sure, if we knew where to look, we could find more at the margins or in the depths of ancient learning. But it remains incontestable that the elements we have described manifest themselves with the force of a dominant tendency, capable of long leaving its mark on intellectual and social attitudes.

So far as we are able to determine, this "dematerialization" of the sensible world in the search for its "first metaphysical causes" was already evident in Ionian thought.[164] Moreover, it culminated in the great classical philosophy of the fifth and fourth centuries B.C., through a process of progressive abandonment whose significance was already apparent to Bacon.[165] It thus took a form that was to greatly influence Western tradition. Its downfall—the large-scale "rematerialization" of the philosophical image of nature—came only with the Renaissance, and, later, with the scientific revolution and modern mechanism and sensism, from Hobbes and Locke to Diderot, d'Holbach, and Leopardi. "Nature loves to hide";[166] "the hidden thread is stronger than the visible one," said Heraclitus.[167] And as Theophrastus wrote, summarizing Anaximander, "the first principle is not water, or any other of the so-called elements, but rather a certain infinite different nature, from which all of the heavens and all of the worlds contained in them arise."[168] The birth of "positive" thought[169] in archaic Ionia has nothing in common with modern research; there was no experimentation, no direct and quantitative observation of nature. Rather, it meant the formation of an abstract rational cosmology which cultivated a spectral vision of the sensible world, and which borrowed from mythic thought the claim that it expressed the most profound form of reality. In the extraordinary crucible and crossroads of culture and knowledge that was the Greek society of Asia Minor, at the same time that the city was being reinvented as a political space—which had no precedent in any oriental tradition—the technical expertise of the Egyptians and Chaldeans in astronomy was transformed not into an experimental science but instead into the Western world's first metaphysics.

It was 213 B.C., and the legions of Marcellus were besieging Syracuse in the crucial phase of the Second Punic War. The Sicilian generals, now despairing of extricating themselves from their difficulties, addressed an appeal to their most illustrious compatriot, the scholar Archimedes, to help them save the city by countering the Roman siege engines with some of his amazing instruments. Archimedes was indeed a gifted inventor—perhaps the greatest in antiquity. In a different context, his talents and flashes of genius would have been considered Leonardesque.

According to Plutarch's account, the Romans had surrounded Syracuse "with sixty quinqueremes filled with all sorts of arms and missiles. [. . .] But all this proved to be of no account in the eyes of Archimedes and in comparison with the engines of Archimedes. To these he had by no means devoted himself as work worthy of his serious effort; most of them were mere offshoots of a geometry he practiced for amusement, since in bygone days Hiero the king had eagerly desired and at last persuaded him to turn his art somewhat from abstract notions to material things, and, by applying his philosophy somehow to the needs which made themselves felt, to render it more evident to the common mind."[170]

Here Plutarch interrupts his narrative to insert a brief excerpt on the history of mechanics.

> The art of mechanics, now so celebrated and admired, was first originated by Eudoxus and Archytas, who embellished geometry with its subtleties and gave to problems incapable of proof by word and diagram a support derived from mechanical illustrations that were patent to the senses. [. . .] But Plato was incensed at this, and inveighed against them as corrupters and destroyers of the pure excellence of geometry, which thus turned her back upon the incorporeal things of abstract thought and descended to the things of sense, making use, moreover, of objects which required much mean and manual labor. For this reason mechanics was made entirely distinct from geometry, and being for a long time ignored by philosophers, came to be regarded as one of the military arts.[171]

Then Plutarch takes up the narration again. Archimedes prepared his implements of war for launching, and put them to use with terrifying effect: "The Romans seemed to be fighting against the gods, now that countlass mischiefs were poured out upon them from an invisible source."[172] Marcellus was forced to suspend all operations, "and thenceforth depended on a long siege."[173] And Plutarch returned to his portrait of the scientist:

> Yet Archimedes possessed such a lofty spirit, so profound a soul, and such a wealth of scientific theory, that although his inventions had won for him a name and fame for superhuman sagacity, he would not consent to leave behind him any treatise on this subject, but, regarding the work of an engineer and every art that ministers to the needs of life as ignoble and vulgar, he devoted his earnest efforts only to those studies whose subtlety

and charm are unaffected by the claims of necessity. [. . .] And although he made many excellent discoveries, he is said to have asked his kinsmen and friends to place over the grave where he would be buried a cylinder enclosing a sphere, with an inscription giving the proportion by which the containing solid exceeds the contained.[174]

It would be pointless to try to determine the trustworthiness of this story. Plutarch's description evokes the profile of an ideal type—the "disinterested" scientist, embodied in the personality of Archimedes—which Roman culture, from the Flavians to the Antonines, condensed in Pliny's example, still proposed as a perfect paradigm. It mattered little (and it mattered little to Plutarch) that this identification required a certain amount of arbitrariness in treating the historical and biographical facts. The convictions of a long tradition, which was considered entirely topical, were reflected in this literary image. It is no coincidence that the imperial patronage system never sought to create a Roman institution comparable to the Museum of Alexandria.

If even the greatest inventor, the true heir to Hellenistic ingenuity and mechanical talents, could be described as if he attached no importance to his discoveries in the field of mechanics, competing with the purest of philosophies, then surely knowledge served only to contemplate the truth and to improve the self: thus believed Plutarch. The passageway between knowledge and the transformation of nature was sealed off; instead, an abyss was being dug. And it was this chasm that expressed a trait of the ancient world.

Perceptible nature remained external to history. Fantasy, first animistic and mythical, then metaphysical, worked constantly to transcend nature, to go beyond it with thought and examination, in order to gain immediate access to a layer of essences and meanings that were considered much more important and that lay beneath surface phenomena, which only cryptically revealed them. Geometry had dignity only to the extent that it was rigorously stripped of *sensibilia* and transformed into an abstract representation of forms.

The perception of physical environment was divided into two distinct images. In the first—the only one considered lofty and respectable—reality was the theater of immaterial presences and forces, remote and mysterious, to be deciphered by means of the bonding of the soul and the careful qualitative identification of details. The solution to the enigma (Heraclitus comes to mind again) was the schema that was most successful in bringing humans closer to the truth. Nature could be assisted in yielding her fruits;[175] one had to respect the system of rules deduced from observing her rhythms and her anthropomorphic appearances (by behaving "according to" nature, never "contrary" to her);[176] one could go below the surface with the acuteness of intelligence in order to reveal the hidden parts of her stage, but one could never hope to defeat and control her. Even the most consistent of "realisms" or the so-called ancient materialisms—from Parmenides ("You will not separate the being from his connection with the being"),[177] to Democritus, Epicurus, and Lucretius—were unfailingly transformed into metaphysical hypotheses. To take inspiration from them, modern sensism will first have to reinterpret them in light of the new science.

According to the second image of physical reality, the "base" and "mechanical" one, nature was raw material, blind and unformed. It was a substance unilluminated by reason that was left to artisans and slaves to manipulate for the sake of practical benefit, or that had to be borne as an unavoidable burden. This cognitive breach—a true schism—was a projection of the dualism at the heart of the Greeks' self-perception, in the primal elaboration of strongly felt psychic experience: the spirit as opposed to the envelope that contains it (temporarily?); the liberty and litheness of thought, in contrast to the shackles and heaviness of the body (as Heraclitus said, "By walking, you will be unable to find the boundaries of the soul, even if you go down every street—so profound is its *logos*").[178] But the imprisoned mind found ways to vindicate its inferiority. Beyond the screen of the material, metaphysics revealed a world of essences and forms in which nature appeared completely "spiritualized" and in whose contemplation the philosopher could satisfy his needs, now that he was released from all bodily constraint.

Western Christianity was to work for a long time, and with lasting results, on this schema—which created a gulf between the "spiritual" and the "material," between "body" and "soul," down to the deepest structures of individual identities—and reintroduced it in contexts of ever-increasing complexity. And modern science would inherit it as its starting point (Descartes, and Spinoza in many respects, are examples). We are only now beginning to overcome it, and with great effort. But the original paradigm was already present in Greece, then in Rome. Its origins were the expression of a resolutely antimaterialistic attitude that was to condition ancient civilization as a whole. The famed Roman "pragmatism" was social, not technological. It affected matters of government, politics, law, and military organization, and, to a lesser extent, the techniques of persuasion and consensus (oratory and satire). It derived from an atavistic inclination toward distribution and regulation,[179] as expressed in the ubiquitous ritualistic prescriptiveness of archaic law and religion. The relationship with nature played no role here.

From our own vantage point, what was lacking was the modern discovery that the material world is a "laboratory" whose dimensions and measurements can be precisely calculated and in which the intellect, given the proper keys, can feel at home; whose laws can be interpreted using the language of mathematics; whose principles can be revealed through experimentation and quantitative observation—a revolution that would not eliminate the old dualism between "mind" and "matter" but would lead to progressively more sophisticated and problematic versions of it, until the boundaries separating the two would reach the state of fluid uncertainty to which we are now becoming accustomed.

Ancient philosophy did not conceive of the possibility that the material world could be seen as a field of reason to be dominated and controlled through the verification of experiments, without being allowed to dissolve into metaphysical transcendence. In sum, there was no connection between scientific knowledge and the transformation of external surroundings, or, in other words, between science and power—the association that is so familiar to modern thought. (Even in Renaissance magic and the hermetic tradition of the fifteenth, sixteenth, and seventeenth centuries—the areas of closest contiguity between modern culture and the thinking of the ancients—knowledge was never simply sheer contemplation, but strength and domination.) "Nothing that is not directly produced can truly be understood by reasoning"; "only that which has been made can be true." Such statements have marked Western cognition from Vico to the physicists of the late twentieth century, but they are affirmations that no ancient could ever have consciously formulated.

This lack of any contact between intelligence and transformative production,[180] a link that is first made by experimentation, explains the series of epistemological catastrophes throughout ancient science. We need only mention the incredible refusal of Greek anatomists to admit that blood flowed through a double network of arteries and veins, a refusal which led them to substitute theories as ingenious as they were implausible for the evidence provided by their own observations[181] (not even medicine, despite its spirit of inquiry and the waves of empiricism that periodically affected it, could escape the common trap). And it explains the feelings of satisfaction and completely unfounded saturation that took hold of the Greek and Roman "scientists" early on. Everything has already been discovered, they thought. In the opinion of Vitruvius, architecture had reached a state of unsurpassable perfection.[182] The physicians of the empirical school, according to Celsus, believed their knowledge was fully developed;[183] the brief period when anatomical dissections flourished came rapidly to an end because of the conviction that there was nothing more to explore (and the practice would not resume until the Renaissance).[184] And Pliny wrote that "no new processes can be invented"[185] in agriculture. They all thought they had finished, but in truth they had not even begun.

The exclusively rural character of the ancient world thus becomes apparent, in a much more profound sense than what is usually understood. Ostracized from history, the technological relationship between society and nature was enclosed in a static equilibrium, with no possibility of change. The hidden forces of the land could be assisted in producing nourishment for human beings, but nothing more. If nature was the domain of secret qualities, powers, and relations, using technology to force a way in was futile and dangerous. Her mysteries were to be unlocked through contemplation, not resolved with physics and mechanics. This position brooked no alternatives. Even the restless and curious Posidonius, a wide-ranging intellectual, an attentive and capable astronomer and geographer, had failed to say anything different, though he had attempted in his own way to maintain a connection, however tenuous, between philosophy and technological advances. ("All of these things have been invented by the learned, who, considering their discoveries too lowly for themselves to attend to their execution, entrusted it to more modest men," he said.[186] This statement earned him a sarcastic comment from Seneca: "He comes close to saying that even the shoemaker's craft was invented by the learned.")[187] For Posidonius, even penetrating the depths of the earth to extract its metals was morally reprehensible:[188] according to an ancient historical tradition, which Seneca later repeated,[189] human beings should not search for what nature had wished to hide by burying it beneath the ground. To be sure, these prohibitions did not impede the development of intensive mining activities, in areas ranging from Greece to Spain, employing particularly advanced extractive technologies and the extensive use of slave labor (as we have seen); but they do allow us to appraise the constraints and idiosyncrasies of the times. Between heaven and earth, the history of mankind could only transpire within inviolable boundaries, in compliance with rhythms and cadences (the weather and seasons in the countryside, the tides, the phases of the moon—again investigated by Posidonius—and the biological sequences of life)[190] whose course almost never corresponded to the open form of progress, but rather reflected the harmonic perfection of repetition and cycles.

Transformational artificiality presupposes instead a disinterested, quantitative vision of nature and a compact, positive idea of matter. The distance between Plato and Descartes represents the space between the "base," traditional expertise inherent in the ancient crafts, and the passion for innovation of modern industrial systems[191] (but this statement does not hold true for Renaissance neo-Platonism, which, as we have already seen, led to very different results). To be sure, classical thought was sometimes able to conceive of the course of technology as a history of innovation and movement: "In technology it is inevitable that what is most recent prevails," we read in a surprising passage in Thucydides (where the Corinthian ambassadors are speaking to the Spartans).[192] But these were isolated bits—fragments of reflections in which the isolated echo of a distant past less influenced by an antimaterialistic perspective (which we have already touched on, and to which we will shortly return) was preserved, then extinguished, without noticeable intellectual or social consequences.

(5)

The picture is coming into focus. The existence of slavery was not the reason the wings of ancient mechanization were clipped. The disjunction between production and machines dated back to a more distant circumstance, whose origins were independent of the subsequent spread of the use of slave labor in the Mediterranean region. Nevertheless, it is true that for a fairly long time the presence of a large number of slaves did conceal, at least in part, the effects of the lack of machines, by providing ample reserves of low-cost energy, employed in the circuits of production as a function of the market. Slavery was thus at the heart of a strange paradox. On the one hand, its existence ensured the functioning of an economy based on exchange, the circulation of commodities, regular patterns of consumption, and urban development—characteristics which gave rise to the aura of singular "modernity" that seemed to accompany the most intensive uses of slave labor (in the mines, *villae*, workshops, and large estates) and has so effectively captured the fancy of certain historians. (This impression has been accentuated by the discovery, confirmed by American revisionists, that the slaves were in no way inefficient in their work and that the businesses using them were not managed "irrationally.")

On the other hand, it was the very duration and efficiency of the organization of slavery that led to the eventual stagnation of the system, blocking off other paths. In short, the use of slaves in production was at the same time the factor that made the most progressive results possible, and an insuperable obstacle to any alternative, more "modern" solution.

To help us understand this apparent contradiction, we would do well to compare the Roman situation with the American one, being careful, however, to avoid overinterpretation. If the Southern plantations were able to keep pace with the North, surviving in a largely capitalist market, and if in a world already transformed by the Industrial Revolution the use of slavery—at least from a narrowly economic point of view—could have been prolonged indefinitely (although in a limited area), there is no reason to doubt that in less competitive situations a well-run system of slavery like the Roman one could have produced consistent and considerable revenues. With regard to the relationship between slave labor and the results of production, therefore, the imperial system cannot in any way be called a "primitive" economic form. The first question we asked at the beginning of this chapter—whether slavery is synonymous with quantitative underdevelopment—must be answered in the negative.

But the slave economy of the Confederate States was functioning in a world already transformed by capitalism, and was developing in its interstices, so to speak. Slavery there was not at all connected with the origin and dynamics of the industrial world, which owed its existence to quite different causes. The modern-day compatibility between "local" structures of slavery and a "worldwide" capitalist economy has much to teach us about the productive capabilities of forced labor in antiquity, but it tells us nothing new about whether a slave-dependent economy—when it is the dominant, "universal" system—can trigger and sustain the transformation to capitalism (the second question we posed). A hypothesis of this kind remains impossible to prove, either historically or conceptually. So far as we know, the association between industrial modernity and free labor is a necessary step in any case.

Precisely because of its decentralized and local roots, slavery in America was in its own way a "parasitic" system, in a world dominated by free labor: it took advantage of technologies and organizations that it could never have produced on its own, using them to reinforce itself and to improve its own performance. Roman slavery instead had no opportunity to procure anything from external sources, because of the very fact that it was a global institution. Thus, in another sense—one that we might ascribe not only to functional and quantitative but also to genetic compatibility with industrial development—the slave system proved to be a singularly "ancient" form. Transplanted into modern times, it was in any case destined to remain intrinsically subordinate, although it was endowed with tenacious (and long undervalued) vitality.

But why in the ancient West did the relationship between nature and society—between materiality and history—harden into the solid cultural and mental block we have seen? Why were the Greek and Roman civilizations so inhibited in their ability to conceive of ways to transform the external environment that they are known for their distinctive and exceptional cultural one-sidedness? Why were they able to nurture extraordinary talent in theorization, fine arts, literature, politics, and the law that was entirely dissociated from their incomparably more limited skill with technology? Were they truly giants with feet of clay?

Why did they feel it necessary to spread a veil over the elements of society dedicated to the transformations of nature that were absolutely essential to ensure the sustenance of the population, the production of a surplus, and the maintenance of a high level of urban life? What were the reasons behind this attitude, which oscillated between contempt and collective repression and which was always incapable of formulating any kind of work ethic?

This had not always been the case in Mediterranean and Near Eastern civilizations. The history of technological advancement in that part of the world followed an irregular course. By the end of the imperial Roman era, in the consciousness of the ancients the distinction between "barbarian" and "civilized" seems to have been reduced to the use of writing and the ethical elaboration of their own behavior, disregarding technology altogether: "If anyone extinguishes the force of our literary expression, we are lowered to the level of the barbarians," wrote Libanius in the middle of the fourth century A.D.[193] (Sidonius later repeated the same idea.)[194] And we can credit Tacitus with being the first to describe the "moral barrier" (not a technological one) on the Rhine and the Danube[195] that Andreas Alföldi discussed.[196] There were, in fact, differences in the ways various populations mastered the techniques, but these disparities concerned circumscribed elements from which it would be difficult to generalize. For example, the Celtic and Roman methods of ironwork and salt mining[197] could be considered virtually equal from the point of view of their productivity. The diversity in their methods arose from their social organization, not the development and application of their skills.

But if we go back farther in time, we find another state of affairs. During the Neolithic Age and the Iron Age, there was a definite leap forward in technology in the area extending from the eastern Mediterranean to western Asia[198]—although it was diluted by the long scansions of the prehistoric era. Its most significant results consisted of the changeover to agriculture and the diffusion of metallurgy. Radiocarbon tests date the existence of permanent agricultural communities in southwest Asia from the ninth to the seventh millennia B.C.[199] In the fifth millennium grain was regularly cultivated in the Nile Valley; and between 4500 and 2000 B.C. a stable agricultural economy evolved on the Mediterranean coast and in many regions of the European hinterland, reaching as far as Germany and Scandinavia.

In Anatolia there are traces of copperwork dating from as early as the seventh millennium B.C.; in the Aegean, from the beginning of the third. People in Europe and Asia had already long been building wheels and carts for labor and battle. At the end of the second millennium, from the thirteenth to the eleventh centuries, the technique of hammering bronze for vases, helmets, cuirasses, and shields was widely practiced in Western Asia and the Aegean: that point marks the threshold of the world made familiar by the *Iliad*. Then the advances came to a halt. From the Iron Age to the economic renaissance of the late Middle Ages, there were no significant developments in the West. If we compare the state of technology in Europe just after the year 1000 A.D. with that of China or the Arab world, either of the latter could be shown to have been in the lead; and this was to remain the case until at least the middle of the fourteenth century.

What importance should we ascribe to this standstill? If we measured it on the scale of the preceding periods, a pause of slightly more than 2,000 years might even seem of little account: between the first signs of the agricultural revolution and the peak of the Bronze Age, surely no less time had passed. But the point is that within the same span of centuries the course of the "rest" of history on the shores of the Mediterranean—the history of politics, society, literature, taste, customs, the arts, and the law—had acquired a very different tempo and rhythm, and had rapidly achieved spectacular results. In this sense—to indicate the obvious disparity of rhythms within the environment under consideration—it may not be inappropriate to speak of technological "stagnation." It was as if the sudden acceleration which had transformed the patterns of time and the quality of life in that corner of the world at the end of the first millennium had come to a halt without affecting the relation between humans, nature, and technology. This aspect seems to have been precociously dominated by an immutable set of attitudes inherited from a past of which no traces remained.

Why was this so?

Let us return once more to the world of archaic Greece. We have seen that the rejection of technology and physical labor was less deep-rooted at that time than in the eras that followed. The myth of Prometheus, the ancient Stoic doctrine of the divinization of the hero-benefactors,[200] the Platonic image of God as craftsman are signs that point to layers of thought and social experience in which technological ability and skill had more prestige.

Now let us try to go even further back in time, before the so-called Hellenic Middle Ages. As far as we can determine, even in the Minoan and Mycenaean civilizations the relationship between the artisans and the elites was closer then than it was later on (and in Etruscan Italy, the situation must have been similar). What appeared, from the point of view of classical Greece and republican Rome, to be indigenous characteristics—the refusal of manual labor and the exclusion of technical knowledge from high culture—now reveal themselves to have been the results of a process and a transformation. Results, not archetypes.

In the Greek cities of the eastern Mediterranean between the beginning of the first millennium and the eighth to sixth centuries B.C., the conditions produced by improvements in the functioning of organizations, the accumulated technological progress in Europe and Asia, the frequency of travel and commerce, and the new kinds of relationships between civic bodies and urban spaces—the same ones that were to lead to the birth of politics and "isonomy"—had laid the groundwork for an unprecedented change. One portion of the community had been "mentally liberated" in a strong and (relatively) rapid manner from the ancient routines imposed by the older, more severe conditions of life and the exercise of power.

At the heart of the new equilibrium was the belief that the immateriality of thought and the emotional, ethical, and political aspects of reality were superior to the dark and constrictive materiality of the physical world. An aristocracy took shape which was able to add to arms and domination the ever-increasing exercise of speech, the memory of poetry and music, the contemplative observation of the heavens, and the intoxicating discovery that the "soul" ("I have looked into myself")[201] was a limitless psychic spirituality: "one of the soul's properties is a logos that expands itself."[202] Philosophy was invented, along with what Bruno Snell[203] and Jean-Pierre Vernant[204] have called "the discovery of the spirit" in the West. The introduction of the alphabet and the resulting conquest—through the "fission" of syllables—achieved by the expressive omnipotence of writing played a part in the same cultural surge.[205]

The new polity was marked by the primacy of the interior self and of political ties over the material aspects of life. What resulted can be described as the anthropological structure of the Mediterranean aristocracies. The heroic individualism of the *Iliad*—which already marked a step along this road—would soon become the self-perception revealed through lyric poetry and the tragic retellings of myth. Later, it would mean the development of rational and abstract discursiveness and the skillful practice of politics—and, in Rome, a military posture, a talent for organization, and juridical sophistication.

Running the risk of adopting a deterministic standpoint,[206] we might maintain that this was the specifically Greek or Ionic outcome of the cycle that began with the "agricultural revolution" which had inaugurated the history of Europe. The long development of technology from the late Neolithic period to the Mycenaean era had created, for the first time, the conditions necessary to liberate the thought processes of whole generations of people—in the Aegean cities of the Orient and the Occident—from the ties imposed by earlier restrictions and old stereotypes of behavior. At the heart of this open and expanding world a reserve of intellectual potential was now available, which could turn in a number of directions. From among the various possible paths (the course taken in Egypt and Mesopotamia was quite different), what was chosen was the flight of the more evolved mind from the prison that had confined it up to that point.

The essence of the "new man" was expressed in politics, war, civic life, the poetic and metaphysical transformation of the world, and the analysis of the forms of rational thought. The rest—the realities of subsistence and production, the mechanical and instrumental conception of nature—was transformed in the mnemonic surge of an ancient servitude, as the memory of a dependency, now dissolved, on the materiality of the earth and the body. Freedom consisted of mastering the techniques of social intercourse in the *polis:* writing and its precepts, music and poetry, rhetoric, self-awareness, travel and the conquest of new lands, the exercise of arms as a virtue at first reserved for the aristocracy, but later permitted to every good citizen—with labor in the fields considered, at most, a guarantee of autonomy and civic independence.

The evolving texture of Mediterranean culture manifested from the time of its origin—and preserved from Greece to Rome (but Rome itself was a "Greek" city in its own way)[207]—a peculiarly "spiritual" imbalance, to use the term employed by Snell and Vernant. This was clearly visible, for example, in the ritualistic mantle of Roman religious practice and archaic law. The technological advances that allowed the creation of that civilization were now disregarded, becoming the shadowy side of this world. To ignore them was the revenge of thought that was finally liberated from distant constraints, of minds which, no longer imprisoned, were now able to probe the expanses they were discovering within themselves.

Moreover, it is precisely in this holistic triumph of the "spirit," which, as we have said, is also clearly visible in all ancient forms of naturalism and realism and even in the recurring legend (so fascinating to the moderns) of the original Golden Age—with respect to which time and history had led to nothing but retrogression—that the genesis of the myth of the "classical" resides. It was the discovery of a charmed state in which a disincarnate perfection never ceases to bring delight and gratification and which is still capable of entrancing us, on the condition that we value it for what it really is—the result of societies only partially developed—and not try to transport it artificially into modernity, for that would be an entirely different matter.

In the history of Greece and then Rome, this asymmetry—which in time assumed the character of an anthropological structure—soon took on definitively aristocratic shadings (which even the most radical manifestations of Athenian democracy did not abandon). The aristocracy emerged with increasing success as the "universal class" in that civilization,[208] the social expression of its cultural one-sidedness, we might say. We are now able to understand more clearly the reasons for the consequence of this (which we have already described in our account): all of the elements that came together to form the obscure foundation of this world—technology, cooperative production, the various kinds of manual labor that were different from the solitary exertions of the peasant on his lands—could not but end up socially and intellectually abandoned to the lowliest members of the community, in direct contact with the exploitation of the slaves, for whom the necessity and demand increased out of all proportion. The circle between the spread of slavery, the rejection of labor, and the absence of machines, from which we began our analysis, then closed: the labor of slaves was in symmetry with and concealed behind (so to speak) the freedom of aristocratic thought, while this in its turn was in symmetry with the flight from a mechanical and quantitative vision of nature. It would have been quite difficult to interrupt this kind of spiral without completely disrupting the era.

Through a coincidence that can be explained in various ways but not denied, the crisis of Roman slavery, beginning in the early years of the third century A.D., took place at the same time as the collapse of the entire imperial economic system. Its definitive decline (for it languished in Europe long after the fall of the empire, fading away particularly slowly) marked an irreversible breach in the history of the Western world. Never again in this region of the world would slavery play a role even remotely comparable to the one it had in Rome.[209]

The stage was laboriously being set for a major innovation: the historical separation between production and personal domination, as labor made its way from coercion into the orbit of individual freedom. The changeover has been progressive, and in many ways is still far from complete (in fact, today we are in the midst of another revolutionary phase). At the beginning, it was made possible not by advances in ethics but by a series of economic circumstances related to the downfall of the ancient world, and later it was helped along more and more by changes in technology.

Even the medieval economy would know about and use forms of dependent labor, especially in the countryside. To designate a person who performed such labor, the word for "slave" in Latin was still used: *servus* (and its derivatives *servile, servitus;* and later the French *serf* and the Italian *servo*). But as Marc Bloch has shown,[210] the lack of lexical differentiation masked a growing semantic one, indicative of the profound modifications in its economic, social, institutional, and juridical connotations. From the fourth to the ninth centuries, a process was under way that would completely transform the history of labor in Europe and the social landscape of the countryside. The changes were so striking, and the new "serfs" had so little in common with the ancient "slaves," that in order to designate the original form of slavery (we can call it "Roman slavery") where it still survived in a peripheral way, a new word was necessary. Probably starting in the tenth century, the word *sclavus* (*esclave, sklave, slave, schiavo*) was used to refer unequivocally to the ethnic origins of the victims of the slave trade. Thus, even in its very name, "modern" slavery had racial connotations that had been more in the background (if not entirely absent) in the ancient practice. For this reason we translate the word *servus* in ancient texts with "slave," not "servant" or *Knecht, serf, servo*—words which preserve the medieval resonance of *servus* in European languages, instead of the meaning of the classical Latin term. This semantic asymmetry conceals, and almost erases, the traces of a change of civilization.

Chapter Ten

Ancient and Modern Work:
Three Philosophers

(1)

Let us take another look at these problems before coming to the epilogue.

In the first book of the *Politics,* in the same context as the passages we have already cited, Aristotle writes:

> A possession is spoken of in the same way as a part. For a part is not only part of another but belongs to another wholly; and so too, similarly, does a possession. Accordingly, whereas the master is only the master of his slave but does not belong to him, the slave is not only the slave of his master, but belongs to him wholly. These considerations make clear what the nature and capacity of the slave are. Anyone who, though human, belongs by nature not to himself but to another is by nature a slave; and a human being belongs to another if, in spite of being human, he is a possession; and a possession is a tool for action and has a separate existence.[1]

Aristotle revealed the pattern of an insurmountable asymmetry between master and slave. The ties of dependency so effectively erased every vestige of autonomy in the actions of the subordinate that these activities seemed to be produced by a mere tool already present in nature, and not constructed by the skill of a craftsman. For Aristotle the labor of slaves, like that of hammers or shuttles or oxen, could not have a history. It nullified itself in the sheer materiality of its existence. History was present only in the models of organization and subordination imposed by the masters.

The condition of the slaves thus lacked any possibility of transformation. It was petrified in a timeless immobility. There was no way to change it. The slave was entirely reduced to a single dimension—the "natural" one proper to objects and things. His role as producer did not set any liberating forces in motion. On the contrary, it was this very function—with its intrinsic relationship to the ties of dependence—that degraded him and drove him out of the community.

Aristotle's analysis reflected the conceptual essence of the condition of a chattel slave, recognizing its total annihilation. We cannot expect his vision to account as well for all of the directions in which Roman slavery developed. We would find it difficult to reconcile the social status of slaves as described by jurists in the period between the late republic and the Severan age—who acted as buyers and sellers, ran ships and plantations, conducted business negotiations, and held administrative posts reaching to the courts—with the implacable scheme of the *Politics*. Some of the jurists during the principate (including Mela and Africanus, a student of the great Julian)[2] even refused to extend to slaves the generic title of "commodities," so strong was the perception that their special economic status called for a specific juridical designation that would go beyond inadequate simplifications. Cicero, in *De republica,* had already distanced himself from the Aristotelian model (as we have noted),[3] stressing the aspect of discipline and punishment inherent in the masters' domination (in other words, underlining what we might call slavery's "historical" and "sociological" side), and deemphasizing its importance as a purely naturalistic phenomenon.

Nevertheless, even the most audacious Roman innovations could not succeed in obliterating the institutional specificity of the mechanisms of slavery, which had always remained true to the philosopher's description. No matter how conspicuous they may have been, all of the variations were seen as functional exceptions or conceptual nuances, never as evidence of a new regimen.

More than twenty centuries after Aristotle's remarks, the same relationship of subjection would return, illuminated by a light which, although no less crude, was completely different. The passage—equally famous— seems to be a gloss that completely overwhelms the text of the *Politics*:

> The lord relates himself mediately to the bondsman through a being [a thing] that is independent, for it is just this which holds the bondsman in bondage; it is his chain from which he could not break free in the strug-

gle, thus proving himself to be dependent, to possess his independence in thinghood. But the lord is the power over this thing, for he proved in the struggle that it is something merely negative. Since he is the power over this thing and this again is the power over the other [the bondsman], it follows that he holds the other in subjection. Equally, the lord relates himself mediately to the thing through the bondsman. The bondsman *qua* self-consciousness in general also relates himself negatively to the thing, and takes away its independence. But at the same time the thing is independent *vis-à-vis* the bondsman, whose negating of it, therefore, cannot go the length of being altogether done with it to the point of annihilation; in other words, he only *works* on it. For the lord, on the other hand, the *immediate* relation becomes through this mediation the sheer negation of the thing, or the enjoyment of it. What desire failed to achieve, he succeeds in doing—namely to have done with the thing altogether, and to achieve satisfaction in the enjoyment of it. Desire failed to do this because of the thing's independence; but the lord, who has interposed the bondsman between it and himself, takes to himself only the dependent aspect of the thing and has the pure enjoyment of it. The aspect of its independence he leaves to the bondsman, who works on it. [. . .] But this satisfaction [on the lord's part] is itself only a fleeting one, for it lacks the side of objectivity and permanence. Work [of the bondsman], on the other hand, is desire held in check, fleetingness staved off; in other words, work forms and shapes the thing. The negative relation to the object becomes its *form* and something *permanent*, because it is precisely for the worker that the object has independence.[4]

This is Hegel writing in the second section of his *Phenomenology of Spirit*, published for the first time in 1807. To all appearances the scene has not changed, with the master on one side and his slave on the other. But the identification of the protagonist has been transposed: the hand of history has completely shifted; here the slave is the real victor, not the master. How can this be? As a modern, Hegel has simply realized something that Aristotle had obfuscated (or rather, something that his world had obfuscated for him): the transforming power of labor.

Hegel explains why the relationship—when considered from the master's point of view, as in Aristotle—cannot but be immobile and fixed (just as it seemed to the ancient philosopher). The master is rigidly inserted in his dominion, as Alexandre Kojève remarks:[5] the relationship cannot go forward, change, or develop. The master, who does not work, does not create anything substantial outside himself; he can only destroy the products of the slave's labor. His existence consists of a sterile short-circuit between desire and possession: he lives in an "existential blind alley," as Kojève put it.[6] (The obsession with the corrupting influence of wealth and dissipation that constantly hung over the great ancient aristocracies was condensed here by Hegel in a flash of inspiration. We know that philosophers do not relate the facts in a narrative fashion, but instead are able at will to distill their essence, as if by a concentration of thought.)

On the contrary, the germination and development of history depends entirely on the slave at work. Aristotle could not have been aware of this—and not for lack of analytic ability or ethical awareness. What he failed to perceive was precisely the relationship between labor and history: that the history of mankind is nothing but the history of their labor—an association that is dominant from Hegel's perspective. Aristotle did not understand it (and neither did Cicero), because in his world labor—and not only the labor of slaves—was confined to a purely naturalistic and repetitive dimension. Between intellectual ability and production an insurmountable gulf had already opened. The ties of personal dependence only reinforced this condition of exclusion and subordination.

Hegel, on the other hand, examined the activities of slaves from the viewpoint of someone capable of appreciating the explosive elements inherent in the social sphere of modern production, where the fracture between intelligence and materiality of action had been overcome, and the disruptive force of the self-emancipation of labor could assert itself by means of the new "civil society" in Europe. The reduction of human beings to "articles of property," a topic on which the *Politics* and the *Phenomenology of Spirit* both dwell, was thus open to contradictory interpretations: for Aristotle it led to the destruction of the status of the slave as a person ("a possession may be defined as an instrument of action"); for Hegel it laid the foundations for the possibility of the slave's liberation ("thus proving himself [. . .] to possess his independence [by means of work] in thinghood").

This contrast, which I would not hesitate to describe as dramatic, has the depth of an abyss. It clearly demonstrates, with no softening of reality, the enormous distance between the ancient and the modern.

(2)

Several decades after Hegel's reflections, Marx presented the same antithesis from a different but no less edifying point of view: "In slave labor, even that part of the workday in which the slave is only replacing the value of his own means of existence—in which he thus, in fact, works for himself alone—appears as labor for his master. All the slave's labor appears as unpaid labor. In wage labor, on the contrary, even surplus labor, or unpaid labor, appears as paid. There the property relation conceals the labor of the slave for himself; here the money relation conceals the unrequited labor of the wage-labourer." And he adds in a footnote: "The *Morning Star*, a London free-trade organ, naive to silliness, protested again and again during the American Civil War, with all the moral indignation of which man is capable, that the negro in the 'Confederate states' worked for absolutely nothing. It should have compared the daily cost of such a negro with that of the free workman in the East End of London."[7] This comes from the section on wages in the first book of *Das Kapital*. The subject is the relationship between labor and time— a crucial matter for the economies and the consciences of the modern era.

Moses Finley has observed that, in our world, "when one hires labour, one purchases an abstraction, labour-power (which is separated from both his person and the product of his work), which the purchaser then uses at a time and under conditions which he, the purchaser, not the 'owner' of the labour-power, determines (and for which he normally pays after he has consumed it)." But in addition to the abstraction of labor-power, "the wage-labour system requires the establishment of a method of measuring the labour one has purchased, for the purposes of payment, commonly by introducing a second abstraction, namely, labour-time."[8] Finley does not refer to Marx here (for the passage from Marx, unlike the one from Hegel, is not well known). But he does touch on the most important nucleus: the sharp contrast in the ways in which systems based on slave labor and those based on wage labor divide the labor-time into "necessary labor" (necessary, that is, to compensate for the value of the goods consumed by the worker required to restore his proper level of subsistence) and "surplus labor" rendered once the level of "necessary labor" has been exceeded.

To establish this comparison, Marx therefore used the concept of "surplus labor": the difference between the total quantity of labor performed by the worker over a certain time period (for example, in one day) and the quantity of work contained in what he consumed in that same time period, either as wages or in other ways. This notion, which has been at the heart of a long dispute in contemporary economic thought, caused rivers of ink to flow during the golden years of Marxism. The discussions concerned the manner in which this concept was connected with the "theory of value" (which states that in a market in equilibrium the ratios of exchange between commodities are equal to the ratios between the quantities of labor contained in the commodities themselves)—a doctrine which turned out to be unfounded—and with the very possibility of scientifically demonstrating the existence of capitalistic "exploitation."

We have no desire to venture down these now dusty roads. Marx's interpretation of the differences between the ancient and modern economies lies before the boundary beyond which the historicization of capitalism (an indisputable virtue that remains topical) was transformed into an analysis of its alleged contradictions, and a prediction of its collapse. For this reason, let us confine our attention here to the wording of the text. What does it have to say? First of all, it claims not only that the division of labor time into necessary and surplus—the relationship between labor and time of which Finley spoke—is at the heart of the calculations of capitalist economics, but also (as Marx implicitly maintained) that any system based on dependent labor and the production of commodities must use this separation. If we wished, we could say as well that in this sense "surplus labor" can be perceived as a totally neutral concept (even if it was not what Marx had in mind), without any particular social or historical connotation (in the same way that Piero Sraffa later used the concept of "surplus"),[9] and therefore without necessarily deducing from it the existence of any form of exploitation.

But with this constant as his starting point, Marx discovered that the division of labor time was concealed in opposite ways in slave and free societies. In the workday of the slave, the division of labor time was covered up by the omnipresence of the personal relationship of dependence—a precondition which functioned outside the economic process as such, although it reflected it in a crucial way. During part of the day, the slave worked for himself, as if he were not a slave; that is, he "paid" with his labor for his own sustenance (which the master provided to him in the form of goods, services, or even money). But this reality was never clearly disclosed. The relationship of dependence made it invisible, because in formal terms the slave always worked for the master, never for himself. Cato, Varro, the Sasernae, and Columella were obviously successful in cutting through the fog and grasping the essence of the matter—otherwise, they could not have correctly performed their business calculations. And the plantation owners of Georgia and Louisiana were equally successful. But it seems that the hapless editors of the *Morning Star*, so blinded by the abolitionist struggle that they attracted Marx's sarcasm, did not properly understand this state of affairs.

In the case of salaried industrial labor, on the other hand, the situation was exactly the contrary. The division of labor time was concealed by the equal legal status of the two protagonists in the exchange (the salaried worker and the capitalist entrepreneur). In the contract they agreed to, labor as a commodity seemed to be sold at its full market value.

It does not matter whether we concur with Marx's argument that the modern division of labor time was the source of all capitalistic exploitation and the "fetishistic" nature of industrialized societies. From a theoretical point of view, it is rash to conclude that by definition any capitalistic organization of labor involves exploitation. (Surprisingly, Marx himself seems to have been aware of this, as is evidenced by a truly prophetic unpublished passage that critics for some reason have overlooked: "But to the degree that large industry develops, the creation of real wealth comes to depend less on labor time and on the amount of labor employed than on the power of the agencies set in motion during labor time."[10] Here is a case where Marx has already gone beyond Marxism!)

We find that circumstances are different if we shift our attention from economic theory to social history. It has been demonstrated historically (without requiring recourse to any particular theory) that between the Industrial Revolution and Marx's time the English working class was subject to quite severe exploitation—just as it has been historically demonstrated that the ancient (or modern American) slaves were subject to exploitation at least as harsh. We can thus infer that, independently of the theory that Marx believed he was demonstrating, he was analyzing two historical forms of exploitation: the exploitation of slavery (in Rome and America) and that of the English workers in the eighteenth and nineteenth centuries. The difference between these forms lies in the roles played in the respective systems by two opposing formal models: the one that determines the personal relationship of dependence, and the one that determines the exchange between persons of equal juridical status.

In the case of slavery the formalism of the relationship of dependence so crushed the slave that the portion of his labor which served to sustain his own life was lost from view, and it seemed that all of his work went to support his master. In the case of wage labor, the formalism of the contractual relationship between legally equal individuals so exalted the freedom of the worker that even labor which was extorted, and in large part reinvested as a surplus in order to increase capital, was made to seem properly compensated.

Ancient formalism—by status—rested its power on personal domination, not on capital (or even less on labor). As Hegel said, it was on the side of the person who had staked his life and won. Here, the slave's identity as a person was obliterated, putting him at the mercy of his master and obscuring the exploitative nature of his labor by blurring it in the shadows of total oppression. In this way, the system made it impossible to differentiate the laborer's personality (in all its manifestations: legal, political, intellectual, and ethical) from the sale of his labor. And since the subjection of the slave was not a result of the productive process, as the abstraction of his labor would have been, but instead remained a prerequisite for it that was historically and sociologically external (in the final analysis, citing Hegel again, a consequence of the military skills of the victor), the economic circuit could never be self-sustaining. Slaves always had to be introduced "from the outside." It was never capable of producing, as results, the conditions that could guarantee its own existence.

In contrast, modern formalism—by contract—rested its power entirely on capital and the market (that is, on the relationship between wage labor and the capitalist enterprise), concealing its own brand of exploitation behind the new shadow of the legal equality of the contracting parties. It thus opened the way for a new, previously impossible connection: the link between subjectivity and productive labor. This confirmed the shift of history toward the relationship between capital and labor, reflecting what had happened in the West between the late Middle Ages and the Industrial Revolution. It was no accident that the complete "liberation" of labor was the utopian dream of the nineteenth century—a theme that Aristotle could not even have imagined, but without which we would not understand so much of modernity, and certainly not Hegel and Marx.

(3)

We should make one final observation, prompted by the comparison just made.

In ancient societies, where the formalism of the personal relationship of dependence made it generally impossible to treat labor as a kind of commodity, there was another, no less important consequence: labor and capital never faced each other directly. Production, distribution, and consumption were never intertwined in the continuous alternation and integration of cycles that would later form the backbone of modern economies. For this reason, the conditions never arose that could have engendered the social realm from which, in the modern world, the antagonism we define as "class struggle" emerged—a phenomenon that has so profoundly marked recent history.

To be sure, in the era of the most tumultuous changes—between the mid-second century B.C. and the decades that immediately followed the Social War, the period between the Gracchi and Catiline—several early signs that could be considered evidence of the formation of "classes" in the modern sense of the term became especially visible in Roman society: the circulation of commodities, merchant capital, trading profits, economic calculations based on the division of labor time, exploitation, the social division of labor, the rise of groups specialized in intellectual activities, and, most of all, a number of political clashes, even including slave revolts, which could be more directly attributed to economic causes.

But it did not take long for the triumph of slavery (which up to a certain point had created the very conditions for the changes), and the completely successful subjugation of the slaves, to cut off any possibility of further evolution. The transformation stopped in its tracks. Merchant capital was self-contained. Reproduction tended to become repetition, not development. Surpluses were increasingly reserved for the consumption of the ruling classes, and were almost never reinvested in the production cycle.

The interruption helps to clarify why, in comparison to other factors (which at various times included kinship, politics and appointed offices, military ties, and bureaucratic power), the economy played an important role, but not the exclusive one, in the formation of social hierarchies in Rome. And it also explains why Roman society was always structured on the basis of "orders" and "status" rather than "classes." For the development of social classes in a modern sense, the economic sphere would have had to be self-sufficient, and this never came about in Rome. Moreover, it also accounts for the absence of major organized social conflicts in this period, and the almost exclusively patrimonial character of the few truly serious clashes that were recorded[11] and that involved the lowest strata of the population. Those struggles concerned land ownership, the annulment of debts, or tax troubles—nothing to do with labor. It was not yet time for that subject.

Chapter Eleven

A Blind Alley between
Economics and Politics

(1)

We began with a question suggested by the long-established image of perfection and magnificence associated with the Roman Empire. Why was Roman society, after coming to its peak, unable to plunge directly into modernity? Why did the economic and social structures of Western civilization have such a tortuous and remote relationship with their sophisticated ancient past, instead of being its immediate extension? With European civilization already at this high point of development, why was it necessary to begin anew, to start in many ways virtually from zero, after a tremendous catastrophe? Our attempt to respond has led far afield, both in space and in time. Examining the nature of this problem has highlighted some fundamental issues: it has transformed facts into problems that touch the very heart of the history of the Western world, and opened a new vista for our thoughts. But we can now recognize that the question was formulated in a deceptive way. It is time to clear up the misinterpretation.

The uncertainty expressed by Rostovtzeff and Walbank was anchored in their implicit but steadfast conviction not only that the economy of Rome had reached a fairly advanced level, but also, and more important, that the ancient and the modern were markedly compatible—indeed, so similar that it was possible to propose (within an extremely hypothetical fiction) that the imperial society could have fitted readily and directly into the evolution of modern Europe. In other words, they considered the cyclical return of the same forms to be the true message conveyed in the economic history of the West—that the Roman world and the modern-day West are symmetrical in a way that the collapse of the ancient civilization and the rupture caused by the events of the Middle Ages have blurred but not nullified.

This conviction was (and still is) widely held, and seems to reflect deep-rooted historical common sense. From Karl Bücher on, even the theories of primitivist origins, although they place the economies of the Roman world and modern Europe at a greater distance from each other, have defended the existence of a single line of continuity between them—this time a linear relationship, not a cyclical one. To be sure, in order to support their own position, both the old and the new primitivists must emphasize at all costs the unfinished nature of the ancient economy, instead of dwelling, as Rostovtzeff did, on its maturity and on the "political" nature of its final crisis. Nevertheless, this does not cause the thread of continuity to break; instead, it simply renders the course of evolution more gradual and its contours less distinct.

But the assumption that the ancient and the modern are substantially identical is itself the trap concealed in Rostovtzeff's question. Evidence to the contrary has emerged from every viewpoint and every inquiry in our account. The Roman economy and the economy of modern Europe and America are, in their own historical specificity, two different worlds. They are separated by insurmountable qualitative factors, which reflect their drastically divergent mentalities, customs, behaviors, and material and cultural circumstances.

To uncover this misconception is to explain its causes. These consist in assuming that the similarities between most advanced features of the Roman economy and certain aspects of modern economic systems—resemblances that actually exist and that would be impossible to deny—are indications of a precise genealogical derivation. To the modernists, presumption of this line of descent is based on the claim that they have discovered a very clear symmetry and virtually complete overlap between the two systems. This reduces the reason for the distance between them to a mere quirk of chronology, or to the "parenthesis" that was the Middle Ages, or at most to the furious pace of growth experienced in the twentieth century. To the primitivists, the same line of descent, which they too consider indisputable, is attenuated by the recognition that the points of similarity are more limited, and by a greater emphasis on the differences resulting from the improvements which gradually accumulated over the course of the intervening millennium.

Be that as it may, we have found no proof of this assumed filiation. The evidence that is usually presented rests on an incorrect assessment of the comparative relationships between the forms of the two economies, which gives rise either to the mistaken inference that a genealogical link must exist, or (as Rostovtzeff's question implies) to the hypothesis of a fundamental contiguity between the two systems. The whole problem is based on the confusion, in the analysis of the Roman economy, between similarities with modernity which point to the possibility of a genealogical connection, and those which are explained by the fact that common characteristics performed the same functions in different contexts. Thus, a superficial analogy drawn from comparison is mistaken for a rigorous homology determined by derivation. This is an error that must be recognized and avoided.[1]

At times, we can also be misled by the apparent persistence of the juridical forms that cover the economic relationships, in cases in which the modern usage of Roman law seems to be evidence of uninterrupted contact between the ancient and the modern. But this too is illusory, because what has actually been preserved is but a valuable formal syntax—condensed into a rigid specialized vocabulary and a dense network of abstract concepts—which is called on to govern a completely new set of economic and social conditions.

In reality, any comparison between aspects of the economies of Rome and modern or even preindustrial Europe can be considered legitimate only if it succeeds in confronting circumstances that appear as the end result of completely different histories. We are examining neither virtually identical phenomena separated from one another only by the long interval of the Middle Ages, nor a pair of situations in which one must be considered the direct precursor of the other. What we are faced with are two systems that have developed—each following the course of its own history—a not insignificant number of similar characteristics (urban life, navigation, commerce, division of labor, and so on) corresponding to functional requirements that have recurred in the various settings. We cannot find a single modern-day mercantile or financial model that was directly derived from a Roman one. (The same cannot be said of the development of modern from medieval forms.) Moreover, commercial circulation in modern preindustrial societies has proven to be intrinsically different from that of the Roman Empire (as is evident when we consider the labor market, the role of money, the relation between reinvestment and profit, or the relation between production and trade in the two eras). But the fact remains that, since in Roman society there were also relatively widespread and consolidated mechanisms of exchange, we can identify symmetries in the functioning of the ancient and modern systems that lead to certain typological similarities. This is as far as we can go.

The building of economic modernity in the West had its foundations on mental and social characteristics that were totally foreign to the Greeks and Romans: the long and painstaking process of regaining civil and cultural possession of labor, and the invention of a new and untried connection between wage labor and personal liberty, both in renascent medieval cities and in the postfeudal countryside. And later, it meant the reconquest of the physical dimension of nature—matter and movement, in a changed framework of experiments and concepts—as the necessary condition for an alliance between understanding and productivity, and between scientific knowledge, craftsmanship, and technological innovation. After a slow and difficult period of elaboration, these new elements exploded in Europe in the fifteenth to eighteenth centuries. Medieval Christianity and its church played an essential role in this process: their contribution is difficult to overlook, despite the attempts of those who would like to imagine a wall between modernity and Christian teachings.

What is more, the scenario proposed by Rostovtzeff and Walbank did not sufficiently account for another, no less refractory piece of evidence: the difficulty that slave economies faced in reforming themselves, and in redirecting themselves under their own impetus, without trauma or external coercion, toward a model based on wage labor. In other words, the two historians do not seem to appreciate the narrowness of any path (if indeed there was one) that could furnish an untroubled exit from a slave system, once it was completely in place.

(2)

The conclusion seems undeniable. The history of Rome shows no evidence of a true evolutionary fork in the road (as we called it earlier), with one branch pointing toward modernity. This was made impossible by structural constraints and mental obstructions that were never overcome, despite the quantitative success obtained by the imperial economic system.

But, as we noted earlier, Rostovtzeff's hypothesis did contain a striking insight. By conceiving the idea (via a sort of historical short circuit) of a virtual contiguity between the economies of the Roman and modern worlds, his viewpoint correctly emphasized the maturity of the ancient system, and made necessary an unbiased inquiry into its failure to evolve successfully, or at least less disastrously—even before examining the reasons for its downfall.

This, then, is the heart of the question. Although it is unrealistic to conceive of a rapid transition to modernity, could the Romans, at a particular moment of their history, have found another path that might have led to an outcome far different from the one with which we are all familiar—even if it did not immediately move toward the modern world, as Rostovtzeff dreamed? In other words, given this system, was the final catastrophe predetermined from the beginning? Did this civilization contain from the outset the mechanisms for its own breakdown?

We must not be too hasty in our answer. And we must avoid treating the peculiarities of the more mature stage of the Roman economy as if they were not traits outside their time. This is not how we have described them. Indeed, they seem to us to be the result of a complex process, combining explosively brief events with long-enduring constants, elements of slow-moving anthropological continuity interspersed with more eventful and agitated changes in politics, society, culture, and productivity engendered partly by chance. So the question can be reformulated: Could the outcome of such a long historical process—the "classical" structure of the imperial system between the middle of the first century B.C. and the beginning of the second century A.D.—have been so different that the course of its future might have changed, given the cast of actors, the resources available to them, and the potential variations that can reasonably be imagined?

This kind of problem cannot be faced lightly. Although history is a science that leaves no latitude for experimentation and counterevidence, it should not relinquish the opportunity to enrich the horizons of onlookers—whose attention is riveted on what has actually taken place—with hypotheses about what *could* have taken place, so long as these might help shed light on the dynamics and characteristics under discussion.

Therefore, with all due caution, and—if this is not sufficient—inviting readers to contribute even more, I believe that the answer must be in the affirmative. Yes, Rostovtzeff and Walbank were fundamentally correct (at least in this sense). It is likely that another path, one that would have led to a different outcome, actually did exist, although it was closed off almost immediately, within the space of a few decades.

The second century is not the era to which we are alluding. It was no more than a flare at the extreme margin, when all of the various possibilities for transformation had already been exhausted. It represented a mature state to which there were no alternatives. The attention that Rostovtzeff and Walbank paid to this era helped them—and us as well—to describe the problem, but it was not sufficient to arrive at an answer.

We must concentrate instead on a less tranquil time, on a less gilded age during which the "animal spirits" of the imperial economic system were still capable of forging a different route. This is a period that we have already had reason to discuss: when the Roman drive to expansion reached its culmination. In a single vertiginous sequence unequaled in ancient history, these years joined the dissolution of the traditional civic orders—and the culture and social structure that had sustained them—with the municipalization of Italy and with the rapid completion of the system of world domination inaugurated between Zama and Pydna and consolidated after the destruction of Carthage, Corinth, and Numantia.

These were the few decades immediately following the Social War that were crammed with events: Sulla's constitutional and administrative reorganization, the urbanization of south central Italy and Cisalpina (where a major restructuring of the territory took place), Pompey's campaigns in the East and on the seas, the final great slave revolt, Cati-

line's coup, the cultural transformations of Cicero's era, Caesar's conquest of Gaul, right to the end of the civil war, and the *pax Augusta*. If
the film depicting Rome's history were rewound and reprojected from
this period on, there is no guarantee that its outcome would look like the
one that is familiar to us. The sequences of cause and effect that seem so
stable to us are merely the result of lazy retrospective assessment.

Here again, the trail that permits us to understand is more political
than economic, as is almost always the case in Roman history. To our
eyes it takes the form of the extreme dissolution of the old-style aristocratic bloc that had guided the worldwide ascent of the republic, and the
emergence of a Roman-Italic society, with its rough-hewn governance,
at the heart of the empire—a long stream of changes that occupied a
large part of the century and that resonates in the words of Sallust and
Cicero.

The reasons for the crisis of the nobility were deep-seated. They had
to do with the small-mindedness and myopia of its most prominent exponents (if we exclude Sulla and, in part, Pompey); but, more important, they were connected to the consequences of the expansion and
conquests, and to the professionalization of the army. The old senatorial
leadership failed to reformulate its own role in conformity with the new
"municipal Italian state" (to use Emilio Gabba's effective phrase),[2] and
even found it difficult to integrate the new urban elites flexing their
muscles in areas ranging from southern Italy to the Po Valley. Its automatic response was to close the ranks of its own oligarchy, in defense of
now indefensible privileges.

The economic model that we have already described,[3] based on the
cycle proceeding from war to exploitation to contracting to wealth, then
to war again, and on the interlacing of administrative intervention with
private initiatives, had made available to Italy a large number of resources: land, slave labor, monetary liquidity, technological expertise.
But as a consequence of the mechanisms of social mobility created by
the new forms of military recruitment, it had also introduced a set of
forces, ambitions, expectations, and demands from circles, groups, and
social classes which, in Rome and especially in Romanized Italy, sought
advancement, recognition, and power.

The oscillations of Cicero's political thinking, as reconstructed by

Ettore Lepore in a now classic study, are a faithful reflection of this decisive changeover.[4] In the late Sixties B.C., Cicero proposed his first resolution for the crisis. It was centered on the traditional model of "concord between the orders"[5]—a concept dating back to Greek politics, which had been transplanted to Rome as early as the fourth century B.C. to suggest a direction for mediation in the struggle between the patricians and the plebeians after 367 B.C.[6] Even if Cicero's interpretation of it was dynamic and in no way conservative or oligarchical,[7] his recourse to this ancient parameter clearly demonstrates his faith that the problems could be overcome simply by remaining within the restrictive boundaries of the old urban society of the "orders": senators and knights. But the only possible outcome for this collaboration would have been the rebirth of the hegemony of the old aristocracy—a hypothesis that by now was outmoded.

In the space of a few years, however, pressed by the force of events as well as by the progress of his own reflections, Cicero decisively changed his mind, and drew up a completely different plan. He no longer believed that Roman society could overcome the crisis by remaining faithful to the old political and social order and its practical efficacy. The model of "agreement among all good landholding citizens" replaced that of "concord among the orders."[8] Unlike the senators and knights, the "good landholding citizens" did not constitute a potentially closed group; indeed, they were considered "innumerable,"[9] and lived not only in Rome but in "the whole of Italy."[10] All oligarchic ties were broken. The antimunicipal attitude that had been so widespread in noble circles was thought to be sterile and impotent. The *ancien régime* was dead. It was time to acknowledge this, and to act in such a way that from its ruins would rise a new, completely Roman-Italic order, based on the principle that the masses of citizens—both old and new, inhabiting territories throughout the peninsula, who thanks to the empire (and often to their own long service in the new professional army) had gained property, wealth, and visibility—should fully participate in politics and power. In Cicero's view, this new ruling class, the embodiment of the "middle class" which had been in a state of crisis in Rome since the second century but which was now quite well rooted in the colonies and municipalities of Italy, would fulfill its duty by harmoniously amalgamating its allegiance to "two fatherlands"[11]—the "local" one, or the municipality, and the "universal" one, or Rome—in an equilibrium of memories, functions, and political and economic identification.

This plan was not at all unrealistic. If we link it to the ever-increasing mass of evidence of the new social, economic, and cultural conditions in late-republican Italy assembled by archeological, epigraphic, and historical research—an Italy studded with a hundred cities, from Asisium to Cora, from Florentia to Pompeii, from Ticinum to Verona[12]—we are in a good position to evaluate its plausibility, its concrete foundations, and, most important, the force of its prospects.

A combination of circumstances—the collapse of the old aristocracy, together with the consolidation of the process of Romanization, the concentration in Italy of an amount of wealth and a capacity for production and commerce which had never before been present in the ancient world—was creating an unprecedented period of opportunity. It was the beginning of one of history's rare and precious moments of creativity, in which the potential that had built up during a phase of widespread expansion, though it had already accomplished significant results, had not yet been consolidated into a set order or definitive form. Development in various directions was still possible, even in quite different ones. If radical change was ever possible in the history of Rome, it was then. This was the single occasion when the effects of the dynamics that had been set in motion might have been able to go beyond the limits of the system that had produced them.

Moreover, in the air there was a vague, insistent omen of "new things" and the fall of old boundaries. An unequivocal sign of this was the fear, and not only in conservative circles, of *res novae*, of the risk of venturing into the unknown—so masterfully described by Sallust[13] and analyzed by Antonio La Penna.[14] As was the threatening and inconclusive demagogy of the democratic platforms of the populist factions.

Cicero's projects went as far as conceiving the creation of a politically moderate Roman-Italic democracy, geographically decentralized and regulated by a flexible, up-to-date constitutional system capable of running the empire in all its complexity. This pro-Italic approach corresponded in substance with Sallust's (for which Ventidius was perhaps responsible) and, probably, Caesar's, if we can consider him—as Mazzarino has correctly suggested—the true "urbanizer" of the peninsula.[15]

Cicero, Ventidius, and Sallust proposed restructuring the republic around a broad social coalition of small and medium-sized municipal landowners actively involved in commercial and imperial interests, a coalition which would have been capable of shattering the pernicious (and contradictory) alliance between the nobles and the urban plebs that had led first to the confused events culminating in the Jugurthine War, and later to the Social War and the "devastation of Italy."[16]

If this objective had been reached, the history of Rome would have shifted to an unknown orbital path, with unpredictable results.

Santo Mazzarino has used the word "bourgeois" to characterize the landowning middle class that emerged from the process of Romanization.[17] This term seems excessively modernizing to me. Yet it is undeniable that in the achievements of the members of this social sphere, in both their agricultural and their mercantile endeavors, we can perceive the seeds of entrepreneurial industriousness that in the long run might have come to resemble Mazzarino's description. By the same token, it is indisputable that Cicero's new political program, like Sallust's historiography, brought into relief the contrast—however latent it may have been—between the "fortress mentality" of the aristocrats, who were now incapable of actively dominating the course of events, and the rationality of the Italian municipalities, under the influence of small landholders and commercial interests, which were poised to provide vitality, energy, and ideas to the republic.

Cicero's political platform certainly incorporated no element that could be called fully "bourgeois"; and we must not forget that in this same period Cicero was also designing an ideal model of society and a hierarchy of values (mentioned earlier) whose outcome would not have been even remotely similar. Furthermore, a victorious "municipal revolution" would not have been sufficient; for it would also have been necessary to put into effect the economic and cultural premises of a change of this kind. But as we have seen, none of this was even close to being realized. The Roman economic system—including the municipal one—was restrained by weighty ties, inherited even from the anthropology of the ancient Western world. It demonstrated its need for uninterrupted political support at every step. The intensive use of slaves and, from another point of view, the role of public intervention in provisioning the capital city were unmistakable signs of this dependence. And even the rise of urbanization of the Italian countryside between the second and first centuries B.C. clearly had institutional rather than narrowly economic origins.[18]

Nevertheless, despite such a large number of obstacles, the very existence of a special relationship between economics and politics leads one to believe that if the government had exerted its influence more forcefully, and above all for a longer period of time, in the direction of incorporating the average Italian municipality fully into the heart of the empire, making the best use of its spirit of initiative in politics and production—if, in sum, the "municipal revolution" had actually triumphed during those years and if the "identity of Italy" (to repeat Andrea Giardina's felicitous expression)[19] had been perfected—this thrust might have made enough of an impression on events to trigger a set of changes whose outcome was unpredictable. In all probability, more balanced economic ties between the cities and the countryside, and tighter links between agriculture and the markets, would have resulted. The propensity to invest would have increased, the agrarian landscape would have been repopulated with free wage laborers—a focal point of every "democratic" program, from the Gracchi to the last Caesar—and the importance of urban manufacturing would have grown. Although the conditions necessary for the "agrarian capitalism" of preindustrial France or England would still not have existed, the economy of Rome would at least have resembled the state of "potential capitalism" so suggestively discussed by Fernand Braudel.[20] It would have come close to vanquishing the paralyzing preference commonly demonstrated by the aristocrats for revenue in the place of productivity.

A new state of affairs could have been established, loosening the bonds imposed by the long and generalized use of slave labor, which henceforth would have served only as a fly-wheel for growth based on other factors. The entire system would have had a new configuration: capital and labor would have competed directly in manufacturing and farming, and the historical dependence on war booty would have been overcome. It is impossible to conceive of the consequences—including the cultural ones—of such a scenario, had it been realized. The future of Rome would have acquired an Italic coloring even before worldly and ecumenical tones, and the entire history of Europe would have taken an unknown tack.

But at the very moment that this new order seemed to be most within reach—between Sulla's time and that of Caesar—in the space of a few years the conquests first by Pompey and then by Caesar and the newly regained security of the seas permitted an unprecedented influx of slaves (at least one million, it is said), and put an unusual amount of new land (in Gaul) and new resources (in the East) at the disposal of the empire, thus definitively shifting its axis away from the Italian peninsula. The picture suddenly changed. The outcome was determined as much by fortuitous circumstances as by structural causes. The Italian municipalities failed to find a true leader. And insofar as the victory of Octavian accentuated the purely localistic and administrative aspects—rather than the thoroughly political and federative nature—of the autonomy and organization of the peninsula, it furthered a completely different arrangement, consistent with the economic tendencies that had already manifested themselves. Rome, now even more isolated from the rest of Italy, extended its universalistic vocation; and instead of reforming itself, the imperial system drowned in its own success, so to speak, and in the ephemeral abundance that had produced it. In the short run, well-being increased and opportunities multiplied, and the newfound peace made everything easier. But the time for discovering alternative solutions had forever slipped away.

(3)

There is one additional indication of how, in the space of a few short years, the economic situation reached a critical threshold from which transformations along various lines were possible. We return again to slavery.

In the doctrines of late-republican jurists, the use of slaves is portrayed in an unexpectedly ambiguous light.[21] Not only was it considered beneficial, in that it made possible the total utilization of labor at a very low cost, but it was also a constraint, a sort of obstacle to be overcome in order for the society to achieve a combination of human resources and mercantile cycles that never would have been possible with the "classical" form of chattel slavery, where slaves were considered only commodities.

This evidence is very important—perhaps the most progressive statement of its era; but for some reason it has not attracted the notice of historians. From the middle of the second century B.C. to the age of Augustus—when the expansion of slave labor in Italy reached its culmination—jurists and magistrates who administered civil justice addressed issues of slavery with an intensity never to be equaled in succeeding periods. Their work resulted in a sort of "commercial law of slavery" without parallel in any other slaveholding society, whether ancient or modern. The aim they lucidly pursued was—as much as seemed possible without completely obliterating the ties of personal subordination—to integrate the best slaves into superior management positions. This was achievable only through the concession of numerous forms of juridical and patrimonial autonomy. As a result, the regulation of slavery came under a kind of dual regime: one continued to be centered on the personal tie between slave and master, and the other involved the limited but increasingly disruptive state of patrimonial and commercial independence in which the slaves were placed, so long as it remained within the field of production and trade. The jurists faced this extremely difficult task, which created a tangle of problems, with subtlety and skill. Soon such a dense web of circumventions and regulations was spread over the original form of chattel slavery that, sociologically and juridically speaking, it held a unique place among slave societies in history.

The slaves continued to be treated essentially as human tools, as commodities (although of a particular kind). Aristotle's definition was never belied. But at the same time, through the subtle mechanics of legal fictions and transpositions, they were indirectly allowed to play active and even leading roles in commerce, maritime trade, and the administration of farms and workshops. Numerous and detailed legal cases point to examples of slaves ordered by their masters to supervise merchant vessels, run shops, administer estates, and participate in joint enterprises.[22] The masters generally retained civil responsibility for the slave transactions, but in many cases the slaves almost found themselves the owners of their own patrimonies, thanks to the earnings or conferments assigned to them. Although their property (the *peculium*, meticulously defined by the jurists of the first century B.C.),[23] which could consist of money or goods—or even other slaves—formally belonged to the master, the slaves had virtually complete autonomy in managing it, to the point of being able to use it to buy their own freedom.

Thus, among the slaves, there arose a group who lived in comfortable or even opulent circumstances, free of physical coercion, with complete license over their own bodies. They fit into two, potentially antithetical categories: one concerned with "status," and the other with the economy. On the one hand, the bond of personal dependence, which was still decisive, prevented them from being considered autonomous in the juridical sense. On the other hand, this obstacle was partly circumvented (but never eliminated): slaves were afforded significant latitude in entrepreneurial activities and in amassing possessions, although this was always legalized in a rather oblique manner.

Not only did the dualism of their situation alter the relations between slaves and third parties, but it also transformed those between slaves and their masters, reaching the very core of the ties of dependency. In a passage no less important for being unique, Servius Sulpicius Rufus, the greatest jurist of Caesar's time, describes a master who "grants a lease" to an estate to one of his slaves, who is to farm it. (But this attribution is not completely sure; the text may have been written by his student Alfenus Varus.)[24] The passage reveals an extant situation that has a certain form of juridical recognition, in which the slave and the master are portrayed as two economically and juridically distinct entities, almost like a landlord and a tenant farmer, facing each other on the same level of reciprocal autonomy. It was a ruinous hypothesis, if considered in the light of the typical form of chattel slavery. In the few words of this text ("a certain person leases to one of his slaves a piece of land to be farmed") two different worlds are evoked: the discriminatory one of "status" and the inclusive one of the contract.

Making property available to slaves usually went hand in hand with acknowledging the integrity of their family units. At the same time, the minutely detailed laws on manumission opened up further perspectives. In many cases they brought nearer a freedom that could mean the attainment—even in the space of a single generation—of a station in society that would shield former slaves from the most serious dangers.

By all appearances, the decisive step seemed close at hand: slavery seemed to be ready to give way from the inside out, so to speak—devoured by a sort of "protocapitalist" maturation unleashed by economic cycles that required the labor force to be more highly valued. But this leap was never made, and the breakthrough was not widespread enough to bring about a general transformation in Roman slavery. The institution did not eliminate itself progressively, in a smooth transition to the generalized use of free wage labor. It was also a matter of quantity: the changeover, even at its peak, concerned only a minority, almost totally urban, of the millions of slaves who lived and worked in Italy between the era of the Gracchi and the rule of Augustus. For the majority—divided among the slave-gangs of the *villae* and of large landholdings, the hellish conditions in the mines, and the unrelieved toil of the most humiliating domestic service in the cities—prospects for the future did not extend beyond the level of pure survival.

The internal logic of the mechanisms of slavery—exclusion and total exploitation—eventually regained the upper hand. The creative and original efforts of the jurists and republican magistrates were exhausted within the space of a few generations; and their period of maximum effectiveness coincided almost exactly with the time when the "tilt toward Italy" mentioned earlier seemed most likely. Then it all came to a halt, lacking the foundations it would have needed in order to survive. Later jurisprudence did not erase what had been achieved; indeed, it perfected and fine-tuned those results. Nor did judicial edicts during the principate modify the ones that had already been issued. But no further significant progress was made. All of the examples of imperial legislation aimed at improving the lot of the slaves, particularly in the second century,[25] were the consequence of a vague philanthropic attitude, determined by the intellectual opinion of the time and not by strictly economic considerations. (But the effectiveness of these interventions should not be exaggerated. The conditions under which the majority of the slaves lived continued to resemble those described by Galen, who wrote about a master, "in other respects not a despicable person," who habitually assailed his slaves "with his hands, and sometimes also with his feet, but most of the time with his whip or some piece of wood that was within his reach.")[26] The "distinguished slaves" of Hadrian's and Antoninus' times—Epictetus, Phlegon—were isolated cases. And when the Severan jurists, overturning the naturalism of Aristotle's views on slavery, stated that all men were by nature free and that slavery was based on the *ius gentium* rather than on the *ius naturale*, they were not indulging in a revolutionary assertion but simply assembling and conceptually rearranging ideas inherited from their late-republican predecessors (and from Cicero). Indeed, these earlier thinkers already understood the unique character of Roman slavery, basing their explanations and their theoretical profile of the phenomenon on the more flexible scaffolding of human society, instead of on the rigid structure of the unchangeable laws of nature.[27]

In the attitudes of republican jurisprudence we find no philanthropically related motivation. Neither the effort to integrate slave resources and commercial capital nor the attention given to the expansion of urban artisan production required the ruling class to alter its traditional outlook (these jurists were themselves nobles who were proud of their condition), and there were no plans for ethical reform. The rigid value judgments critical of the universe of labor that Cicero was propounding in those same years were never repudiated, and no dogma asserting the intransigence of the institution of slavery was ever repealed. These principles were simply put aside, so to speak, and transferred to another level in the name of the ultimate goals of the "economic functionality" of Roman society: operational efficiency in producing profits, and a community that was juridically well organized. It was a result that demonstrably contained some of the elements of a "protocapitalist" culture, but no class was predisposed to seize it and appropriate it for its own purposes.

(4)

Instead of giving impetus to municipalization, which would have built on the successes of Romanization in Italy, the crisis of the first century led, with Augustus, to a great neo-aristocratic stabilization which recast the role of Italy in accordance with the pluralistic and multicentric geometry of a world government. Imperial universalism—which we glimpsed in the writings of Aristides—was the most spectacular consequence of this choice,[28] and into it flowed resources that a more specifically Italic solution would have put to different use. The pattern from conquest to submission, fidelity, and finally Romanization began to mark the relationships between Rome and every population of the empire, both inside and outside Italy, with no ethnic or territorial limits on the process of integration.[29] "What was the germ of the decline of Sparta and Athens, so powerful in war, if it was not that the victors banished the conquered like foreigners?" Thus (according to Tacitus) spoke the emperor Claudius, in a document that is essential for the understanding of the politics of the principate, as early as the first century.[30] The magnificence of the edifice that was being constructed—mythical in Western memory from the early Middle Ages on—was to contribute in no small degree to its own demise. But both the length of its life—which ran from the era of Augustus at least until that of Constantine—and the catastrophe that marked its finish made an indelible impression on the history of Europe: the very phenomenon that Rostovtzeff and Walbank were examining.

The unequal diarchy of the senatorial and equestrian orders peculiar to the old republican city, having survived only as an empty shell that marked the progression of political and administrative careers, was replaced by the revivified and expanded agrarian and bureaucratic elites. The expression not only of the Italic aristocracies but more and more of the emerging realities of the provinces, the newly configured ruling classes were aligned with the mercantile interests but were now far removed from specifically protocapitalist affinities. Through a network of subsidies and privileges, the urban plebs and the army joined the consensus in their turn, becoming "twin pillars" (in Syme's words)[31] of the new order. The economic circuits established themselves on a worldwide scale in their dual form. Consumption became more widespread without showing a decisive increase; and where production and commercial capital were concerned, the "external" mechanisms of cooperation and reciprocal influence that had already developed in Italy were preserved and put into practice in many provincial settings, from southern Gaul to Spain and Africa. The slaveholding *villae* of Etruria, whose structure and daily life has been revealed by stratigraphic archeology, can serve as an example.

Thus the Roman "miracle" reached its full worldwide extension. Although the empire did not unify the economies of the provinces, an unprecedented network of relationships and various forms of interdependence was established. In the short term, the failure to take advantage of a unique opportunity for development did not cause a collapse of any kind. Rather, the *pax Augusta* cleared the way for the full maturity of the system, even though it was in a state of equilibrium that held no prospects. The Romans did not invent the quest for the greatest degree of compatibility between profiting from the provinces, using slaves in production, and commercial expansion—Athens had already served as a laboratory for this kind of trial. But it was the ruling classes of the Roman Empire who were responsible for carrying the experiment to the point of building the first "world economy" in history. The noose of poverty that inevitably tightens around preindustrial societies was not untied. But the large agrarian estates, the financial and commercial nexus, the political and cultural integration of the elites, and the various forms of urban autonomy all formed very solid foundations. They were the enduring constructs of imperial Romanization. In particular, agricultural production—of cereals, wine, and oil—became standardized at relatively advanced levels, which led to the slow but inexorable economic (as well as political and cultural) ascendancy of the provinces. Their success resulted from the fact that the agricultural estates, which were quite differentiated in type from one region to another, were particularly adept at selling on favorable terms especially over long distances—although it is almost impossible for us to determine the parameters of their economic situation, considering that not all of the goods produced were sold in the broader markets.

If the missed opportunity did not immediately propel the empire into a state of crisis, it nevertheless soon had an effect on the future of Italy. Indeed, the beginning of the decline in the economic and political preeminence of Italy that was to become unmistakable toward the end of the first century A.D. (eventually leading to the dramatic marginalization of the entire area) can be traced to the very years of the failed "municipal revolution." Augustus' "institutional localism" shattered the process of unification (which in any case was still in the draft stage) at its outset, closing off all of its prospects for the future. Up to a certain point the "worldwide" triumphs of the principate concealed the signs of the untimely decay of its ancient core; but when it was all over, the full extent of the trauma was revealed.

The economic stabilization based on agriculture and slavery was therefore first and foremost the result of a complex set of political events. To understand its significance, a short digression is necessary.

The history of the clash between the late-republican factions presents the surprising image of a ferocious dispute between political camps with no well-defined ideas or truly contrasting programs—a struggle behind which no wide-reaching themes or cogent alternatives can be found. Even the idea of a revolution of Italic municipalities did not surface in the minds of the protagonists with any more definition than in Cicero's writings (he being the first to recognize the lack of genuine leaders, and of any appreciable mobilization of the directly interested parties) and perhaps in Caesar's fleeting thoughts. In any case, it was nothing but a transitory perception on the most distant horizon of their world.

This opacity has weighed on a century of modern historiographers—from Theodor Mommsen[32] to Matthias Gelzer[33] and Ronald Syme[34]—who all fought with the risks of considering prosopography the only key to understanding and recounting these conflicts. To explain the cause of this shortcoming would take us far from the matter at hand. It is a long-established phenomenon that in part can be attributed to the persistence of the oligarchic form throughout the history of Rome—unlike the situation in Athens (or medieval Florence, where the classicist aspects were stronger), in which the long and radical political struggle between the nobles and the *demos* (between the "magnates" and the "common people" of medieval Florence) caused a confrontation more easily grasped by modern sensibilities. The shadow of a similar "antidemocratic" Roman tendency can clearly be felt in Sallust, and is transformed into a sort of negative anthropology of political action. "Only a few prefer liberty—the majority seek nothing more than fair masters," we read in his *Histories*.[35] The naturalistic model of Aristotle's *Politics*—proclaiming the existence of "who naturally rules and is ruled"[36]—was reinterpreted in the light of a pessimistic historicization.

The harshness of the conflict thus seemed to close in on itself. There was never any prospect of real transformation or clear-cut innovation in the locus of power and the composition of the ruling classes. Since the idea for change could not be rooted in class conflict (which never arose), when it did occur it was immediately transmuted into pure negativity, a danger to be exorcised.

If they had been successful in their struggle, the middle classes of the Italic municipalities would probably have transformed the government more radically than even Cicero had imagined. But the impetus for this project dissipated before it had completely formed. And Caesar's death threatened to bring matters back to their untenable starting point—that is, wedged between the old aristocracy's obstinate efforts to promote the straightforward conservation of an outdated political and institutional model, and the inability of the opposing forces to design and realize a plan for true reform or to ally themselves with the only groups—outside Rome—who were actually in a position to break away from the oligarchic past. This incapacity is understandable, of course; at the least, a different political program would have needed a base of social support prepared to recognize it and adopt it as its own, and a coalition of economic interests in opposition to the aristocratic bloc. But the requisite elements were never mobilized. There were no alternatives to the economy of the nobility, with its wars and slaveholdings, and its commerce, taxation, and contracts all subordinated to the revenues from agriculture. There might have been a different outcome, perhaps, if the municipal transformation had progressed far enough to usher the "new Italic men" onto the scene *en masse*. But this did not happen. And the political struggle, increasingly subject to the influence of military patronage, turned into a ferocious clash among the factions, all of which were expressions of the same institutional confusion and the same economic mechanisms.

The ingeniousness of Augustus' solution lay in its ability to transform, paradoxically, the very fragility of the alternatives into the strength of the chosen strategy. If a reform program based on new social protagonists who were not part of the aristocracy was out of the question, the only practicable path consisted of promoting and organizing a skillful "passive revolution" by the old ruling classes.[37] They spontaneously renounced a portion of their power and privileges, thereby opening themselves cautiously to the new Italic elites—the local aristocracies, not the "middle classes." They accepted the idea that the prince embodied a level of leadership substantially above that of the traditional "orders" and the senate itself. Thus, they succeeded—in the eyes of the urban plebs, the army, the very Italic municipalities, and the most important provincial circles—in reviving the legitimacy of their former superiority without actually opening it up to discussion; they procured peace and security in exchange for the prerogatives they had lost. In short, the old nobility surrendered its power monopoly, but, after such a fearsome period, reopened its "salons" (Ronald Syme's image is effective, but overly evocative of the eighteenth century or the Directoire).[38]

These political efforts at containment and the cooling down of innovation in the first century B.C. played a major role in determining the parameters of what we have called the economic stabilization of the principate. At an earlier time, politics had offered a glimmer of hope that further evolution was possible; and now it was politics that rescinded this hope. Once again, the economy could not manage to stand up and keep its footing on its own.

In a crucial passage from a famous text—a terse political testament of rare fascination and efficacy—Augustus told how he had made himself central to a worldwide consensus. He said that in 32 B.C. "all Italy swore allegiance to me, [. . .] and the provinces of Gaul, Spain, Africa, Sicily, and Sardinia made the same oath."[39] This act, which had no constitutional precedents (if we exclude a few vague gestures by Julius Caesar),[40] made the emperor the object of a plebiscitarian and mass proxy that had no equivalent in any ancient civilization. In remembering the episode at the end of his life, Augustus emphasized the fact that at the decisive moment he was invested not only by Italy but also by the provinces. This was a sign of unquestionable ideological and programmatic relevance.[41] And even if we must consider it likely that during his struggle with Mark Antony, both before and immediately after Actium, he had still (while the events were taking place) aspired to reawaken a specifically Italic form of "patriotism" for anti-oriental purposes, it is impossible to disregard the fact that when he later returned to the situation to hold up its memory as an example to posterity, he presented it in something of a different light. By associating the oaths taken by Italy with those of the provinces—to great narrative effect and perhaps with a touch of exaggeration—the emperor placed Italy and the world (temporarily limited to the West, for reasons of war) on the same level with himself and Rome; and he positioned himself at the center of recognition and proxy granted not only by Italy but also by the rest of the empire. This was the source of the "universal consensus" which Augustus mentions later in the same text.[42] It was the surge of support that also determined the outlines—at least in the ideal sense—of a new institutional architecture.

A single common theme linked the project of Augustus and the statement quoted above, which Claudius, according to Tacitus, made in order to convince the Roman senators to admit the notables of "long-haired

Gaul" (Gaul north of Provence) to their ranks. Allegiance to Rome—and to the emperor—united the Gauls and the Italics over time: they swore the same oath (in the era of Augustus), and they demonstrated the same secular loyalty and the same degree of integration (in Claudius' message). The first threads of the tapestry of imperial universalism were being interwoven ("I am the ruler of the world," Antoninus Pius would later proclaim),[43] a successful alliance between political stability and economic preservation, without which the very birth of the principate would have been incomprehensible.

(5)

We must nevertheless not be deceived by the long time spans involved here. The fate of the imperial system was decided at the very moment it was unable to create the conditions necessary for the qualitative leap that would have set it on a different course. But understanding the momentous crossroads at which it stood does not mean that one should describe the history of the principate as a general stagnation, or even as a premature recession, as many commentators have done, expanding on Weber's model.[44]

The end of the age of conquests certainly entailed a profound readjustment for the system, since without the particular form of heightened growth ensured by the spoils of war and the influx of large masses of slaves, the periods of marked expansion could not continue. Given these conditions, it was impossible to make the transition from a war economy to a peacetime economy without losing forward impetus. But the search for a new compatibility between tax collection, economic dualism, and the use of slaves led to such marked growth in trade, the circulation of money, and urban life that the zones where subsistence economy remained were reduced to dimensions that were long unrepeated in the history of Europe. Even the end of Italy's economic supremacy did not immediately have globally negative consequences; indeed, it triggered a movement toward reequilibration (especially with respect to the western provinces) which had partially beneficial results. In any case, maturity did not change the fundamental state of affairs. Once the decisive opportunity had been missed, all that was left was a blind alley leading toward a society without growth, structurally incapable of producing innovation and development. It was like a dead letter in history.

The path that was taken—the weaker branch of the fork—led literally nowhere. By holding fast to its dependence on slaves and by refusing to elaborate any kind of social and intellectual frame of labor, thereby continuing to marginalize production irremediably, this civilization managed to detach itself from the future. The late republican period had concentrated such a large quantity of resources, and liberated such a flood of social and cultural energy, that there was a real possibility of finding a political solution that could have overcome at least some of these constraints. But the establishment of the principate had quashed this opportunity by dispersing material resources in the construction, at a very high cost, of a multicontinental order, and by steering mentalities and cultures toward the diffusion and exaltation of a model of a prominent "Mediterranean" elite, which was motivated less and less by "virtue" (that is to say, it was less acquisitive and less attached to warlike routine than before) and more and more by conservative concerns for opulence and income.

The momentum in the direction of a "worldwide" economy was thus provided more by political unification than by any real expansion of Roman production or commerce. Unlike modern-day systems, the functioning of the worldwide system of the imperial economy was always dependent on the close political ties of the regions and connected areas. The extent of this integration—civic and cultural in nature—between east and west and between north and south has no parallel in the history of the geopolitical blocs around the Mediterranean. It was also facilitated by the sparse population of whole countries, no less than by the Hellenistic and Roman *koinē* instituted early on by the ruling classes of the empire, which was built on the long-standing foundations of the uninterrupted relationship between Rome and Greece.

When political unity dissolved, the network of economic connections could no longer survive; the system was a fragile consequence of the empire, not a bulwark of it. Catastrophe was the only way out of the stalemate—even if, in some ways, it happened in slow motion (compared to the speed to which our own era has accustomed us). History took another tack, and destruction—at least in the West—proved to be the only evolutionary path for a civilization unable to break loose from its chains in any other manner.

Could we imagine some other way out? One alternative, perhaps, might have been long-term stagnation. But too many obstacles stood in the way, too many local and heterogeneous influences everywhere set in motion by the very process of Romanization—not to mention the pressure exerted by external forces. The imperial regime had ventured so far forward and created systems of such complexity, whose proper operation required so many resources and so much information that it would have been impossible for any form of stabilization, which by this time would have become recessive, to hold out for long or to turn into anything other than a lengthy and tedious crisis. In the rhythms of the history of Rome, which became the history of Europe, disaster was more congruous than a long period of "Asiatic" immobility.

Until the end of the principate of the Flavian emperors, the advantages of "worldwide" range—the contacts between far-flung producers and markets, and the existence of a still virtuous spiral between trade and taxation—continued to be greater than its costs; the economic accounts of the empire were still in balance. But in the course of the second century, the values on the balance sheet were inverted. In the absence of new technologies that might have permitted long-term savings, the costs of political unification—the army, bureaucracy, transportation, communications—began to be higher than the profits earned through economic integration. In order to keep growing, the system would have first and foremost needed more sustained demand, supported by a significant increase in the quantity and variety of consumption, as well as by a network of better differentiated and more elastic markets. Only a changeover to the extensive use of wage labor could have made this happen.

Instead, the perpetuation of slavery and other forms of dependence, especially in rural areas—however subtly the jurists treated them—bound the entire production cycle to a rigid set of constraints that were out of its control. Inelasticity seems to have been the most predominant feature in the whole structure, and in the long run it was this disconnectedness that caused the decline of the slave-dependent *villae*. From at least the end of the first century A.D., the course of the imperial economy tended to assume a pattern characteristic of the history of a society that had posited the terms of its existence as a limit to its expansion. Reserves were so close to exhaustion that not even the political alimentation of the economy (to use Weber's concept)[45] was capable of remedying the situation. There were no more external resources to draw on at the boundaries of the empire; in outposts far from the Mediterranean there were no stores of wealth to be found, no masses of men and women to reduce to slavery. Wars ceased to be investments, becoming solely defensive in nature (with the lone exception of Trajan's Dacian campaign, which was a very costly undertaking).

The provinces continued to be used as a regular and plentiful source of wealth, but the administrative and military costs of managing an immense empire, now inhabited almost entirely by subjects to whom Roman citizenship had been granted, relentlessly absorbed huge quantities of money and goods. The imperial universalism—which, as we have seen, was itself born of an evolutionary blockage, and incapable of overcoming it along the way—became increasingly untenable, as ever more onerous expenses accumulated. Politics, which had always supported the economy, now remained crushed by its inertia. The economic disintegration fed on the political breakdown, and vice versa.

In the course of the first half of the third century, the imbalance between resources and requirements was beginning to resemble a true epochal collapse, even in the minds of contemporaries, although their diagnosis of the problem remained confused and clouded.

You must in the first place know this, that the world has now grown old, and does not abide in that strength in which it formerly stood; nor has it that vigor and force which it formerly possessed. [...] This [...] world itself is now announcing and bearing witness to its decline by the testimony of its failing estate. In the winter, there is not such an abundance of showers for nourishing the seeds; in the summer, the sun has not so much heat for cherishing the harvest; nor in the spring season are the cornfields so joyous; nor are the autumnal seasons so fruitful in their leafy products. The layers of marble are dug out in less quantity from the disemboweled and wearied mountains; the diminished quantities of gold and silver suggest the early exhaustion of the metals, and the impoverished veins are straitened and decreased day by day. The husbandman is failing in the fields, the sailor at sea, the soldier in the camp, innocence in the market, justice in the tribunal, concord in friendships, skillfulness in the arts, discipline in morals. [. . .] Moreover, that wars continue frequently to prevail, that death and famine accumulate anxiety, that health is shattered by raging diseases, that the human race is wasted by the desolation of pestilence—know that this was foretold; that evils should be multiplied in the last times, and that misfortunes should be varied; and that as the day of judgment is now drawing nigh, the censure of an indignant God should be more and more aroused for the scourging of the human race.

So wrote St. Cyprian, bishop of Carthage.[46] A hundred years had passed since Aristides had expressed his luminous vision, and the whole world seemed turned upside down. The crisis of the economy and the deterioration of living conditions led Cyprian to formulate a judgment that fused the ancient theme of the world grown old (a theme derived from Florus and Seneca) together with the apocalyptic side of the Christian message. History and eschatology, realism and prophecy[47]—all seemed to converge at a horrific intersection.

From the time of the Severan emperors to the reigns of Diocletian and Constantine, the ruling classes of the empire (the majority of whom now came from the provinces), in an effort to stem the catastrophe and avoid breakdown, implemented a series of unprecedented realignments in the power structure, which had become quite militarized. They made changes in its ideologies, its social alliances, and the ways sovereignty was exercised. The result was a dramatic new "passive revolution," which took place in various phases, not all of which were homogeneous. Like that of Augustus, its goal was to save the empire from ruin; and in its final stage, Christianity readily became its source of support.

But in contrast to the conditions that had prevailed during the early principate, the margins for maneuver were almost nonexistent. The imperial system had exhausted all its reserves, and ominous fault lines were already in place. The crisis involved production, society, and finances simultaneously; and at the same time, the army, the bureaucracy, and taxes kept growing. In an attempt to put an end to the disaster through political means, the central government intervened more and more directly in the economy, trying to control the results from above through markedly dirigistic yet still empirical methods. The tactics ranged from radically redistributive fiscal measures, to price freezes, to the search by means of laws for the proper equilibrium between liquidity, inflation, and tendencies to return to the widespread practice of barter economy. As always, the reaction was solely a political one: even in its final hour the ancient economy could not escape from its congenitally subordinate station.

The attempt was unsuccessful, at least so far as Europe and the West were concerned—although on more than one occasion it seemed that collapse had successfully been forestalled. The economy of the fourth century showed various signs of recovery. But the situations and destinies of the two parts of the empire took definitively separate paths. From the end of the third century on, the economic interdependence of the individual regions ceased to be a global phenomenon, though commercial ties persisted throughout late antiquity. Once political unity was dissolved, after Constantine, the contact between the Orient and the Occident (and between the North and the South), stabilized and maintained for centuries by the Romanized ruling classes around the Mediterranean—who had assumed and broadened the ancient Greek role—was permanently broken off. The precious patrimony of integration and pluralism was lost, never to be recovered. The history of the Orient and Africa was now distant from that of western and northern Europe, separated as they had not been since the time of Polybius. The Occident was headed for catastrophe, and, later, for its medieval and modern rebirth; the Orient was to turn to Islam and the long continuity of Byzantium. The different forms taken by the crisis of late antiquity in the various regions set two styles of history: in one, the rupture was emphasized; in the other, transition was mediated by the survival of Byzantium. Only the first would later experience the renaissance of modernity.

Nevertheless, the length of the period of resistance made possible a complete transformation in the political organization of the empire. The metamorphosis gave rise to a political arrangement that was new to this part of the world: the absolutist state, in an almost perfect model. The lean administration of the republic and the early principate—with its handful of men and very few resources, with its thin layer of apparatus, almost free of bureaucracy, had been capable of ruling an empire stretching from Mesopotamia to the North Sea. But now economic interventionism, tax increases, and military buildup all contributed to the genesis of a new structure: a true "state machine" unparalleled among ancient societies, rising from the ruins of Hadrian's civic autonomy and destined soon to assume the autocratic and (Christian) paternalistic visage of the despotism of late antiquity.[48]

The changeover was once again directed by the jurists[49]—the last great generation, between Caracalla and Alexander Severus. All subsequent measures bore the imprint of their initial actions, even in the military and bureaucratic complex that rapidly took shape. Juridical legalism, economic control, fiscal voracity, military intrusiveness, and strict ethical and social discipline administered by the widespread power of the bishops became the hallmarks of government in late antiquity. And it is no coincidence that many of these characteristics would resurface centuries later, although in entirely different circumstances, when modern national states arose, from France to England, in the sixteenth and seventeenth centuries.

(6)

This interpretation elucidates another knotty point in our account: the so-called modernity of the Roman economy. Was this idea, therefore, simply an illusion that captivated Gibbon and Rostovtzeff—not to mention Mommsen and Walbank—and found itself repeated in all later antiprimitivist histories? We saw earlier that this impression incorporated a mistake induced by the fascination of contemporary capitalism. It is possible that the same explanation is valid in Gibbon's case, although he witnessed only the earliest years of the Industrial Revolution; the feverish state of late eighteenth-century England certainly could have led to the same stimuli.

But now we can see that the "modernity" attributed to the ancients was also the expression of something different from error. The image contained the remnants, eroded but still perceptible, of what the opportunity for a precocious but suddenly botched evolution had imprinted on the environment in which it had taken shape. What was visible was the inert but unmistakable fossilization of a minimally sketched-out and unexpectedly uncompleted configuration—the muffled yet still distinguishable resonance of an explosion smothered at birth. The phantom of modernity was discernible, not its substance—but it still counted for something, because every new possibility that history presents, no matter how fragile or fleeting, transforms history as a whole in some way. It was the glow of a disembodied one-dimensional form suspended in the void—an incandescent meteor speeding through cold space.

This was not simply a matter of economic structures, such as the circulation of goods, the development of cities and commerce, the concentration of capital, the accumulation of profits, the rational use of slaves, and the quantity of consumption. No less intensely, failed modernity also involved social roles, institutions, and cultural and mental attitudes: the division of labor (in agriculture and urban workshops); the formation of new social classes, which resulted from municipalization; the transformation of intellectual activities into professions (in the case of legal specialists, for example); daily life in the cities (the lifestyle that Gibbon and Rostovtzeff found charming); power, money, manipulation of the masses, and the mechanisms of corruption (Caesar's career comes to mind). It even embraced the inner landscape of religious intimacy, feelings, and emotions—from love to pessimism (as in Lucretius, Catullus, and Seneca).

Despite the fact that the losing fork of the road was selected, this proving ground was not entirely demolished. It was preserved in sealed-off areas, islands from which no impulse toward change arose—in urban centers (especially coastal ones), in the administrative and mercantile organization that serviced the capital and the major imperial cities, in the economy of the ruling classes, in intellectual activities and great literature—but no further expansion was possible. It represented a mature state that was already preparing its own end, capable only of a crude anticipation of standardized production and stereotypes (urban, cultural, and behavioral) that were easily exported through worldwide Romanization—the index fossils, so to speak, of an aborted experiment. What remained was an indelible imprint of the material and mental limits that had been reached: the shadow of a missed opportunity, surviving in a world that had denied it existence.

Chapter Twelve

How History Works

(1)

Our survey is now complete. At the outset, we said that the tour would take the form of an ellipsis. Thus, here in the epilogue we find ourselves back where we began, at the time of Aelius Aristides.

What Gibbon, Rostovtzeff, and Walbank, following Aristides, had considered to be the spectacular modernity of the era was therefore nothing more than fossilized remains, enhanced by the deceptive light of the consummate maturity of that world—"a celebration that marks the end of the adventure, a sky ablaze at the end of the day"[1]—where every path not leading to ruin was now definitively blocked.

But Aristides, as we have seen, was also an extremely anxious man, like other second-century intellectuals, who tended to reduce life to a state of mind. Their apprehensions reflected the fears and neuroses of a time capable of recognizing no goals beyond self-preservation and no satisfaction except in the greatness it had already achieved; it lacked new scopes and distant objectives to pursue. With all desires now fulfilled, the unwelcome stillness allowed an indefinable world-weariness to come to the surface, as if history had reached the point of acute exhaustion. It was the mental reflex of a civilization that believed it had conquered everything but that transformed the conditions of its existence and success into an insurmountable limit, blocking the way to any further prospects of change: mass enslavement, the social and cultural obscurity of labor, the disarticulation between technology and productive activities, or the persistent dualism between self-consumption and markets. This suspended torpor—which Gibbon labeled "indolence"—represented the emotional resonance of an impasse in history. Once the opportunity for successful change had been lost, in the course of a few centuries the

Roman system reached the most extreme point to which it could venture without obliterating the configuration it had assumed. But since it was also a world system, global and all-encompassing, from within nothing could be seen that was not its own closure.

The finite was everywhere—there were limits in every direction. Valleys and walls: immensity, but in a fixed form. Moreover, what else was the irresistible ancient inclination to conceive of history in terms of cycles, if not an expression—almost metaphysical—of the idea of the insuperability of boundaries, limits, and endings?

A passage in one of Marx's unpublished notebooks, written between December 1857 and February 1858, reads: "This is why the childlike world of antiquity appears on one side as loftier. On the other side, it really is loftier in all matters where closed shapes, forms, and given limits are sought. It is satisfaction from a limited standpoint; while the modern gives no satisfaction, or, where it appears satisfied with itself, it is vulgar."[2] The adjective "childlike"[3] can be deceptive, leading one to think of an implicit, mechanically evolutionist hypothesis, as if Marx's pen had made an inadvertent slip. But a different interpretation is possible. The childlike universe is a circumscribed space, closed in itself, and profoundly self-referential; it is the realm of the immediate and the present. In using this metaphor, Marx probably wished to attribute to the ancient world this very element of enclosure, together with pure, complete self-fulfillment—almost as if he perceived in it the sign of a measurement that contains its own limit and is satisfied with it. In other words, as if he thought the ancients confused the intellectual and material boundaries (even the geographic ones)[4] of their own civilization with the extreme margins of time and history, and mistook the one-sidedness of their own perspective for natural or metaphysical constraints. Their satisfaction—"from a limited standpoint," as Marx wrote (Hegel's comment, discussed earlier, about the "enjoyment" derived by the master from the labor of the servant, comes to mind)—was "lofty" because it corresponded to the maximum visibility realizable under these conditions, and was born from their ability to impose form on time passing, which is the true demand of beauty.[5]

The revolution of European modernity meant, above all, abolishing limits—sweeping away not only the obstacles that had blocked ancient

civilizations, but also the very nature of limit as an insuperable barrier
and the belief that cyclicality was destiny. Boundaries were transformed
into movable frontiers, continually shifted forward. The new forms of
labor and science set potentialities in motion, ensuring that the history
of the Western world would never again attempt "to remain something
it has become"[6] (as in Aristides' idea of an eternal empire). Instead, it
would begin to be identified with the "absolute movement of becoming"[7] (as in our commonsense notion that there is nothing lasting that
does not change).

In short, modernity is infinity that has become history—or the
infinite productivity of human labor and intelligence, in the circumstances made possible by the new course of events. It is also the unlimited growth of needs, desires, and individualities, with dissatisfaction
as its justification and battle standard. To the moderns, satisfaction is
"vulgar," because it is blind, and, although capable of doing so, it does
not reach the point of self-surpassing and thus of a higher form of dissatisfaction. The preoccupations of Aristides' day did not—and could
not—embrace this expectancy of the new. The ancients' sense of whole-
ness, after reaching its peak, dissolved into melancholy and fear—even
as early as Seneca. In a memorable letter, he spoke of the widespread
"voluptuousness of death," which took hold of people who were victims
of "a surfeit of seeings and doings,"[8] fearful of discovering a terrifying
void within themselves.

Once the crisis had begun, the ancients' inability to change direction
and conceive of a different future outside their collapsing world was to
assume psychologically devastating aspects. The apocalypticism of the
early Christians and the Gnostics took root in this insufficiency; their
solutions found favor because they went beyond the scope of the events
of this world, on the contrary basing the salvation of the faithful on its
complete annihilation. This was the same agonizing expectation of the
end, the shipwreck in God, that was later so widespread in the mentality
of the desolate early Middle Ages in the West. Only the "new men" who
issued from Europe's cities after the eleventh century, and, later, the generations of the Renaissance, were able to find meaning and value in their
own history once again, by discovering principles and perspectives unthinkable for ancient civilizations.

*   *   *

We have been seeking an explanation for a state of mind that was half-buried in the heart of the imperial grandeur of Rome. We have had to go on a long journey to uncover it. If hope is the perception of the infinite—if it is the discovery of how the unlimited possibilities of our species emerge in history through a series of trials and experiments—sometimes the work of the historian can come very close to it.

(2)

The laborious unfolding of a civilization that extended over three continents, a development which recapitulated a millennium-long continuity, beginning with Archaic Greece and the early flourishing of the Etruscans in Italy; the political unification of an immense physical expanse; a considerable degree of economic development, which eventually was paralyzed by the social and mental disjunction between knowledge, labor, and moral life, and which was not overcome when an unrepeatable opportunity perhaps presented itself; entrapment in a blind alley, leading to catastrophe; and then, after its outcome was assimilated, a new beginning, based on entirely different principles, which was to initiate a sequence of events that has never again been interrupted:[9] all this takes place in the history of the West.

It is a history that proceeds by trial and error, making choices over time, irregularly and discontinuously, among different attitudes and lines of development, connecting chance and necessity, and sweeping away unsuccessful attempts, when their stratifications form an obstacle to the path to be taken. It is a succession of standstills and accelerations, and, most of all, it is not irreversible: there is always a possibility of failure and regression—in human terms, of tragedy.

To begin again, however, does not mean to repeat. Reversibility exists, as the result of the disappearance of an unsuccessful form; but it never entails mere return. This sliding between levels—which resembles a totally unpredictable oscillation—is actually the intermittence of history. The genetic memory of the earlier "error" is concealed in the modes of resumption, to prevent the same trajectory from being followed: "You will never do it that way again." History begins all over again; it does not repeat itself, even if people sometimes try to repeat it.

But Europe's journey was more than this. The rebirth of social and economic life in the Middle Ages was not only a witness to the complete obliteration of the economy and material civilization of Rome.[10] It also was responsible for the extraordinary conservation of a portion of the cultural patrimony that the same foundations and social ties, now effaced, had made it possible to construct. In the twelfth to nineteenth centuries, while an ever more rapid series of innovations lacking all connection to the Greeks or the Romans was changing the face of the Western world, Europeans achieved a new and coherent reinterpretation of classical philosophy, political thought, art, and law. In these fields it was so clear that no new ideas without Greek and Roman precursors were conceivable, that on many occasions the moderns were led to ask whether the ancients had not been matchlessly superior, as appears in the debates of the famous *Querelle*[11] (not to mention those of the hermetic extremists)[12] or in the enduring metaphor of dwarfs on the shoulders of giants.[13]

This symmetry of abandonment and revival—virtually a contrapuntal movement between deprivation and recovery, in which the loss is the more drastic the greater the length of time needed to offset it—this series of vacillations and confirmations, never foreseeable in advance, has proven to be (as we might say) the style of the Western world. This is how history works; this is the rhythm of its breathing.

Italian culture from the Renaissance to the Counter-Reformation displayed an early intuition of this kind of juncture (or, at least, of some of its aspects). For example, scholars immediately perceived that Greece and Rome made it possible to establish an anthropology of politics and power that was resistant to all temporal change: passions, relationships, and characteristics that persisted, albeit through the changes in the forms of subjectivity from the ancient world up to Christianity, until the new era took hold. There even remained an immutable elementary grammar of institutional forms.[14] But at the same time, they understood that the ancients had not handed down acceptable views on the interpretation of nature, or on the relationship between society and environment.

"Prudent men are wont to say—and this not rashly or without good ground—that he who would foresee what has to be should reflect on what has been, for everything that happens in the world at any time has a genuine resemblance to what happened in ancient times. This is due to the fact that the agents who bring such things about are men, and that men have, and always have had, the same passions, whence it necessarily comes about that the same effects are produced."[15] These words by Machiavelli date from the early sixteenth century (probably sometime between 1513 and 1519), and a distant echo of a verse from Ecclesiastes runs through them ("That which is, already has been; that which is to be, already has been").[16] Livy and his history are a precious laboratory, indispensable "in constituting republics, in maintaining states, in governing kingdoms, in forming an army or conducting a war, in dealing with subjects, in extending the empire,"[17] because "the world was always to the same extent inhabited by men, who always had the same passions."[18] Soon thereafter, Francesco Guicciardini[19] (although with certain significant differences in emphasis) and, later, Giordano Bruno[20] were to make similar statements.

Let us remain in Florence, moving forward to less than a century later.

"So put forward the arguments and demonstrations, Simplicio—either yours or Aristotle's—but not just texts and bare authorities, because our discourses must relate to the sensory world and not a world of paper."[21] This is the voice of Salviati in Galileo's famous *Dialogo*. By now the domination of the ancients has come to an end—that "antiquity pounding on almost every line," in Eugenio Garin's words.[22] They did nothing that needs to be "imitated."[23] "We need guides in forests and in unknown lands, but on plains and in open places only the blind need guides. It is better for such people to stay at home; but anyone with eyes in his head and his wits about him could serve as a guide for them."[24]

The relationship has been turned upside down. In politics the guidance of the ancients is essential, because "in all cities and in all peoples there are the same desires and the same passions that have always existed. So that if one examines the past with diligence, it is easy to foresee the future of any commonwealth and to apply those remedies which were used of old."[25] But in the face of the power of new scientific thought and the revolutionary connection between technology and knowledge, those masters of antiquity—and all of their doings—became nothing more than "a world of paper." Moreover, as Bacon had already noted, "In general, it is necessary to obtain knowledge from the light of nature and not try to call it back from the shadows of antiquity. What has been done is not important. What is necessary is to see what can still be done."[26]

The outlines of a twofold—or rather, two-sided—perspective were taking shape. On one side stood the closed and defined antiquity of human social character, the eternal theater of history and power, the elemental anatomy of the "nature" of politics. On the other side was the open and unlimited modernity of the sciences, of technology, of labor constantly transformed. This ambiguity has, right up to the present, been typical of the manner in which the West has faced its own past: the only way of recalling it.

NOTES

INDEX

Notes

There is an enormous bibliography on the topics discussed in this book. The notes that follow are not a complete list of the works the author consulted in the course of his research, but rather should be considered only as reference points that are closely associated with the interpretations being proposed. The same criterion has been used for ancient sources: citations have been provided only for those to which direct reference is made. This is but a small part of everything it has been necessary to keep in mind, which serves as a silent (but—one hopes—perceptible) backdrop for the development of the argument.

1. A Golden Age

1. For the year 143, see J. H. Oliver, "The Ruling Power: A Study of the Roman Empire in the Second Century after Christ through the Roman Oration of Aelius Aristides," *Transactions of the American Philosophical Society,* 43, part 4 (1953): 871ff. For the year 144 (the most widely accepted date), see A. Boulanger, *Aelius Aristides et la sophistique dans la province d'Asie au IIe siècle de notre ère* (Paris, 1923), pp. 480 and 495. For the year 155, see Charles A. Behr, *P. Aelius Aristides: The Complete Works* (Leiden, 1981), vol. 2, p. 373; and Charles A. Behr, *Aelius Aristides and the Sacred Tales* (Amsterdam, 1968), pp. 88–90. For a later study by Behr, see "Studies in the Biography of Aelius Aristides," in H. Temporini, ed., *Aufsteig und Niedergang der Römischen Welt* (Berlin, 1972–), vol. 2, 34, 2, pp. 1140ff., which includes a full bibliography. But see also the sound observations in R. Klein, "Zur Datierung der Romrede des Aelius Aristides," *Historia,* 30 (1981): 337ff.; and idem, *Die Romrede des Aelius Aristides,* vol. 1 (Darmstadt, Germany, 1981), p. 77.
2. Alexander of Phrygia, referred to as *grammaticus* by Marcus Aurelius in his *Meditationes,* 1, 10 (ed. Schenkel). See also *Scriptores historiae augustae: Vita Marc. Aur.* (ed. Hohl) 2, 3. Alexander is also recalled by Aristides himself, in a funeral oration in his honor; see *Aelii Aristidis quae supersunt omnia,* ed. Bruno Keil, oration 32. All of the citations from Aristides come from this edition. With-

out exception, on the points that concern us, see R. Klein, *Die Romrede des Aelius Aristides,* 2 vols. (Darmstadt, Germany, 1981). Alexander is also mentioned in two passages in the *Sacred Discourses:* I, 23 and IV, 62 (ed. Keil); I use this title because it is customary, but E. R. Dodds, *Pagan and Christian in an Age of Anxiety: Some Aspects of Religious Experience from Marcus Aurelius to Constantine* (Cambridge, 1965), p. 40, note 3, makes a valid point.

3. M. Tagliaferro Boatwright, *Hadrian and the City of Rome* (Princeton, 1987), pp. 202, 207–208, 270–271; Sextus Aurelius Victor, *Liber de Caesaribus,* ed. F. Pichlmayr (Leipzig, 1966), 14, 1–4.

4. XLVII, 23 (ed. Keil).

5. Philostratus, *Vitae sophistarum,* ed. Kayser (Hildesheim, 1971), 2, 9, 2 (582).

6. Dodds, *Pagan and Christian,* p. 41. See also E. D. Phillips, "A Hypochondriac and His God," *Greece and Rome,* 21 (1952): 23ff.; and M. and D. Gourevitch, "Le cas Aelius Aristides, ou Mémoires d'un hystérique au IIe siècle," *L'Information psychiatrique,* 10 (1968): 897ff.

7. Mentioned in XLVIII, 3 (ed. Keil).

8. As in Synesius, *De insomnia,* 18 (ἐπινυκτίδες, or "acta nocturna"); cf. Philostratus, *Vitae sophistarum,* 2, 9, 1 (581).

9. Artemidorus Daldianus, *Oneirocritica,* ed. R. A. Pack (Leipzig, 1963).

10. D. Sohlberg, "Aelius Aristides und Diogenes von Babylon: Zur Geschichte des rednerischen Ideals," *Museum Helveticum,* 29 (1972): 177ff., 256ff.; Dodds, *Pagan and Christian,* pp. 39–45; S. Nicosia, *Elio Aristide nell'Asclepieio di Pergamo e la retorica recuperata* (Palermo, 1979). U. von Wilamowitz-Moellendorff, *Der Rhetor Aristeides* (1925), remains important; it is reprinted in Wilamowitz-Moellendorff, *Kleine Schriften,* vol. 3, *Griechische Prosa* (Berlin, 1969), pp. 426ff.

11. As in Philostratus, *Vitae sophistarum,* 1 (481).

12. Klein, *Die Romrede,* vol. 1, esp. pp. 160ff., and vol. 2 (Darmstadt, 1983). Cf. C. Moreschini, "Elio Aristide tra retorica e filosofia," in *Aufsteig und Niedergang der Römischen Welt,* vol. 2, 34, 2, pp. 1234ff.; and S. A. Stertz, "Aelius Aristides' Political Ideas," *Aufsteig und Niedergang der Römischen Welt,* vol. 2, 34, 2, pp. 1248ff. The observations of G. W. Bowersock, *Greek Sophists in the Roman Empire* (Oxford, 1969), pp. 16, 45, are perspicacious but too severe. See also G. W. Bowersock, *Fiction as History: Nero to Julian* (Berkeley, 1994), p. 68. The editions of Keil and Klein have superseded Dindorf's old edition: *Aristides,* 3 vols. (Leipzig, 1829; rpt. Hildesheim, 1964). In Dindorf, the oration is in vol. 1, XIV.

13. *Corpus Inscriptionum Latinarum* (Berlin, 1863), IV, suppl. 3, 8297. The same palindrome later returns in third-century graffiti. See P. Castrén, in F. Magi, *Il calendario dipinto sotto Santa Maria Maggiore con appendice sui graffiti del vano XVI* (Vatican City, 1972), p. 79, n. 25, table 66, 1: ROMA SUMMUS AMOR; and p. 77, n. 18, table 65, 1: ROMA / OLIM / MILO/ AMOR.

14. XXVI, 99 (ed. Keil). All English-language citations from "Regarding Rome"

come from Behr, ed., *Aristides in Four Volumes* (Cambridge, 1973), vol. 2, pp. 73–97.

15. Ibid., 101.

16. Ibid., 94.

17. Ibid., 99.

18. Ibid.

19. Ibid., 105.

20. Ibid., 97.

21. Ibid., 59.

22. Ibid., 65.

23. Ibid., 57.

24. Ibid., 103.

25. Ibid., 9, 10, 11, 16, 29, 33, 36, 105.

26. Ibid., 11–13.

27. Ibid., 99.

28. Cf., for example, XXVI, 29 (ed. Keil); and H. Mattingly and E. A. Sydenham, *The Roman Imperial Coinage,* vol. 3 (London, 1930), esp. pp. 28, 33, 36, 40, 42 (αἰών/ *aeternitas*).

29. E. Gabba, "I municipi e l'Italia augustea," in M. Pani, ed., *Continuità e trasformazioni fra repubblica e principato* (Bari, 1991), p. 80, is correct here; this reference can also be found in Gabba, *Italia romana* (Como, 1994), p. 143. Significant statements on the subject are made by D. Magie, *Roman Rule in Asia Minor to the End of the Third Century after Christ* (Princeton, 1950; rpt. New York, 1975), esp. vol. 1, pp. 630ff., and vol. 2, pp. 1491ff.; Oliver, "The Ruling Power"; A. H. M. Jones, *The Cities of the Eastern Roman Provinces* (Oxford, 1971); F. Grelle, *L'autonomia cittadina fra Traiano e Adriano* (Naples, 1972); A. Kuhrt and S. Sherwin-White, eds., *Hellenism in the East* (London, 1987).

30. Tertullian, *De anima,* ed. Waszink (Amsterdam, 1947), 47, 2. Of the three citations that follow, the first is from Aristides, L, 102 (ed. Keil), and the third is from Marcus Aurelius, *Meditationes,* 2, 17. The second is a modern-day restatement of extraordinary interpretative power, from H. Broch, *Der Tod des Virgil* (1945), translated as *The Death of Virgil* (San Francisco, 1983), p. 161. See D. Meinert, *Die Darstellung der Dimensionen menschlicher Existenz in Brochs "Tod des Vergil"* (Bern, 1962).

31. Plotinus, III, 2, 15 (but see Marcus Aurelius, *Meditationes,* 4, 3, 2; 7, 59; and 9, 13). A. J. Festugière, *Personal Religion among the Greeks* (Berkeley, 1954), pp. 85ff.; Festugière, "Sur les 'Discours sacrés' d'Aelius Aristide," *Revue des études grecques,* 82 (1969): 117ff.

32. Synesius, *De insomnia,* 3–4; Dodds, *Pagan and Christian,* pp. 38–45; Behr, *Aelius Aristides and the Sacred Tales,* pp. 171ff.; G. Michenaud and J. Dierkens, *Les rêves dans les "Discours sacrés" d'Aelius Aristide, IIe siècle ap. J.-C.: Essai d'analyse*

psychologique (Mons, 1972); D. Del Corno, "I sogni e la loro interpretazione nell'età dell'impero," in *Aufstieg und Niedergang der Römischen Welt,* vol. 2, 16, 2, pp. 1605ff.

33. L. Cracco Ruggini, "Imperatori e uomini divini, I–VI secolo," in Ruggini et al., *Governanti e intellettuali: Popolo di Roma e popolo di Dio, I–VI secolo* (Turin, 1982), pp. 9ff.; F. E. Brenk, "In the Light of the Moon: Demonology in the Early Imperial Period," in *Aufstieg und Niedergang der Römischen Welt,* vol. 2, 16, 3, pp. 2068ff.; G. Cambiano, "Le filosofie tra l'impero e il cielo," in A. Schiavone, ed., *Storia di Roma,* vol. 2, part 3 (Turin, 1992), pp. 349ff.

34. F. Regen, *Apuleius Philosophus Platonicus* (Berlin, 1971), trans. A. Darby (Baltimore, 1998); A. D. Nock, *Conversion* (Oxford, 1933; rpt. 1961), pp. 138–155.

35. C. P. Jones, *Culture and Society in Lucian* (Cambridge, Mass., 1986).

36. O. Deubner, *Das Asklepeion von Pergamon: Kurze vorläufige Beschreibung* (Berlin, 1938); E. J. L. Edelstein, *Asclepius: A Collection and Interpretation of the Testimonies* (Baltimore, 1945; rpt. New York, 1975).

37. G. R. S. Mead, *Apollonius of Tyana: The Philosopher-Reformer of the First Century A.D.* (New Hyde Park, N.Y., 1966); Bowersock, *Greek Sophists,* pp. 4ff., 101ff.

38. F. S. Krauss, *Artemidorus aus Daldis: Symbolik der Träume* (Vienna, 1881) is important (although "pre-Freudian"). This was the translation of the *Oneirocritica* familiar to Freud; now in a new edition: *Traumkunst Artemidor* (Leipzig, 1991). See also W. Kurth, "Das Traumbuch des Artemidoros im Lichte der Freudschen Traumlehre," *Psyche,* 4 (1950): 488ff.

39. P. A. Brunt, "Marcus Aurelius in His Meditations," *Journal of Roman Studies,* 64 (1974): 1ff.

40. Including Momigliano, in a brief early study: "Aspetti di Michele Rostovzev" (1933), reprinted in *Contributo alla storia degli studi classici* (Rome, 1955), pp. 330–331. But the notion of Aristides' "insincerity" is deep-rooted; see H. Baumgart, *Aelius Aristides als Repräsentant der sophistischen Rhetorik des zweiten Jahrhunderts der Kaiserzeit* (Leipzig, 1874).

41. Dodds, *Pagan and Christian,* pp. 3–4. For what follows, see also pp. 40–45.

42. Pliny, *Historia naturalis,* 27, 1, 3; for Favorinus, see Aulus Gellius, *Noctes Atticae,* ed. P. K. Marshall (Oxford, 1968), 20, 1.

43. Sextus Caecilius Africanus: "opulentia civitatis," in *Noctes Atticae,* 20, 1, 23 (Gellius is a faithful intermediary). But from Celsus to Julian, all Hadrianic jurisprudence reflected an awareness of living in an era of unequaled wealth and civility. See also Tertullian, *De anima,* 30, 3.

44. G. Sasso, *Tramonto di un mito: L'idea di "progresso" fra Ottocento e Novecento* (Bologna, 1984), esp. pp. 109ff.

45. P. Rossi, *Naufragi senza spettatore: L'idea di progresso* (Bologna, 1995), esp. pp. 45ff. Also R. V. Sampson, *Progress in the Age of Reason: The Seventeenth Century to the Present Day* (London, 1956).

46. Santo Mazzarino's massive note 555—a monograph in itself at the end of Mazzarino, *Il pensiero storico classico,* vol. 2, part 2 (Bari, 1966), pp. 412ff.—is now considered classic. See also L. Edelstein, *The Idea of Progress in Classical Antiquity* (Baltimore, 1967).

47. A good example of this is Kant, *Beantwortung der Frage: Was ist Aufklärung?* (1784); in English, *What Is Enlightenment?* trans. L. W. Beck (New York, 1959). See also Edelstein, *The Idea of Progress;* and E. R. Dodds, *The Ancient Concept of Progress* (Oxford, 1973).

48. XXVI, 99 (ed. Keil). Cf. Gellius, *Noctes Atticae,* 2, 20, 4.

49. XXVI, 80.

50. Ibid., 83.

51. See below, Chapter 7.

52. *Epitome bellorum omnium annorum DCC,* "Praefatio," 4–8 (ed. Jal). There are ten paintings by Tiepolo after Lucius Annaeus Florus (five in the Hermitage in St. Petersburg, three in the Metropolitan Museum of Art in New York, and two in the Kunsthistorisches Museum in Vienna).

53. Lactantius Firmianus, *Divinae institutiones* (ed. Brandt), 7, 15, 14–19. See also Cassius Dio, *Roman History,* 72, 36, 4.

2. Why Not Then?

1. E. Gibbon, *History of the Decline and Fall of the Roman Empire* (1776), ed. Bury (London, 1896–1900), vol. 1, p. 1.

2. Ibid., p. 78.

3. Peter Brown, *The Making of Late Antiquity* (Cambridge, Mass., 1978; rpt. 1993), p. 27.

4. P. Gay, *Style in History* (New York, 1974), pp. 19ff.; J. Clive, "Gibbon's Humor," in G. W. Bowersock, J. Clive, and R. Graubard, eds., *Edward Gibbon and the Decline and Fall of the Roman Empire* (Cambridge, Mass., 1977), pp. 183ff.; D. Womersley, *The Transformation of "The Decline and Fall of the Roman Empire"* (Cambridge, 1988), pp. 51ff., 89ff.

5. Gibbon, *History,* p. 78.

6. Leonardo Bruni, *Historiarum Florentini Populi libri XII* (1415–1440), in L. A. Muratori, ed., *Rerum Italicarum Scriptores,* vol. 19, part 3 (Città di Castello, 1926), pp. 14–15; P. Burke, "Tradition and Experience: The Idea of Decline from Bruni to Gibbon," in Bowersock, Clive, and Graubard, eds., *Edward Gibbon and the Decline,* pp. 87ff.

7. Gibbon, *History,* p. 57.

8. In a note in the margin of the *incipit* of his *History* written during the winter of 1790–1791; reprinted in *The English Essays of Edward Gibbon,* ed. Craddock (Oxford, 1972), p. 338. See also Womersley, *The Transformation,* pp. 44–45.

9. Arnaldo Momigliano, "La formazione della moderna storiografia sull'impero romano" (1936), reprinted in Momigliano, *Contributo alla storia degli studi classici* (Rome, 1955), pp. 107ff., 125f., 139ff.; Momigliano, "Gibbon's Contribution to Historical Method" (1954), reprinted in *Contributo*, pp. 195ff. See also Momigliano, "Ancient History and the Antiquarian" (1950), reprinted in *Contributo*, pp. 67ff. G. Giarrizzo, *Edward Gibbon e la cultura europea del Settecento* (Naples, 1954), is still important.

10. Montesquieu, *Considérations sur les causes de la grandeur des Romains et de leur décadence*, ed. Truc (Paris, 1945), pp. 83ff. This work appeared anonymously in 1734 in Amsterdam, and went through six editions prior to 1746. Gibbon's library contained the Parisian edition of 1755; see G. Keynes, *The Library of Edward Gibbon* (Dorchester, 1980), p. 201. But Machiavelli had already expressed a clearly positive opinion about the Antonine monarchy in *Discorsi sopra la prima deca di Tito Livio*, ed. Vivanti (Turin, 1983), p. 62 (Book 1, ch. 10); in English in *The Discourses of Niccolò Machiavelli*, trans. L. J. Walker (New Haven, 1950), vol. 1, pp. 237f.

11. Condorcet, "Esquisse d'un tableau historique des progrès de l'esprit humain" (1795), in Condorcet, *Oeuvres*, vol. 6 (Paris, 1847), p. 97, clearly derived from Montesquieu.

12. M. Baridon, *Edward Gibbon et le mythe de Rome: Histoire et idéologie au Siècle des Lumières* (Paris, 1977), pp. 328ff., 472ff., 482ff.; J. G. A. Pocock, "Between Machiavelli and Hume: Gibbon as Civic Humanist and Philosophical Historian," in Bowersock, Clive, and Graubard, eds., *Edward Gibbon and the Decline*, pp. 103ff.; Womersley, *The Transformation*, pp. 9ff., 20ff.

13. Keynes, *The Library of Edward Gibbon*, p. 55. Jebb's edition of Aristides was published at Oxford in two volumes, in 1722 and 1730. Dindorf's reference is in *Aristides*, 3 vols. (Leipzig, 1829), vol. 1, p. vii.

14. J. J. Reiske and J. E. Faber, *Opuscula Medica ex Monimentis Arabum et Ebraeorum* (Halle, 1776; ed. posthumously by C. G. Gruner), pp. 4–5.

15. Gibbon, *History*, vol. 1, p. 36, n. 37, and p. 56, n. 114.

16. D. P. Jordan, *Gibbon and His Roman Empire* (Urbana, Ill., 1971), pp. 70ff.; P. Ducrey, ed., *Gibbon et Rome à la lumière de l'historiographie moderne* (Geneva, 1977); P. B. Craddock, *Young Edward Gibbon* (Baltimore, 1989); Craddock, *Edward Gibbon, Luminous Historian* (Baltimore, 1989); R. Porter, *Edward Gibbon: Making History* (London, 1988), pp. 67ff.

17. J. E. Norton, ed., *The Letters of Edward Gibbon*, vol. 2: *1774–1784* (New York, 1956), p. 218: "La décadence des Deux Empires, le Romain et le Britannique, s'avancent à pas égaux."

18. G. W. Bowersock, "Gibbon on Civil War and Rebellion in the Decline of the Roman Empire," in Bowersock, Clive, and Graubard, eds., *Edward Gibbon and the Decline*, pp. 27ff.

19. Michael Rostovtzeff, *The Social and Economic History of the Roman Empire*, ed. M. Fraser (Oxford, 1957); all citations are from this edition. A. M. Wes, *Michael Rostovtzeff: Historian in Exile* (Stuttgart, 1990).

20. T. Mommsen, *Römische Kaisergeschichte: Nach den Vorlesungs-Mitschriften von Sebastian und Paul Hensel*, ed. B. and A. Demandt (Munich, 1992). K. Christ, "Theodor Mommsen und die *Römische Geschichte*," in vol. 8 of the Munich, 1976, edition of the *Römische Geschichte*. See also S. Mazzarino, "Vindice e il 'separatismo' gallico (con lezioni inedite di Th. Mommsen)," now in Mazzarino, *Antico, tardoantico ed era costantiniana*, vol. 2 (Bari, 1980), pp. 163ff.

21. K. Christ, *Von Gibbon zu Rostovtzeff: Leben und Werk Führender Althistoriker der Neuzeit* (Darmstadt, 1972), pp. 8ff., 84ff., 334ff.

22. Rostovtzeff, *History*, pp. 130ff. (quotation is from p. 139).

23. A. Momigliano, "Aspetti di Michele Rostovzev" (1933), "Rostovtzeff's Twofold History of the Hellenistic World" (1943), "M. I. Rostovtzeff" (1954), all in Momigliano, *Contributo*, pp. 327ff., 335ff., 341ff.

24. Rostovtzeff, *History*, vol. 2, pp. 710 and 748, and vol. 1, p. 532.

25. Ibid., vol. 1, p. 371.

26. See, for example, the statements on pp. 143, 153, and 173–174.

27. A. Momigliano, ed., *The Conflict between Paganism and Christianity in the Fourth Century* (Oxford, 1963), p. 2.

28. Rostovtzeff, *History*, p. 534.

29. Ibid., pp. 534–535.

30. F. W. Walbank, *The Decline of the Roman Empire in the West* (London, 1946; rpt. 1953), p. 19; later republished, substantially unchanged, as *The Awful Revolution: The Decline of the Roman Empire in the West* (Toronto, 1969). The citation is on p. 36.

31. Rostovtzeff was already critical of this concept; see *History*, vol. 2, pp. 748–749 (but see also vol. 1, pp. 531ff.). See also Rostovtzeff, "The Decay of the Ancient World and Its Economic Explanations," *Economic History Review*, 2 (1930), pp. 197ff., reprinted in *Scripta varia: Ellenismo e impero romano*, ed. A. Marcone (Bari, 1995), pp. 215ff.; and Rostovtzeff, "Cities in the Ancient World," in *Urban Land Economics* (Ann Arbor, 1922), pp. 17ff., reprinted in *Scripta varia*, pp. 101ff. S. Mazzarino, *The End of the Ancient World*, trans. G. Holmes (Westport, Conn., 1966), is still important.

32. H. Pirenne, *Mahomet et Charlemagne* (Paris, 1937), p. 14; in English in *Mohammed and Charlemagne* (New York, 1939), p. 31.

33. A. Carandini, L. Cracco Ruggini, and A. Giardina, eds., *L'età Tardoantica*, in A. Schiavone, *Storia di Roma*, vol. 3, parts 1 and 2 (Turin, 1993), contains an effective synthesis of this discussion.

34. The work of Peter Brown has been exemplary here. We need mention only *The World of Late Antiquity: From Marcus Aurelius to Muhammed* (London, 1971);

The Making of Late Antiquity (Cambridge, Mass., 1978); *Power and Persuasion in Late Antiquity: Towards a Christian Empire* (Madison, 1992); and *The Rise of Western Christendom* (Oxford, 1995). See also A. Giardina, "Esplosione di Tardo-antico," *Studi Storici*, 40 (1999): 157ff.

35. Henri Pirenne, *Medieval Cities: Their Origins and the Revival of Trade,* trans. F. D. Halsey (Princeton, 1925); French version, *Les villes du Moyen Age: Essai d'histoire économique et sociale* (Brussels, 1927). See also idem, *Mahomet et Charlemagne,* p. 260, translated as *Mohammed and Charlemagne.* Pirenne's familiarity with re-search on antiquity was spotty. *Mahomet et Charlemagne,* the first draft of which he completed in May 1935, makes no mention of Rostovtzeff's *History,* which had been published nine years before; and it overlooks the whole contemporary debate on the Roman economy (to be discussed in Chapter 4, below).

36. Pirenne, *Mahomet et Charlemagne,* p. 260; English translation, p. 284.

37. Ambrose, *Epistulae,* ed. Faller, 8, 3–4 (*Patrologia Latina,* 16, *Epistulae,* 39, 3). The image is borrowed from a letter by Servius Sulpicius Rufus, preserved in Cicero's collection of letters, *Epistulae ad familiares,* 4, 5, 4.

38. For example, *Rerum gestarum libri,* ed. W. Seyfarth (Leipzig, 1978), 15, 7, 1–5. See J. Matthews, *The Roman Empire of Ammianus* (London, 1989).

39. See also Henri Pirenne, *L'origine des constitutions urbaines au Moyen Age* (1893–1898), and idem, *Villes, marchés et marchands au Moyen Age* (1893–1898), re-printed in *Les villes et les institutions urbaines,* vol. 1 (Paris, 1939), pp. 1ff., 111ff. Pirenne also maintains that urban history after the year 1000 was disconnected from its Roman heritage; see Pirenne, *Medieval Cities,* pp. 82ff, 101ff.

40. By the end of the tenth century the cities of Germany, England, France, and even Italy had just a few hundred or at most a few thousand inhabitants. In Arab Spain the situation was a little better: Cordoba had a population of 100,000; To-ledo, 37,000; Granada, 26,000; Valencia, 15,000. See F. Vercauteren, "La ville en Europe du IVe au XIe siècle," in *Città, mercanti, dottrine nell'economia europea dal IV al XVIII secolo: Saggi in memoria di G. Luzzatto* (Milan, 1964), pp. 15ff.; and G. Duby, *L'économie rurale et la vie des campagnes dans l'Occident médiéval: France, Angleterre, Empire, IXe–XVe siècles* (Paris, 1962; rpt. 1977), esp. pp. 63ff.; in English in Duby, *Rural Economy and Country Life in the Medieval West* (Lon-don, 1968), pp. 5ff. See also V. Fumagalli, *Quando il cielo s'oscura* (Bologna, 1987), esp. pp. 9ff.; and Fumagalli, *L'alba del Medioevo* (Bologna, 1993), esp. pp. 11ff.

41. This expression is borrowed from R. Sennett, *Flesh and Stone: The Body and the City in Western Civilization* (New York, 1994).

42. As in R. S. Lopez, "La città dell'Europa postcarolingia," in Lopez, *Le città nell'Alto Medioevo* (Spoleto, 1959), p. 742. See also A. Molho, K. Raaflaub, and J. Emilien, eds., *City-States in Classical Antiquity and Medieval Italy* (Ann Arbor, 1991).

43. As in E. Garin, *La cultura del Rinascimento* (Bari, 1967), p. 47.

44. For an overall view, see F. Krantz and P. M. Hohenberg, eds., *Failed Transition to Modern Industrial Society: Renaissance Italy and Seventeenth Century Holland* (Montreal, 1975). In particular, see C. Cipolla, "The Italian Failure," pp. 8ff., originally published as "The Decline of Italy: The Case of a Fully Matured Economy" (1952), and reprinted in *"Le tre rivoluzioni" e altri saggi di storia economica e sociale* (Bologna, 1989), pp. 85ff. See also I. Wallerstein, "Failed Transition or Inevitable Decline of the Leader? The Workings of the Capitalist World-Economy: General Comments," ibid., pp. 75ff.

3. The Hidden Form

1. D. C. North, "The State of Economic History," *American Economic Review,* 55 (1965): 86ff.; F. Redlich, "'New' and Traditional Approaches to Economic History and Their Interdependence," *Journal of Economic History,* 25 (1965): 480ff.; J. Hicks, *A Theory of Economic History* (Oxford, 1969); T. C. Cochran, "Economic History, Old and New," *American Historical Review,* 74 (1968–1969): 1561ff.; W. O. Aydelotte, A. G. Bogue, and R. W. Fogel, eds., *The Dimensions of Quantitative Research in History* (Princeton, 1972); R. Floud, *An Introduction to Quantitative Methods for Historians* (Princeton, 1975); D. C. Coleman, *History and the Economic Past: An Account of the Rise and Decline of Economic History in Britain* (Oxford, 1987); C. M. Cipolla, *Tra due culture: Introduzione alla storia economica* (Bologna, 1989). See also N. Lamoreaux, "Economic History and the Cliometric Revolution," in A. Molho and G. S. Woods, eds., *Imagined Histories: American Historians Interpret the Past* (Princeton, 1998), pp. 59ff.

2. See the surveys of E. Will, "Trois quarts de siècle de recherches sur l'économie grecque antique," *Annales: Economies, sociétés, civilisations,* 9 (1954): 7ff. (useful, though now out of date); and especially E. Lepore, "Economia antica e storiografia moderna: Appunti per un bilancio di generazioni," in L. De Rosa, ed., *Ricerche storiche ed economiche in memoria di Corrado Barbagallo,* vol. 1 (Naples, 1970), pp. 1ff. See also H. W. Pearson, "The Secular Debate on Economic Primitivism," in K. Polanyi, C. M. Arensberg, and H. W. Pearson, eds., *Trade and Market in the Early Empires: Economies in History and Theory* (Glencoe, Ill., 1957; rpt. Chicago, 1971), pp. 3ff. E. Cicotti, "L'evoluzione della storiografia e la storia economica del mondo antico," in *Biblioteca di storia economica,* vol. 1, part 1 (Milan, 1903; rpt. Bologna, 1976), pp. xviiff., is interesting.

3. I will cite their works individually in the course of my text. But it is opportune to mention here the important studies by C. Nicolet collected in *Rendre à César: Economie et société dans la Rome antique* (Paris, 1988); and H. W. Pleket, "Wirtschaft des Imperium Romanum," in W. Fischer, J. A. Van Houtte, H. Kellenbenz, I. Mieck, and F. Vittinghoff, eds., *Handbuch der Europäischen*

Wirtschafts- und Sozialgeschichte (Stuttgart, 1990), vol. 1, pp. 25ff., a study rich in observations with which I agree, although it is almost entirely dedicated to historiographic and methodological topics.

4. See notes for Chapter 4, below.

5. M. Finley, *The Ancient Economy* (Berkeley, 1985), pp. 24–25. See also Finley, "Le document et l'histoire économique de l'antiquité," *Annales: Economies, sociétés, civilisations,* 37 (1982): 697ff.; Finley, *Ancient History: Evidence and Models* (New York, 1985), pp. 7ff., 27ff.; A. H. M. Jones, *Ancient Economic History* (London, 1948), esp. pp. 1ff. (with which I do not entirely concur); F. Furet, "L'histoire quantitative et la construction du fait historique," *Annales: Economies, sociétés, civilisations,* 26 (1971): 63ff., rpt. as F. Furet, "Le quantitatif en histoire," in J. Le Goff and P. Nora, eds., *Faire l'histoire,* vol. 1 (Paris, 1984), pp. 42ff., in English in *Constructing the Past: Essays in Historical Methodology* (Cambridge, 1985), pp. 12ff.; and E. Le Roy Ladurie, *Le territoire de l'historien* (Paris, 1973), pp. 15ff., 23ff., in English in *The Territory of the Historian,* trans. B. and S. Reynolds (Chicago, 1979), pp. 7ff., 17ff. Additionally, see M. Frederiksen, "Theory, Evidence, and the Ancient Economy," *Journal of Roman Studies,* 65 (1975): 164ff.

6. Cipolla, *Tra due culture,* p. 31.

7. Both the *Nicomachean Ethics* (*Aristoteles Ethica Nicomachea,* ed. I. Bywater [Oxford, 1890]) and the *Economics* (*Oeconomica,* ed. F. Susemihl [Leipzig, 1887]) have tangled textual histories. In particular, the three books composing the treatise on economics seem to have different provenances. Only the first has an unequivocally peripatetic derivation, reworking Aristotle's *Politics* and Xenophon's *Economics;* the second was perhaps written independently (according to an old hypothesis of Niebuhr's); and the third has survived only in two Latin versions. Xenophon's *Economics* (ed. S. Pomeroy [Oxford, 1994]) was translated into Latin by Cicero (Pliny, *Historia naturalis,* 18, 60, 224; cf. also Cicero, *De officiis,* 2, 24, 87). Sixteenth-century commentaries were written on Cato, Varro, and Columella as a group: F. Ursinus, *Notae ad M. Catonem, M. Varronem, L. Columellam "De re rustica"* (Rome, 1587). See R. Martin, *Recherches sur les agronomes latins* (Paris, 1971), esp. pp. 31ff., 211ff.

8. [Aristotle], *Oeconomica,* 2, 1 (1345b): "Of such administrations there are four main types [. . .]: the administration of a King; of the governors under him; of a free state; and of a private citizen" (trans. G. C. Armstrong, Loeb edition [Cambridge, Mass., 1935], p. 345). This phrase is found in the introduction to the second book, which was probably written in the second half of the third century B.C. See B. A. Van Groningen, *Aristote: Le deuxième livre de l'"Economique"* (Leiden, 1933), pp. 11ff., 37ff., 53ff.; and U. Victor, [*Aristoteles*] *Oikonomikos: Das erste Buch der Ökonomik-Handschriften* (Königstein im Taunus, 1983), pp. 15ff., 75ff., 107ff. However, at the beginning of Book I (1, 1, 1343a), the two words appear separately: "economics" is dissociated from "politics." See also

C. Ampolo, "*Oikonomia:* Tre osservazioni sui rapporti tra la finanza e l'economia greca," *Annali dell'Istituto Orientale di Napoli: Sezione di archeologia e storia antica—Seminario di studi mondo classico,* 1 (1979): 119ff.

9. Antoyne de Montchrétien, *Traicté de l'oeconomie politique, dédié en 1615 au Roy et à la Reine mère du Roy,* ed. T. Funk-Brentano (Paris, 1889).

10. The texts of greatest relevance to this study will be cited below, in the course of the discussion. Here, see Plato, *Republic,* 2, 11 (369 b–c); and Thucydides, 1, 2, 2.

11. W. Harvey, *Exercitatio anatomica de motu cordis et sanguinis in animalibus* (Frankfurt, 1628), reprinted in *The Anatomical Exercises: De motu cordis and De circulatione sanguinis,* ed. G. Keynes (London, 1928; rpt. New York, 1995). G. Whitteridge, *William Harvey and the Circulation of the Blood* (London, 1971). See also J. J. Bylebyl, ed., *William Harvey and His Age: The Professional and Social Context of the Discovery of the Circulation* (Baltimore, 1979).

12. H. von Arnim, *Stoicorum veterum fragmenta* (Leipzig, 1903–1924), vol. 2, p. 338, n. 1176.

13. Quintilian, *Instituto oratoria,* 1, 8, 9 and 3, 3, 9.

14. Karl Bücher, *Die Entstehung der Volkswirtschaft* (1893), vol. 1 (Tübingen, 1920), p. 114, n. 21; in English in idem, *Industrial Evolution,* trans. S. M. Wickett (New York, 1968), p. 112, n. 22.

15. As in Lefebvre de Noëttes, "L'Esclavage antique devant l'Histoire," *Mercure de France,* 44, no. 241 (1933), 1, 2, p. 574.

16. The excavations of the Tuscan villa of Settefinestre, near Cosa-Ansedonia, are now justly considered a model of the new Italian archeology. See A. Carandini and S. Settis, *Schiavi e padroni nell'Etruria romana: La villa di Settefinestre dallo scavo alla mostra* (Bari, 1979); A. Carandini and A. Ricci, eds., *Settefinestre: Una villa schiavistica nell'Etruria romana* (Modena, 1985); A. Carandini, *Schiavi in Italia: Gli strumenti pensanti dei Romani fra tarda repubblica e medio impero* (Rome, 1988), pp. 109ff. Another important book is J. Kolendo, *L'agricoltura nell'Italia romana: Tecniche agrarie e progresso economico dalla tarda repubblica al principato* (Rome, 1980).

17. Cato, *De agri cultura,* ed. A. Mazzarino (Leipzig, 1962), 2, 7; 5, 1–5; 56–59.

18. Columella, *Res rustica,* ed. Lundström, Josephson, and Hedberg, 1, 7–8; 1, 9, 1–5.

19. See, for example, the typology used by Varro at the end of the Republican era: *De re rustica,* ed. Goetz, 1, 17, 2.

20. Aristotle, *Politics,* ed. W. D. Ross, 1, 2 (1252a).

21. Cicero, *De officiis,* 1, 42, 150. Also *De oratore,* 3, 32, 127–128; *Pro Sexto Roscio Amerino,* 46, 134.

22. Seneca, *Epistulae,* 88, 21.

23. Libanius, *Orationes,* ed. Foerster, 58, 4.

24. A. de Tocqueville, *Voyage aux Etats-Unis,* reprinted in Tocqueville, *Oeuvres complètes,* vol. 5 (Paris, 1957), pp. 59–387; in English in Tocqueville, *Journey to*

America, ed. J. P. Mayer, trans. G. Lawrence (Garden City, N.Y., 1971)—this is a notebook dating from 1831–1832. See also D. B. Davis, *Slavery and Human Progress* (New York, 1984), esp. pp. 51ff., 168ff.

25. John Saffin, "A Brief and Candid Answer to a Late Printed Sheet, Entitled 'The Selling of Joseph,' Whereunto Is Vindication of the Author's Dealing with and Prosecution of His Negro Man Servant for His Vile and Exorbitant Behavior towards His Master and His Tenant, Thomas Shepard; which Hath Been Wrongfully Represented to Their Prejudice and Defamation," in G. H. Moore, *Notes on the History of Slavery in Massachusetts* (New York, 1866; rpt. 1968), pp. 251–256; and in A. C. Goodell, "John Saffrin and His Slave Adam," *Colonial Society of Massachusetts Publications,* 1 (1895): 103–112. See also L. W. Towner, "The Sewall-Saffin Dialogue on Slavery," *William and Mary Quarterly,* 21 (1964): 40ff. An important document is T. Parsons and E. Pearson, eds., *A Forensic Dispute on the Legality of Enslaving the Africans, Held at the Public Commencement in Cambridge, New England, July 21, 1773, By Two Candidates for the Bachelor's Degree* (Boston, 1773).

26. L. E. Tise, *Proslavery: A History of the Defense of Slavery in America, 1701–1840* (Athens, Ga., 1987), pp. 45, 356, 358 (see also the American prints reproduced on pp. 244–245). See also P. Finkelman, *Slavery and the Founders: Race and Liberty in the Age of Jefferson* (New York, 1996); and R. Blackburn, *The Making of New World Slavery* (London, 1997), esp. pp. 217ff., 371ff.

27. Its most important exponent was probably Robert Walsh, *An Appeal from the Judgments of Great Britain Respecting the United States of America* (Philadelphia, 1819; rpt. New York, 1969), esp. p. 409. See W. S. Jenkins, *Pro-Slavery Thought in the Old South* (Chapel Hill, 1935), pp. 65ff., 76ff. See also Tise, *Proslavery,* pp. 97ff.; and the important book by I. Berlin, *Many Thousands Gone: The First Two Centuries of Slavery in North America* (Cambridge, Mass., 1998).

28. Aristotle mentions them in *Politics,* 1, 3 (1253b): "Others think that it is contrary to nature to be a master, because the fact that one man is a slave and another free is by convention, whereas in nature they do not differ at all, which is why it is not just either; for it is the result of force." In English in T. J. Saunders, *Aristotle: Politics, Books I and II* (Oxford, 1995), p. 5. Efforts to identify these opponents of slavery have been based on conjecture; see G. Cambiano, "Aristotle and the Anonymous Opponents of Slavery," in M. Finley, ed., *Classical Slavery* (Totowa, N.J., 1987), pp. 21ff. The contrast between "nature" and "law" is a major motif in the cultural history of the late fifth century. See F. Heinimann, *Nomos und Physis: Herkunft und Bedeutung einer Antithese im griechischen Denken des 5. Jahrhunderts* (Basel, 1945). The name of Antiphon is often mentioned, probably correctly; see *The Oxyrhynchus Papyri,* ed. and trans. B. P. Grenfell and A. S. Hunt (London, 1898), 11, 1364, F2, col. 2: "since by nature we are all, whether Greek or Barbarian, equal in every way." According to this line of thinking, the

theme of slavery is inextricably linked with that of the relationship between the Greeks and the Barbarians; it even appears in Euripides' *Hecuba*. The integrations in the *Oxyrhynchus Papyri* (52, 3647 [ed. Cockle]) should also be kept in mind. See A. Momigliano, "Sul pensiero di Antifonte il sofista" (1930), reprinted in *Quarto Contributo alla storia degli studi classici e del mondo antico* (Rome, 1969), pp. 135ff.; D. J. Furley, "Antiphon's Case against Justice," in G. B. Kerferd, ed., *The Sophists and Their Legacy* (Wiesbaden, 1981), pp. 81ff. On the dialectics between "nature" and "law" in Roman juridical thinking on slavery, see below, Chapters 9 and 11.

29. This expression is borrowed from the title of a well-known book: K. M. Stampp: *The Peculiar Institution: Slavery in the Ante-bellum South* (New York, 1956; rpt. 1989).

30. Hesiod, *Works and Days*, 42.

31. The problem facing us, in other words, is how to exploit the conceptual richness of modern economic theory in such a way that its use does not take us down a historiographic blind alley (by establishing that its methods, such as they are, are completely inapplicable), and does not lead—along with the whole network of analogies that its indiscriminate utilization would inevitably imply—to the arbitrary modernization of the ancient economy, distorting its original features.

An examination of the period during which the great categories of modern economic science were being defined—from the *Tableau économique* to the neoclassical school, and Kalecki and Keynes—points up the strongly self-centered nature of the entire construct, from a historical standpoint. Except in brief fragments or entirely vague hypotheses, modern economics almost never makes reference to anything external to the ever more clearly defined contours of industrialized societies. This is a very unusual situation, peculiar to the discipline. Indeed, this was not true of the two other social sciences that accompanied the progress of modernity in the West: modern political theory and new European juridical thought from the Renaissance on. The latter were formed by means of a coherent reworking of their ancient heritage, making constant reference to its historical and theoretical richness in the course of a dialogue that economic thought could not imitate.

It would be hard to believe that such an intensive and pervasive use of the modern industrialized world as a reference point (the sole exceptions perhaps being Smith, in his historical digressions and, later, Marx, for whom history was everything) would not have particular consequences, if this analytic system (or a piece of it) were to be projected outside its context. For this reason, historians of ancient economies are forced to limit themselves to referring to it indirectly, or reflectedly, so to speak—not with immediacy, in order to convey a description, but rather in order to give shape to the concepts that make description possible. Only in this way can the inevitable comparisons between ancient and modern be expressed through a meticulous analysis of their differences (for historical knowledge is nothing but knowledge by means of difference), rather than through a muddled and sterile process of assimilation.

This explanation intersects with another proposition—and it, too, has a wealth of implications for economic historiography, not to mention other disciplines. We can call it the rule stating that "the more complex" (in our case, the theory of industrialized economies) is always capable of explaining "the less complex" (that is to say, preindustrial economies). This principle is paraphrased from Marx, where it appears precisely in a passage on the history of precapitalist economies, in the famous metaphor about how the anatomy of man explains that of the monkey, and not vice versa (as a faintly historicist interpretation of Darwinian evolutionism would maintain). But nowadays any statement of this kind, made without further clarification, would be ambiguous. The cognitive preeminence of the "more complex" is undeniable. Nevertheless, it remains to be seen how this position of cognitive advantage can be translated into rigorous historiography, avoiding the distortions of the shortcut by which the same frame of reference is mechanically transposed from one system to the other. The important example presented by the methodology of anthropology and paleontology in the second half of the twentieth century (thanks to Stephen J. Gould as well as to Claude Lévi-Strauss) is a constant demonstration that something which appears to be less complex in evolutionary terms—simply because it is radically different from ourselves—is not necessarily easier to understand, unless we are prepared to make an effort of intellectual adaptation that is proportional to the differences (and the distances) in question. At the very least, then, our principle should be modified to read "the more complex does not directly explain the less complex, but enables us to draw up a list of categories suitable for interpreting it."

32. Nothing on this has been published yet. The statement is based on private discussions and presentations at conferences (for example, a 1990 symposium in Aquileia).

4. Optical Effects

1. *Opus*, 1 (1982): 195ff., 201ff.; A. Carandini, *Schiavi in Italia: Gli strumenti pensanti dei Romani fra tarda repubblica e medio impero* (Rome, 1988), pp. 11ff., 291ff.

2. These works appeared in the *Jahrbücher für Nationalökonomie und Statistik*, with the comprehensive title *Untersuchungen auf dem Gebiete der Nationalökonomie des klassichen Alterthums*. The first was J. K. Rodbertus, "Zur Geschichte der agrarischen Entwicklung Rom unter den Kaisern oder die Adscriptier,

Inquilinen und Colonen," 2 (1864): 206ff. The second—more relevant to the discussion—was Rodbertus, "Zur Geschichte der römischen Tributsteuern seit Augustus." It was published in five installments: 4 (1865): 341ff.; 5 (1865): 13ff., 241ff.; 8 (1867): 81ff., 385ff. It has been reprinted in Rodbertus, *Gesammelte Werke und Briefe,* vol. 3 (Osnabrück, 1971), pp. 1ff., 67ff., 157ff., 196ff., 271ff., 319ff. In addition, see Rodbertus, "Zur Frage des Sachwertes des Geldes im Altertum," *Jahrbücher für Nationalökonomie und Statistik,* 14 (1870): 341ff., 15 (1870): 182ff. (also in *Gesammelte Werke und Briefe,* vol. 3, pp. 411ff.).

3. K. Bücher, *Die Entstehung der Volkswirtschaft* (Tübingen, 1920–1921), esp. vol. 1, pp. 85ff.; in English in *Industrial Evolution,* trans. S. M. Wickett (New York, 1968), pp. 83ff. See also Bücher, "Zur griechischen Wirtschaftsgeschichte," in *Festgabe A. Schäffle* (Tübingen, 1901), pp. 193ff., reprinted with several additions in *Beiträge zur Wirtschaftsgeschichte* (Tübingen, 1922), pp. 1ff. A brief summary of the first work and all of the second were published in M. Finley, ed., *The Bücher-Meyer Controversy* (New York, 1979).

4. See Bruno Hildebrand, *Die Nationalökonomie der Gegenwart und Zukunft* (Frankfurt-am-Main, 1848); and idem, "Naturalwirtschaft, Geldwirtschaft und Creditwirtschaft," in *Jahrbücher für Nationalökonomie und Statistik,* 2 (1864): 1ff. Both have been reprinted in Hildebrand, *"Die Nationalökonomie der Gegenwart und Zukunft" und andere gesammelte Schriften,* ed. H. Gehrig (Jena, 1922). There is a well-founded hypothesis that Hildebrand's work is based partly on J. K. Rodbertus, *Zur Erkenntnis unserer Staatswirtschaftlichen Zustände: Fünf Theoreme* (1842), reprinted in Rodbertus, *Gesammelte Werke,* vol. 1 (Osnabrück, 1972), part 1, pp. 33ff., esp. 189ff. So states B. F. Hoselitz, "Theories of Stages of Economic Growth," in Hoselitz, *Theories of Economic Growth* (Glencoe, Ill., 1960), pp. 193ff., 210ff., and 218, n. 53. If this is the case, the relationship between Rodbertus and Bücher would turn out to be even closer, albeit indirectly. The reader should keep in mind two works by Friedrich List. The first is *Das nationale System der politischen Ökonomie* (Stuttgart, 1844), reprinted in List, *Werke,* vol. 6 (Berlin, 1930); in English, *The National System of Political Economy* (Fairfield, N.J., 1991). The second is *Le système naturel d'économie politique* (1837; written in French), reprinted in List, *Werke,* vol. 4; in English, *The Natural System of Political Economy* (London, 1983).

5. J. K. Rodbertus, "Zur Geschichte der römischen Tributsteuern," *Jahrbücher für Nationalökonomie und Statistik,* 4 (1865): 344ff.; reprinted in Rodbertus, *Gesammelte Werke,* pp. 72ff.

6. G. von Below, "Über Theorien der Wirtschaftlichen Entwicklung der Völker," *Historische Zeitschrift,* 86 (1901): 22ff.; and idem, *Probleme der Wirtschaftsgeschichte* (Tübingen, 1920), p. 153 and n. 2. There is a substantially correct appraisal of Bücher's writings (although it is tinged with partiality) in M. I.

Finley, *The Ancient City: From Fustel de Coulanges to Max Weber and Beyond;* reprinted in Finley, *Economy and Society in Ancient Greece* (New York, 1982), pp. 12ff.

7. Arnaldo Momigliano, "Dopo Max Weber?" (1978), in *Sesto contributo alla storia degli studi classici e del mondo antico,* 1 (Rome, 1980), p. 299; reprinted in Momigliano, *Sui fondamenti della storia antica* (Turin, 1981), pp. 441–442. There are three relevant works by Meyer. The first is "Die wirtschaftliche Entwicklung des Altertums," *Jahrbücher für Nationalökonomie und Statistik,* 64 (1895): 696ff.; reprinted in Meyer, *Kleine Schriften,* vol. 1 (Halle, 1924), pp. 79ff. (this contains the first extreme attack on Bücher). The second is Meyer, "Die Sklaverei in Altertum" (1898), reprinted in Meyer, *Kleine Schriften,* vol. 1, pp. 169ff.—quite deserving of the pitiless demolition it received from Finley in *Ancient Slavery and Modern Ideology* (New York, 1980), pp. 44ff. (updated and expanded edition edited by B. D. Shaw [Princeton, 1998], but all of my quotations come from the 1980 edition). The third is Meyer, *Geschichte des Alterthums,* vol. 2 (Stuttgart, 1893), pp. 547ff.; reprinted in 3rd ed., vol. 3 (Stuttgart, 1954), pp. 504ff. See also M. Calder and A. Demandt, eds., *Eduard Meyer: Leben und Leistung eines Universalhistorikers* (Leiden, 1990), esp. the essay by H. Schneider, "Die Bücher-Meyer Kontroverse," pp. 417ff.

8. L. Canfora, *Ideologie del classicismo* (Turin, 1980), pp. 164ff.; following in the footsteps of H. Delbrück, *Weltgeschichte: Vorlesungen gehalten an der Universität Berlin, 1896–1920,* vol. 1, *Das Altertum* (Berlin, 1924), p. 14. But to which interpretation of Hegel did Meyer ascribe? Evidently, this was the Hegel who was considered a direct precursor of Bismarck—the Hegel of Rudolf Haym, certainly not that of Franz Rosenzweig, Friedrich Meinecke, or Wilhelm Dilthey—reflecting the reading that was so popular in Germany between 1870 and 1914.

9. R. von Pöhlman, *Geschichte der sozialen Frage und des Sozialismus in der antiken Welt, 1893–1901* (Munich, 1925; rpt. Darmstadt, 1984).

10. G. Salvioli, *Le capitalisme dans le monde antique: Etudes sur l'histoire de l'économie romaine* (Paris, 1906; rpt. New York, 1979); Italian edition edited by A. Giardina (Rome, 1985). See also E. Ciccotti, "Tratti caratteristici dell'economia antica," in *Biblioteca di storia economica,* vol. 2, 1 (Milan, 1905; rpt. Bologna, 1977), pp. viiff.

11. In addition to his social and economic history of the Roman Empire, in 1941 Rostovtzeff wrote *The Social and Economic History of the Hellenistic World* (Oxford, 1953).

12. Friedrich Oertel, "Anhang," in Robert von Pöhlman, *Geschichte der sozialen Frage,* vol. 2, p. 516. See also Oertel, "Zur Frage der Attischen Grossindustrie," *Rheinisches Museum für Philologie,* 79 (1930): 230ff.

13. Max Weber, "Agrarverhältnisse im Altertum," in *Handwörterbuch der Staatswissenschaften,* vol. 1, 2nd and 3rd editions (Jena, 1898, 1909), the section

of the entry "Agrargeschichte" dealing with the classical period; reprinted in Weber, *Gesammelte Aufsätze zur Sozial- und Wirtschaftsgeschichte* (Tübingen, 1924), pp. 1–228; in English, *The Agrarian Sociology of Ancient Civilizations* (London, 1976; rpt. 1998).

14. J. Hasebroek, "Zum griechischen Bankwesen der klassischen Zeit," in *Hermes,* 55 (1920): 113ff.; idem, "Die Betriebsformen des griechischen Handels im IV. Jahrhundert," in *Hermes,* 58 (1923): 393ff.; idem, *Staat und Handel im alten Griechenland* (Tübingen, 1928; rpt. Hildesheim, 1966), translated into English, with modifications (London, 1933); idem, *Griechische Wirtschafts- und Gesellschaftsgeschichte bis zur Perserzeit* (Tübingen, 1931; rpt. Hildesheim, 1966).

15. Rostovtzeff wrote this in a review of Hasebroek, *Griechische Wirtschafts- und Gesellschaftsgeschichte.* The review appeared in *Zeitschrift für die gesamte Staatswissenschaften,* 92 (1932): 333ff.; reprinted in Rostovtzeff, *Scripta varia: Ellenismo e impero romano,* ed. A. Marcone (Bari, 1995), pp. 459ff. (This is an important passage for Rostovtzeff's thinking, to which we shall return below.) See also Rostovtzeff, *The Social and Economic History of the Hellenistic World,* vol. 3 (Oxford, 1941), pp. 1327–1328, n. 25.

16. F. Heichelheim, *Wirtschaftsgeschichte des Altertums* (Leiden, 1938); in English, *An Ancient Economic History* (Leiden, 1958–1970).

17. U. von Wilamowitz-Moellendorff, *Staat und Gesellschaft der Griechen und Römer* (Berlin, 1910; rpt. New York, 1979), esp. pp. 32, 36, 93ff. Wilamowitz was actually the one who first suggested to Rostovtzeff that he undertake a social and economic history of the ancient world; see G. W. Bowersock, "*The Social and Economic History of the Roman Empire,* by Michael Ivanovich Rostovtzeff," *Daedalus,* 102 (1973): 17.

18. Eduard Meyer, "Die wirtschaftliche Entwicklung des Altertums"; and idem, "Die Sklaverei in Altertum."

19. See Werner Wilhelm Jaeger, *Paideia: Die Formung des griechischen Menschen,* 3 vols. (Berlin, 1934–1937); in English, *Paideia: The Ideals of Greek Culture,* trans. G. Highet (New York, 1986). The indexes to this work make no mention of the word "slave," as Finley observed (*Ancient Slavery,* p. 57).

20. Keith Hopkins, "Models, Ships, and Staples," in P. Garnsey and C. R. Whittaker, eds., *Trade and Famine in Classical Antiquity* (Cambridge, 1983), p. 84.

21. At virtually the same time as the above-mentioned debate was taking place, the ancient economies were being viewed from new angles created by the successful intersection of various specializations. Their conclusions went a great deal further. What these inquiries had in common—since they were connected not by a single lineage, but rather by the same deep-seated inspiration—was the realization that the study of the ancient economic systems called for quite specific conceptualizations and approaches, not doctrinaire rigidity. I am referring specifically to three scholars: Karl Marx, Max Weber, and Karl Polanyi—three

names that we are not used to seeing in the same place but that will often appear in each other's company in the following pages. I do not seek to confuse the ideas of these three authors; rather, I would like to integrate them in a way that has long been desirable. Only the ideological traumas of the past century have made them wait so long.

5. The Rhythms of the Economy

1. The expression (and the concept of) "imperial system" can be traced back to Edward Gibbon, *History of the Decline and Fall of the Roman Empire,* ed. Bury (London, 1896–1900), vol. 1, p. 68.

2. In the sense employed by E. Gellner, *Plough, Sword, and Book: The Structure of Human History* (London, 1988), pp. 43ff. In my perspective, it is an implicit reference to K. Polanyi, "Aristotle Discovers the Economy," in K. Polanyi, C. M. Arensberg, and H. W. Pearson, eds., *Trade and Market in the Early Empires: Economies in History and Theory* (Glencoe, Ill., 1957; rpt. Chicago, 1971), pp. 64ff., 243ff.; K. Polanyi, *The Livelihood of Man,* ed. H. W. Pearson (New York, 1977), pp. 47ff.; K. Polanyi, *Primitive, Archaic, and Modern Economies: Essays of Karl Polanyi,* ed. G. Dalton (Garden City, N.Y., 1968; rpt. Boston, 1971), pp. 3ff., 26ff., 139ff., 306ff. Polanyi, in turn, was reworking H. S. Maine, *Ancient Law: Its Connection with the Early History of Society, and Its Relation to Modern Ideas* (1st ed. 1861; 2nd ed. London, 1863; rpt. Tucson, 1986); and F. Tönnies, *Gemeinschaft und Gesellschaft: Grundbegriffe der reinen Sociologie* (1887; 2nd ed. Berlin, 1922), in English as Tönnies, *Community and Society* (East Lansing, Mich., 1957; rpt. New York, 1963). Polanyi embraced the functional aspects of Maine's theories, not their substratum of Romanticism or their ideological consequences.

3. P. A. Brunt, *Italian Manpower, 225 B.C.–A.D. 14,* 2nd ed. (Oxford, 1987), pp. 54, 59 n. 3, 67 n. 2, and 121; W. V. Harris, *War and Imperialism in Republican Rome, 327–70 B.C.* (Oxford, 1979; rpt. 1992), pp. 81ff.; K. Hopkins, *Conquerors and Slaves* (Cambridge, 1978), p. 101. See also Livy, 26, 40, 13; 27, 16, 7; 45, 34, 5–6; and Polybius, 30, 15 (Strabo, 7, 7, 3, ed. A. Meineke).

4. K. J. Beloch, *Historische Beiträge zur Bevölkerungslehre, I: Die Bevölkerung der griechisch-römischen Welt* (1886; rpt. Rome, 1968), pp. 339ff., 389ff.; A. Afzelius, *Die römische Eroberung Italiens, 340–264 v. Chr.* (Copenhagen, 1942), pp. 98ff., 133ff., reprinted in Afzelius, *Two Studies on Roman Expansion* (New York, 1975); Brunt, *Italian Manpower,* pp. 27–28, 30, 384; Frontinus, *De aquaeductu urbis Romae,* ed. Kunderewicz, 1–12. F. Coarelli, "Demografia e territorio," in A. Momigliano and A. Schiavone, eds., *Storia di Roma,* vol. 1 (Turin, 1988), p. 339, has a different opinion on the subject.

5. P. A. Brunt, "The Roman Mob," *Past and Present,* 35 (1966): 3ff., esp. 13ff.

6. F 20 Peter = *Fragmente der Griechischen Historiker,* 809 F 27 (Strabo 5, 3, 1); F. Cassola, *I gruppi politici romani nel III secolo a. C.* (Trieste, 1962), pp. 93–94; Harris, *War and Imperialism in Republican Rome,* p. 67; D. Musti, "I due volti della Sabina: Sulla rappresentazione dei Sabini in Varrone, Dionigi, Strabone, Plutarco," *Dialoghi di Archeologia,* 3 (1985): 77ff.; E. Gabba, "Allora i Romani conobbero per la prima volta la ricchezza" (1988), reprinted in Gabba, *Del buon uso della ricchezza: Saggi di storia economica e sociale del mondo antico* (Milan, 1988), pp. 19ff.

7. This is one of the most crowded chapters in the history of twentieth-century economic theory. Some of the classic studies include M. Kalecki, *Studies in the Theory of Business Cycles, 1933–1939* (New York, 1966); idem, *Selected Essays on the Dynamics of the Capitalist Economy, 1933–1970* (Cambridge, 1971; rpt. 1980); J. M. Keynes, *The General Theory of Employment, Interest, and Money* (London, 1936; rpt. New York, 1964), pp. 313ff.; J. A. Schumpeter, *Business Cycles: A Theoretical, Historical, and Statistical Analysis of the Capitalist Process* (New York, 1939; rpt. Philadelphia, 1982), esp. vol. 1, pp. 72ff., 130ff., 252ff.; W. Röpke, *Crises and Cycles* (London, n.d. [1936]), esp. pp. 14ff., 38ff.; A. H. Hansen, *Business Cycles and National Income* (New York, 1964).

8. The most significant of these are represented by the studies of R. Duncan-Jones: *The Economy of the Roman Empire: Quantitative Studies* (Cambridge, 1982); *Structure and Scale in the Roman Economy* (Cambridge, 1990; rpt. 1992); and *Money and Government in the Roman Empire* (Cambridge, 1994).

9. The statistics that follow come from three sources: B. R. Mitchell, *European Historical Statistics, 1750–1970* (New York, 1976); C. Cipolla, *Storia economica dell' Europa pre-industriale* (Bologna, 1990), in English as *Before the Industrial Revolution: European Society and Economy, 1000–1700* (rpt. New York, 1993); and R. Duncan-Jones, *The Economy of the Roman Empire.* See also the numbers presented in C. Vivanti, "Note per una discussione sull'assolutismo (1550–1650)," Atti del III Convegno degli studi italiani e sovietici, *Quaderni di Rassegna sovietica,* 3 (1969): 11–12.

10. A. Smith, *An Inquiry into the Nature and Causes of the Wealth of Nations* (1776; 5th ed. 1789), ed. E. Cannan (New York, 1937; rpt. 1994), pp. 314ff. (book 2, ch. 3); D. Ricardo, "On the Principles of Political Economy and Taxation," in *The Works and Correspondence of David Ricardo* (1821), ed. P. Sraffa, vol. 1 (Cambridge, 1966), pp. 110ff.; and D. Ricardo, "An Essay on the Influence of a Low Price of Corn on the Profits of Stock" (1815), in *The Works and Correspondence of David Ricardo,* vol. 4 (Cambridge, 1962), pp. 1ff.

11. W. A. Lewis, *The Theory of Economic Growth* (1955; rpt. New York, 1970); A. O. Hirschman, *The Strategy of Economic Development* (New Haven, 1958), esp. pp. 1ff., 29ff.; N. Kaldor, *Essays on Economic Stability and Growth* (1960; rpt. New

York, 1980), esp. pp. 177ff., 213ff.; W. W. Rostow, *The Stages of Economic Growth: A Non-Communist Manifesto* (1960; rpt. Cambridge, 1990), esp. pp. 4ff., 17ff.; W. W. Rostow, *Rich Countries and Poor Countries: Reflections on the Past, Lessons for the Future* (Boulder, Colo., 1987), esp. pp. 1ff., 49ff.; J. D. Gould, *Economic Growth in History: Survey and Analysis* (London, 1972); C. Owen Paepke, *The Evolution of Progress: The End of Economic Growth and the Beginning of Human Transformation* (New York, 1993). It must be added that classical economic thought also developed a special model of time, different from the one shared by the other social sciences ranging from law to political theory. But this is a subject we cannot elaborate on here.

6. Dual Equilibria

1. See, for example, Moses Finley, *The Ancient Economy* (Berkeley, 1985), pp. 43ff.

2. As in Fernand Braudel, *Civilisation matérielle, économie et capitalisme: XVe– XVIIIe siècle* (Paris, 1979), vol. 2, *Les jeux de l'échange* (Paris, 1979), pp. 142ff. In English: *Civilization and Capitalism, 15th–18th Century*, vol. 2, *The Wheels of Commerce*, trans. S. Reynolds (New York, 1982), pp. 168ff. The French expression is *plus-value marchande*.

3. But even here this was not always the case. See the well-founded statements in A. Giardina, "Uomini e spazi aperti," in A. Schiavone, ed., *Storia di Roma*, vol. 4 (Turin, 1989), pp. 71ff., esp. 78ff. Also P. Garnsey, "Mountain Economy in Southern Europe: Thoughts on the Early History, Continuity, and Individuality of Mediterranean Upland Pastoralism," in C. R. Whittaker, ed., *Pastoral Economies in Classical Antiquity* (Cambridge, 1988), pp. 196ff.; E. T. Salmon, *Samnium and the Samnites* (Cambridge, 1967); C. Nicolet, *Rome et la conquête du monde méditerranéen: 264–27 avant J.-C.*, vol. 1, *Les structures de l'Italie romaine* (Paris, 1977); E. Gabba and M. Pasquinucci, *Strutture agrarie e allevamento transumante nell'Italia romana (III–I sec. A. C.)* (Pisa, 1979), esp. pp. 79ff. There are precious glimpses in Strabo's *Geographical Sketches:* for example, 3, 3, 5–7; 4, 4, 3; 5, 1–4; 6, 1–4; 11, 5, 6–7. A theoretical model for this kind of production is presented in P. Sraffa, *Production of Commodities by Means of Commodities: Prelude to a Critique of Economic Theory* (Cambridge, 1960), pp. 3ff. ("production for subsistence").

4. Keith Hopkins, "Taxes and Trade in the Roman Empire, 200 B.C.–A.D. 400," *Journal of Roman Studies*, 70 (1980): 101ff.; also R. P. Duncan-Jones, *Structure and Scale in the Roman Economy* (Cambridge, 1990), pp. 30ff. See also M. Crawford, ed., *L'impero romano e le strutture economiche e sociali delle province* (Como, 1986), esp. the essays by E. Lo Cascio, pp. 29ff., M. Crawford, pp. 61ff., D. Foraboschi, pp. 109ff., and M. Benabou, pp. 127ff.

5. W. W. Rostow, *The Stages of Economic Growth: A Non-Communist Manifesto* (1960; rpt. Cambridge, 1990), pp. 4ff.

6. J. H. Boeke, *Economics and Economic Policy of Dual Societies, as Exemplified by Indonesia* (1953; rpt. New York, 1978); I. Wallerstein, *The Modern World-System: Capitalist Agriculture and the Origins of the European World-Economy in the Sixteenth Century* (New York, 1974), p. 18; I. M. D. Little, *Economic Development: Theory, Policy, and International Relations* (New York, 1982), pp. 86ff. A classic— albeit with a modernizing perspective—is A. Dopsch, *Naturalwirtschaft und Geldwirtschaft in der Weltgeschichte* (Vienna, 1930), esp. pp. 80ff. See also T. F. Carney, *The Economies of Antiquity* (Lawrence, Kansas, 1973), which has a Polanian perspective.

7. Andrea Giardina, "L'identità incompiuta dell'Italia romana," in Ecole Française de Rome, *L'Italie d'Auguste à Dioclétien* (Rome, 1994), 76–77, 87–88, reprinted in Giardina, *L'Italia romana: Storie di un'identità incompiuta* (Rome, 1997), pp. 68–69, 76–77. This is an important work, to which we shall return below. The point mentioned here was given more emphasis in the version presented at the Ecole Française de Rome on March 25, 1992, than in the published text.

8. K. J. Beloch, *Die Bevölkerung der griechisch-römischen Welt* (1886; rpt. Rome, 1968), pp. 491ff., esp. p. 502; P. A. Brunt, *Italian Manpower, 225 B.C.–A.D. 14* (Oxford, 1987), pp. 121ff.; P. Salmon, *Population et dépopulation dans l'Empire romain* (Brussels, 1974), esp. pp. 11ff., 23ff.; Duncan-Jones, *Quantitative Studies*, pp. 2, 8, 259ff.; idem, *Structure and Scale*, pp. 77ff.; T. G. Parkin, *Demography and Roman Society* (Baltimore, 1992), esp. pp. 92ff.

7. The Roman Miracle and Imperial Rationality

1. F. Cassola, *I gruppi politici romani nel III secolo A. C.* (Trieste, 1962), pp. 92ff., 121ff., 161ff. Also, M. Dondin-Payre, "'Homo novus': Un slogan de Caton à César?" *Historia* 30 (1981): 22ff.

2. T. P. Wiseman, *New Men in the Roman Senate, 139 B.C.–14 A.D.* (London, 1971), pp. 3ff.; Cicero, *Philippicae*, 9, 2, 4; Velleius Paterculus, *Historia Romana*, 1, 13, 2. The three consuls were Gnaeus Octavius (consul in 165 B.C.), Lucius Mummius (consul in 146 B.C.), and Quintus Pompeius (consul in 141 B.C.). See T. R. S. Broughton, *The Magistrates of the Roman Republic*, vol. 1 (New York, 1951), pp. 438, 465, 477. See also C. Nicolet, "Economie, société, et institutions au IIe siècle av. J.-C.: De la lex Claudia à l'ager exceptus," *Annales: Economies, sociétés, civilisations*, 35 (1980): 871ff.

3. There were nine between 105 and 94 B.C. alone. See Wiseman, *New Men*, pp. 6, 203, 209ff.

4. Polybius, 6, 11–18.

5. Livy, 5, 25, 7–10.

6. F. Coarelli, "Demografia e territorio," in A. Momigliano and A. Schiavone, eds., *Storia di Roma,* vol. 1 (Turin, 1988), p. 338.

7. Plutarch, *Crassus,* 2; I. Shatzman, *Senatorial Wealth and Roman Politics* (Brussels, 1975), esp. pp. 9ff.

8. Dionysius of Halicarnassus, 2, 7, 4 (on the descent from Romulus). See L. Capogrossi Colognesi, "La città e la sua terra," in *Storia di Roma,* vol. 1, pp. 263ff. There is very important testimony in the statement by Manius Curius Dentatus reported by Pliny in *Historia Naturalis,* 18, 4, 18: "perniciosum intellegi civem, cui septem iugera non essent satis" ("a man not satisfied with seven acres must be deemed a dangerous citizen": A. Rackham, trans. [Cambridge, 1961], p. 201). On Manius Curius Dentatus and his moderation, see also Cicero, *Cato maior,* 16, 55; and Pliny, *Historia Naturalis,* 19, 26, 87.

9. K. Polanyi, "Aristotle Discovers the Economy," in K. Polanyi, C. M. Arensberg, and H. W. Pearson, eds., *Trade and Market in the Early Empires: Economies in History and Theory* (Glencoe, Ill., 1957), pp. 64ff., esp. 68ff.; K. Polanyi, *The Livelihood of Man,* ed. H. W. Pearson (New York, 1977), pp. 47ff.; K. Polanyi, *Primitive, Archaic, and Modern Economies: Essays of Karl Polanyi,* ed. G. Dalton (Garden City, N.Y., 1968), pp. 78ff., 139ff., 306ff.

10. Cato, *De agri cultura,* ed. A. Mazzarino (Leipzig, 1962), "praefatio," 1–4. See E. Gabba, "Riflessioni sulla società romana fra III e II a. C.," reprinted in E. Gabba, *Del buon uso della ricchezza: Saggi di storia economica e sociale del mondo antico* (Milan, 1988), pp. 45ff.

11. Pliny, *Historia Naturalis,* 18, 4, 19–21.

12. This comes from a posthumously published text written between the middle of 1857 and the beginning of 1859: Karl Marx, *Grundrisse der Kritik der politischen Ökonomie* (Berlin, 1974), pp. 379–380. In English in *Foundations of the Critique of Political Economy,* trans. M. Nicolaus (New York, 1973), pp. 475–476.

13. Varro, *De re rustica,* 1, 2, 9; Livy, 5, 30, 8; Columella, *Res rustica,* 1, "praefatio," 14 (but also 1, 3, 10); Valerius Maximus, 4, 3, 5; Pliny, *Historia Naturalis,* 18, 4, 18. There is some degree of confusion in Varro's text—and in Pliny's, which is based on it. This has caused a chain of slip-ups in many of the modern translations.

14. Max Weber, "Agrarverhältnisse im Altertum," in Weber, *Gesammelte Aufsätze zur Sozial- und Wirtschaftsgeschichte* (Tübingen, 1924), p. 41. In English in Weber, *The Agrarian Sociology of Ancient Civilizations* (London, 1976; rpt. 1998), p. 75.

15. Polybius, 3, 24.

16. A. Bernardi, "Incremento demografico di Roma e colonizzazione latina dal 338 a. C. all'età dei Gracchi," *Nuova Rivista Storica,* 30 (1946): 272ff.; A. Toynbee, *Hannibal's Legacy: The Hannibalic War's Effects on Roman Life,* vol. 1 (London, 1965), pp. 159–160; P. A. Brunt, *Italian Manpower, 225 b.c.–a.d. 14* (Oxford, 1987), pp. 29–30, 44ff.

17. "Maecia" and "Scaptia" were formed in 332; "Aniensis" and "Teretina," in 299; "Quirina" and "Velina," in 241.

18. K. J. Beloch, *Die Bevölkerung der griechisch-römischen Welt* (1886; rpt. Rome, 1968), pp. 340ff.

19. W. V. Harris, *War and Imperialism in Republican Rome, 327–70 B.C.* (Oxford, 1979; rpt. 1992), pp. 60, 264. Also, E. T. Salmon, *Roman Colonization under the Republic* (Ithaca, 1970), pp. 55ff., 70ff.; idem, *The Making of Roman Italy* (Ithaca, 1982), esp. pp. 1ff., 57ff.; L. Ross Taylor, *The Voting Districts of the Roman Republic* (Rome, 1960), pp. 47ff.

20. For example, Livy, 4, 47, 6; 4, 48, 2; 4, 51, 5; 4, 53, 6; and Dionysius, 4, 9, 8; 8, 70, 5; 9, 5, 1; 10, 36, 2; 10, 37, 4.

21. Livy, Book 10: 15, 6; 17, 4; 17, 8; 18, 8; 19, 22; 20, 15; 29, 17; 31, 7; 34, 3; 37, 3; 39, 3–4; 42, 5; 43, 8; 45, 11; 45, 14. Harris, *War and Imperialism,* p. 59, n. 4; T. Frank, *Rome and Italy of the Republic* (Baltimore, 1933; rpt. New York, 1975), vol. 1 of Frank, ed., *An Economic Survey of Ancient Rome* (Baltimore, 1933–1940), p. 43, n. 1; H. Volkmann, *Die Massenversklaverungen der Einwohner eroberter Städte in der hellenistisch-römischen Zeit* (1961; rpt. Stuttgart, 1990), pp. 40, 113.

22. Strabo, 3, 2, 10, from Polybius, 34, 9, 8–9 (on the mines, see also Frank, *Rome and Italy,* pp. 152–153). On the indemnification paid by Carthage, see Harris, *War and Imperialism,* p. 69. But a lower amount is suggested in A. H. M. Jones, "Ancient Empire and the Economy: Rome," reprinted in Jones, *The Roman Economy: Studies in Ancient Economic and Administrative History* (Oxford, 1974), p. 114. On the estate of Cornelius Lentulus, see Seneca, *De beneficiis,* 2, 27, 1–2; Suetonius, *Tiberius,* 49, 1; *Prosopographia Imperii Romani,* 2nd ed. (Berlin, 1933), C 1379; Harris, *War and Imperialism,* p. 69.

23. Plutarch, *Aemilius Paulus,* 28.

24. Pliny, *Historia Naturalis,* 7, 43, 139–140, translated by H. Rackham (Cambridge, Mass., 1961), vol. 2, p. 599 (in *Oratorum Romanorum Fragmenta,* pp. 10–11, 535, E. Malcovati reads "primus" for "plurimos"). A. Lippold, *Consules: Untersuchungen zur Geschichte des römischen Konsulates von 264 bis 201 v. Chr.* (Bonn, 1963), pp. 75ff.; E. Gabba, "Ricchezza e classe dirigente romana fra III e I sec. a.C." (1981), in Gabba, *Del buon uso della ricchezza,* pp. 27ff.

25. Livy, 21, 63, 2 (also, Cicero, *Verr.* 2, 5, 18, 45). See G. Rotondi, *Leges publicae populi Romani* (1912; rpt. Hildesheim, 1966), pp. 249–250. Gaius Flaminius continued the policies of Manius Curius Dentatus; his "Lex Flaminia de agro Piceno Gallico viritim dividundo" (I follow the correction of P. Fraccaro, in *Opuscula,* vol. 2 [Pavia, 1957], p. 191) had attracted senatorial opposition. See Polybius, 2, 21, 7–8; Cicero, *De inventione,* 2, 17, 52; idem, *Brutus,* 14, 57; idem, *Cato Maior,* 4, 11; Varro, *De re rustica* 1, 2, 7; Valerius Maximus, 5, 4, 5; Rotondi, *Leges publicae,* pp. 247–248.

26. Asconius, *in orat. in toga cand.* 83, p. 93 (Clark); Cassius Dio, 55, 10, 5; F. De Martino, *Storia della costituzione romana,* vol. 2 (Naples, 1973), p. 308.

27. This regulation is in a *caput* of the "Lex Julia de repetundis" of 59 B.C. (Rotondi, *Leges publicae,* pp. 389–391), still remembered by Cervidius Scevola, at the beginning of the Severian era: 3 *reg.,* in *Digesta* (hereafter abbreviated "D."), 50, 5, 3.

28. Cassola, *I gruppi politici romani,* pp. 215ff.; Gabba, "Riflessioni antiche e moderne sulle attività commerciali a Roma nei secoli II e I a.C.," in Gabba, *Del buon uso della ricchezza,* pp. 89ff.

29. M. Junius Gracchanus, *De potestatibus,* cited in Pliny, *Historia Naturalis,* 33, 9, 36. Ulpian, *Lib. Sing. de off. quaest.,* D., 1, 13, 1 pr.: see C. Nicolet, *L'ordre équestre à l'époque républicaine, 312–43 av. J.C.,* vol. 1 (Paris, 1974), pp. 163ff.; M. Bretone, *Tecniche e ideologie dei giuristi romani* (Naples, 1982), pp. 11ff.

30. K. Hopkins, *Conquerors and Slaves* (Cambridge, 1978), pp. 31ff.

31. Theophrastus, *Historia plantarum,* 5, 8, 1–3 (Wimmer).

32. Polybius, 1, 3, 4; translated by H. W. R. Paton (rpt. Cambridge, Mass., 1960), vol. 1, pp. 7–9.

33. Harris, *War and Imperialism,* pp. 18ff.

34. Sallust, *Historiae,* 4, 69 (Maurenbrecher); translated by J. C. Rolfe (Cambridge, Mass., rpt. 1960), pp. 435–441.

35. Tacitus, *Agricola,* 30; translated by M. Hutton and R. M. Ogilvie (Cambridge, Mass., 1970).

36. "Bella ex bellis": Sallust, *Historiae,* 4, 69, 20. On Rome's so-called imperialism— but the use of this concept, associated as it is with the capitalistic (economic and political) expansion of the nineteenth and twentieth centuries, runs the risk of being excessively modernizing in the context of the ancient world—see J. Carcopino, *Les étapes de l'impérialisme romain* (Paris, 1961); E. Badian, *Roman Imperialism in the Late Republic* (Ithaca, 1968); P. Garnsey and C. R. Whittaker, eds., *Imperialism in the Ancient World* (Cambridge, 1978), esp. the essays by P. A. Brunt, pp. 159ff., and M. Crawford, pp. 193ff.; W. Harris, ed., *The Imperialism of Mid-Republican Rome* (Rome, 1984). See also Y. Garlan, *La guerre dans l'antiquité* (Paris, 1972), esp. pp. 75ff.; and the important essay by P. Veyne, "Y a-t-il un impérialisme romain?" in *Mélanges d'Archéologie et d'Histoire (Ecole Française de Rome),* 87 (1975): 793ff. Many of the works of P. A. Brunt, now collected in Brunt, *Roman Imperial Themes* (Oxford, 1990), are also more or less germane to this subject.

37. As S. Mazzarino suggests; see Mazzarino, *Il pensiero storico classico,* vol. 2, part 1 (Bari, 1966), pp. 367ff. The diametrically opposing view is expressed by A. La Penna, *Sallustio e la "rivoluzione" romana* (Milan, 1968), p. 10. See also R. Syme, *Sallust* (Berkeley, 1964), pp. 223, 228–229; and D. C. Earl, *The Political Thought of Sallust* (Cambridge, 1961).

38. F. Jacoby, ed., *Fragmente der Griechischen Historiker* (rpt. Leiden, 1954–1960), 257 F 36 (the citation is from III, 9), through the mediation of Phlegon of Tralles. It is now virtually certain that the author of the prophetic dream is Publius Cornelius Scipio; Mazzarino, *Il pensiero storico classico*, 2, 1, pp. 156ff., is on the whole correct. See also J.-L. Ferrary, *Philhellénisme et impérialisme: Aspects idéologiques de la conquête romaine du monde hellénistique* (Rome, 1988), pp. 238ff., 362; and the essays by E. Gabba now collected in Gabba, *Aspetti culturali dell'imperialismo romano* (Florence, 1993).

8. Nobles and Merchants

1. *Corpus Inscriptionum Latinarum*, 9, 60, cited in A. Giardina, "Il mercante nel mondo romano," in A. Giardina and A. J. Gurevic, *Il mercante dall'Antichità al Medioevo* (Rome, 1994), pp. 31–32. This essay was originally published in A. Giardina, ed., *L'uomo romano* (Roma, 1989), pp. 269ff. (translated as *The Romans* [Chicago, 1993], pp. 245ff.), in a slightly different form that was itself a reworking of two earlier pieces. See also J. Rougé, *Recherches sur l'organisation du commerce maritime en Méditerranée sous l'empire romain* (Paris, 1966), pp. 47ff., 121ff.; and L. Casson, *Ships and Seamanship in the Ancient World* (Princeton, 1986), esp. pp. 141ff.

2. Plato, *Gorgias*, 23 (467 d).

3. Cicero (*De republica*, 2, 3, 5–6) and Livy (*Ab urbe condita*, 5, 54, 3–4) were already quite aware of this.

4. Keith Hopkins has done this, in "Taxes and Trade in the Roman Empire, 200 B.C.–A.D. 400," *Journal of Roman Studies*, 70 (1980): 105ff., picking up from A. J. Parker, "Ancient Shipwrecks of the Mediterranean and the Roman Provinces," in *British Archaeological Reports, International Series* (1992): esp. 16ff., 39ff.; and also from A. J. Parker, "Shipwrecks and Ancient Trade in the Mediterranean," in *Archaeological Review from Cambridge*, 3 (1984): pp. 99ff. Pertinent observations can be found in C. R. Whittaker, "Amphorae and Trade," in *Amphores romaines et histoire économique: Dix ans de recherche* (Rome, 1989), pp. 537ff.

5. P. Pomey and A. Tchernia, "Le tonnage maximum des navires de commerce romains," in *Archaeonautica*, 2 (1978): 233ff.

6. Cervidius Scaevola, 3 *reg.*, in *Digesta* (hereafter abbreviated "D."), 50, 5, 3 (cited above, Ch. 7, n. 27).

7. Lucian, *Navigium*, 5–6; in English in Lucian, *The Ship or The Wishes*, trans. M. D. Macleod (Cambridge, Mass., 1959), pp. 435–436.

8. Procopius, *De bello Gothico*, 1, 14.

9. Cato, *De agri cultura*, 22, 3; the sum of 172 sesterces for the transport is the result of an unavoidable correction to the text, which reads 72. The change is necessary because the total given by Cato is 100 sesterces greater than the sum of the fac-

tors mentioned. See A. Mazzarino, in his edition of *De agri cultura* published by Teubner (Leipzig, 1982), p. 33, line 16 and note; and F. De Martino, *Storia economica di Roma antica*, vol. 1 (Florence, 1979), p. 90 and n. 8.

10. *Edictum Diocletiani de pretiis rerum venalium*, ed. Lauffer, pp. 95, 118–119, 148–149; R. Duncan-Jones, *The Economy of the Roman Empire: Quantitative Studies* (Cambridge, 1982), pp. 366ff.; K. Hopkins, "Economic Growth and Towns in Classical Antiquity," in P. Abrams and E. A. Wrigley, eds., *Towns in Societies: Essays in Economic History and Historical Sociology* (Cambridge, 1980), pp. 35ff., esp. pp. 42ff. See also A. Burford, "Heavy Transport in Classical Antiquity," in *Economic History Review*, 12 (1960): 1ff.

11. Hopkins, "Economic Growth and Towns," pp. 43–44.

12. Hopkins, "Taxes and Trade," pp. 107ff., esp. p. 109; idem, "Economic Growth and Towns," pp. 39ff.

13. Michael Crawford, *Roman Republican Coinage* (London, 1974); see also idem, *Coinage and Money under the Roman Republic: Italy and the Mediterranean Economy* (Berkeley, 1985); idem, "Money and Exchange in the Roman World," *Journal of Roman Studies*, 60 (1970): 40ff.; idem, "Le problème des liquidités dans l'antiquité classique," in *Annales: Economies, sociétés, civilisations*, 26 (1971): 1228ff.

14. I am referring to Hopkins, "Taxes and Trade." See also the conference volume *Les "dévaluations" à Rome: Epoque républicaine et impériale*, 2 vols. (Rome, 1978–1980); and C. Nicolet, "Les variations de prix et la 'théorie quantitative' de la monnaie à Rome, de Cicéron à Pline l'Ancien," in *Annales: Economies, sociétés, civilisations*, 26 (1971): 1203ff.

15. Fernand Braudel, *Civilisation matérielle, économie et capitalisme: XVe–XVIIIe siècle*, vol. 2, *Les jeux de l'échange* (Paris, 1979), pp. 12ff.; in English, *Civilization and Capitalism, 15th–18th Century*, vol. 2, *The Wheels of Commerce*, trans. S. Reynolds (Berkeley, 1982), pp. 26ff.

16. Daniel Defoe, *A Plan of the English Commerce* (Oxford, 1927; orig. pub. 1728), pp. 76–77.

17. The definitive text is the result of a long series of emendations between 1705 and 1729. See Bernard Mandeville, *The Fable of the Bees; or, Private Vices, Public Benefits*, ed. F. B. Kaye (Oxford, 1966; rpt. Indianapolis, 1988).

18. Karl Polanyi, *The Great Transformation* (New York, 1944; rpt. Boston, 1985), p. 33. "Satanic Mills" is the title of the first section of the second part of the book.

19. From William Blake's "Preface" (second quatrain) to his *Milton* (1804): "And was Jerusalem builded here / Among these dark Satanic Mills?"

20. From the diary of a traveler, *Voyage en Angleterre* (1728), now in the Victoria and Albert Museum (86 NN 2, folios 14, 161), cited in Braudel, *The Wheels of Commerce*, pp. 41–42, 606 (French edition, pp. 27, 539).

21. This is completely the opposite of what Rostovtzeff claimed in his review of

Johannes Hasebroek's *Griechische Wirtschafts- und Gesellschaftsgeschichte*, originally published in *Zeitschrift für die gesamte Staatswissenschaften*, 92 (1932): 335 n. 1; now in Rostovtzeff, *Scripta varia: Ellenismo e impero romano*, ed. A. Marcone (Bari, 1995), p. 460. In this essay he categorically states that the economies in the periods of Hellenism and the early principate "nur quantitativ, nicht qualitativ von der modernen Wirtschaft verschieden war, steht für mich fest" ("I am certain that the differences with respect to the modern economy were only quantitative, not qualitative"). I wonder to what extent the "new orthodoxy" of Moses Finley (*The Ancient Economy* [Berkeley, 1985]) and A. H. M. Jones (*The Later Roman Empire, 284–602: A Social, Economic, and Administrative Survey* [Baltimore, 1964; rpt. 1992], pp. 824ff.)—used in this way by Hopkins, who in "Economic Growth and Towns," p. 43, n. 19, contrasted it with Rostovtzeff's "previous modernizing orthodoxy"—itself ended up prisoner to a solely quantitative schema, by limiting itself to an upward revision of the measurements that Rostovtzeff had too optimistically assessed, and by claiming that all differences between the ancient economy and the modern emanated solely from this greater distance.

22. P. Laslett, *The World We Have Lost* (New York, 1965), p. 50; I. Wallerstein, *The Modern World-System: Capitalist Agriculture and the Origins of the European World-Economy in the Sixteenth Century* (New York, 1974), p. 82.

23. H. Langer, "Zur Rolle der Lohnarbeit im spätmittelalterlichen Zunfthandwerk der Hansestädte: Dargestellt hauptsächlich am Beispiel der Hansestadt Stralsund," *Jahrbücher für Regionalgeschichte*, 3 (1968): 1ff. (cited from an offprint).

24. A. Carandini, *Schiavi in Italia: Gli strumenti pensanti dei romani fra tarda repubblica e medio impero* (Rome, 1988), pp. 235ff., 246ff.

25. Simon Schama, *The Embarrassment of Riches* (Cambridge, Mass., 1987).

26. V. Branca, *Boccaccio medievale* (Florence, 1981), pp. 24ff., 134ff. Also Ph. Jones, *Economia e società nell'Italia medievale* (Turin, 1980), pp. 90ff. Also published in R. Romano and C. Vivanti, eds., *Dal feudalesimo al capitalismo*, vol. 1 of *Storia d'Italia: Annali* (Turin, 1978), pp. 274ff.

27. D. S. Landes, *The Unbound Prometheus: Technological Change and Industrial Development in Western Europe from 1750 to the Present* (London, 1969), p. 5.

28. Ibid., pp. 41–42.

29. This comparison also appears in R. Romano, *Braudel e noi: Riflessioni sulla cultura storica del nostro tempo* (Rome, 1995), p. xi.

30. A. Tchernia, *Le vin de l'Italie romaine: Essai d'histoire économique d'après les Amphores* (Rome, 1986), pp. 21ff. For comparisons, see M. Aymard and H. Bresc, "Nourritures et consommation en Sicilie entre XIVe et XVIIIe siècle," *Annales: Economies, sociétés, civilisations*, 30 (1975): 596; J. Revel, "Les privilèges d'une capitale: L'approvisionnement de Rome à l'époque moderne," ibid., 30 (1975):

571; E. Fiumi, "Economia e vita privata dei Fiorentini nelle rilevazioni statistiche di Giovanni Villani," in C. Cipolla, ed., *Storia dell'economia italiana* (Turin, 1959), pp. 349ff.

31. D. van Berchem, *Les distributions de blé et d'argent à la plèbe romaine sous l'empire* (Geneva, 1939; rpt. New York, 1975); G. Rickman, *The Corn Supply of Ancient Rome* (Oxford, 1980); P. Garnsey, "Grain for Rome," in P. Garnsey, K. Hopkins, and C. R. Whittaker, eds., *Trade in Ancient Economy* (Berkeley, 1983), pp. 118ff.; P. Garnsey, *Famine and Food Supply in the Graeco-Roman World: Responses to Risk and Crisis* (Cambridge, 1989), pp. 167ff.; P. Garnsey, "Famine in Rome," in P. Garnsey and C. R. Whittaker, eds., *Trade and Famine in Classical Antiquity* (Cambridge, 1983), pp. 56ff.; L. Cracco Ruggini, "L'annona di Roma nell'età imperiale," in Rolando Bussi, ed., *Misurare la terra—Centuriazioni e coloni nel mondo romano: Città, agricoltura, commercio—Materiali da Roma e dal suburbio* (Modena, 1985), pp. 232ff.; C. Virlouvet, *Famines et émeutes à Rome des origines de la République à la mort de Néron* (Rome, 1985); and idem, *Tessera frumentaria: Les procédures de la distribution du blé public à Rome* (Rome, 1995).

32. C. Panella, "I commerci di Roma e di Ostia in età imperiale (secoli I–III): Le derrate alimentari," in Bussi, ed., *Misurare la terra*, pp. 180ff.; G. Pucci, "I consumi alimentari," in A. Schiavone, ed., *Storia di Roma*, vol. 4 (Turin, 1989), pp. 374ff., 381ff.

33. Sallust, *Bellum Iugurthinum*, 8, 1.

34. F. Engels, *Die Lage der arbeitenden Klasse in England: Nach eigner Anschauung und authentischen Quellen* (Leipzig, 1845; Berlin, 1952, reproduced from the 2nd German ed., Stuttgart, 1892); in English, *The Condition of the Working Class in England*, trans. W. O. Henderson and W. H. Chaloner (New York, 1958), p. 30.

35. See D. S. Landes, "The Fable of the Dead Horse; or, The Industrial Revolution Revisited" (1993)—a successful anticontinuist provocation. Landes' essay is reprinted in Joel Mokyr, ed., *The British Industrial Revolution: An Economic Perspective* (Boulder, Colo., 1999).

36. Immanuel Wallerstein, *Mercantilism and the Consolidation of the European World-Economy, 1600–1750*, vol. 2 of series entitled *The Modern World-System* (New York, 1980), pp. 31ff.

37. E. Badian, *Publicans and Sinners: Private Enterprise in the Service of the Roman Republic* (Ithaca, 1976); C. Nicolet, "Deux remarques sur l'organisation des sociétés de publicains à la fin de la République romaine," in Henri van Effenterre, ed., *Points de vue sur la fiscalité antique* (Paris, 1979), pp. 69ff. A German translation of Badian's book, with a reply to Nicolet, is *Zöllner und Sünder* (Darmstadt, 1997).

38. This is true even in the case of Arezzo, a major center of "red glaze" ceramics—and its heirs in Gaul, Lezoux, and La Graufesenque—after the decline of the first century A.D. Finley, *Ancient Economy*, p. 137, is in part justified in attacking the

exaggerations of Rostovtzeff, *Social and Economic History of the Roman Empire* (Oxford, 1957), pp. 173ff. (but see also the more carefully worded statement on pp. 35–36). Hopkins, "Economic Growth and Towns," pp. 44–45, also puts the matter in perspective. See also W. Harris, "Roman Terracotta Lamps: The Organisation of an Industry," *Journal of Roman Studies,* 70 (1980): 126ff.

39. Willem Jongman, *The Economy and Society of Pompeii* (Amsterdam, 1988). See also W. O. Moeller, *The Wool Trade of Ancient Pompeii* (Leiden, 1976). For another case, see S. Panciera, *Vita economica di Aquileia in età romana* (Aquileia, 1957).

40. David Hume, "Of the Populousness of Ancient Nations," in Hume, *The Philosophical Works,* vol. 3, 1, *Essays Moral, Political, and Literary* (London, 1882; rpt. Aalen, 1964), pp. 381ff. See also A. Carandini, *Schiavi in Italia,* pp. 333ff. (which overinterprets the data to some degree); and P. Leveau, "La ville antique, 'ville de consommation'? Parasitisme social et économie antique," *Etudes rurales,* 89–91 (1983): 275ff.

41. The adjective *burgensis* appears for the first time in French documents of the latter half of the eleventh century. W. Sombart, *Der Bourgeois* (Munich, 1913), is still worth reading. See also Sombart, *Der Moderne Kapitalismus* (1902; rpt. Munich, 1928), esp. vol. 2, 1.

42. J. Andreau, *La vie financière dans le monde romain: Les métiers de manieurs d'argent, IVe siècle avant J.-C. à IIIe siècle après J.-C.* (Rome, 1987). See J. H. D'Arms, "M. I. Rostovtzeff and M. I. Finley: The Status of Traders in the Roman World," in J. H. D'Arms and J. W. Eadie, eds., *Ancients and Moderns: Essays in Honor of Gerald F. Else* (Ann Arbor, 1977), pp. 159ff.; J. H. D'Arms and E. C. Kopff, *The Seaborne Commerce of Ancient Rome: Studies in Archaeology and History* (Rome, 1980); J. H. D'Arms, *Commerce and Social Standing in Ancient Rome* (Cambridge, Mass., 1981).

43. In an important essay: Paul Veyne, "Mythe et réalité de l'autarchie à Rome," *Revue des études anciennes,* 81 (1979): 261ff.

44. Pliny, *Historia Naturalis,* 18, 60, 224–226.

45. Columella, *Res rusticae,* 1, "praefatio," 8.

46. As in *Corpus Inscriptionum Latinarum,* 9, 3337.

47. Cicero, *De officiis,* 1, 42, 150: "nihil enim proficiant, nisi admodum mentiantur."

48. Cato, *De agri cultura,* "praef.," 1 and 3.

49. Cicero, *De officiis,* 1, 42, 151.

50. C. Cipolla, "I Savary e l'Europa," in Cipolla, *Tre storie extra vaganti* (Bologna, 1994), pp. 75ff., esp. pp. 79ff. See also H. W. Pleket, "Urban Elites and Business in the Greek Part of the Roman Empire," in Garnsey, Hopkins, and Whittaker, eds., *Trade in Ancient Economy,* pp. 131ff.

51. "Mercator urbibus prodest": Seneca, *De beneficiis,* 4, 13, 3.

52. Cicero, *De officiis,* 1, 42, 151.

53. A real "synoptic table" could be mapped out linking Marx's "Formen, die der kapitalistischen Produktion vorhergehn," in Marx, *Grundrisse der Kritik der politischen Ökonomie* (Berlin, 1974), pp. 375ff. (*Grundrisse: Foundations of the Critique of Political Economy,* trans. Martin Nicolaus [New York, 1973], pp. 471ff.), and Weber's "Agrarverhältnisse im Altertum," in Weber, *Gesammelte Aufsätze zur Sozial- und Wirtschaftsgeschichte* (Tübingen, 1924), translated as *The Agrarian Sociology of Ancient Civilizations* (London, 1976; rpt. 1998). This is all the more meaningful in that Weber could not have been familiar with the text of the *Grundrisse,* which was then unpublished. Other works by Weber to be kept in mind include *Die römische Agrargeschichte in ihrer Bedeutung für das Staats- und Privatrecht* (Stuttgart, 1891; rpt. Amsterdam, 1962), now in *Gesamtausgabe,* vol. 1, 2 (Tübingen, 1986); *Die sozialen Gründe des Untergangs der antiken Kultur* (1896), in *Gesammelte Aufsätze,* pp. 289–311 (in English in *The Agrarian Sociology,* pp. 389ff.); and the many references to the ancient world scattered throughout *Wirtschaft und Gesellschaft* (1922; Tübingen, 1956; rpt. 1976), translated as *Economy and Society* (New York, 1968).

54. Karl Marx, *Das Kapital: Dritter Band,* in *Karl Marx, Friedrich Engels: Werke,* vol. 25 (Berlin, 1975), p. 337; trans. D. Fernbach (New York, 1981), p. 442.

55. Duncan-Jones, *The Economy of the Roman Empire,* pp. 32ff., 132ff.

56. P. Veyne, *Le pain et le cirque: Sociologie historique d'un pluralisme politique* (Paris, 1976); abridged English translation London, 1992.

57. Marx, *Grundrisse,* p. 364; English translation (New York, 1973), p. 460.

58. Marx, *Das Kapital,* p. 338; English translation, p. 442.

59. Marx, *Grundrisse,* pp. 434–435; English translation, p. 536.

9. Slaves, Nature, Machines

1. Tacitus, *Annales,* 14, 40, 1.

2. Pliny, *Historia Naturalis,* 10, 16, 35.

3. *Prosopographia Imperii Romani* (Berlin, 1933–), P142–146; R. Syme, *Tacitus* (Oxford, 1958), pp. 247, 479–480, 564, 591, 600ff., 786. Also, *Inscriptiones Latinae Selectae,* 8822; and Pliny, *Epistulae,* 6, 26, 1. R. Syme, *Colonial Elites: Rome, Spain, and the Americas* (London, 1958), pp. 9ff.; and idem, *Ten Studies in Tacitus* (Oxford, 1970), p. 137 and n. 2.

4. Tacitus, *Annales,* 14, 43, 3.

5. Ibid., 14, 42, 1.

6. F. De Marini Avonzo, *La funzione giurisdizionale del senato romano* (Milan, 1957), esp. pp. 76–77; F. Arcaria, *"Senatus censuit": Attività giudiziaria ed attività normativa del senato in età imperiale* (Milan, 1992), esp. pp. 148–149, n. 120.

7. D. Dalla, *Senatus consultum Silanianum* (Milan, 1980), esp. pp. 27ff. Syme, *Tacitus,* p. 564, n. 3, is imprecise (for once) in attributing to Cicero *Epistulae Ad*

Familiares 4, 12, which is actually a letter by Servius Sulpicius Rufus (a slip made by many commentators).

8. Plato, *Leges*, 6, 19 (777b).

9. Ulpian, 50 *Ad edictum*, in *Digesta* (hereafter abbreviated "D."), 29, 5, 1, "principium."

10. Also from Ulpian, 50 *Ad edictum*, in D., 29, 5, 1, 26–27.

11. Tacitus, *Annales*, 14, 44, 4; Syme, *Tacitus*, p. 533; M. Finley, *Ancient Slavery and Modern Ideology* (New York, 1980), pp. 102–103, updated and expanded edition, ed. B. D. Shaw (Princeton, 1998), pp. 170–171.

12. F. D'Ippolito, *Ideologia e diritto in Gaio Cassio Longino* (Naples, 1969), esp. pp. 41ff.; J. G. Wolf, *Das Senatusconsultum Silanianum und die Senatsrede des C. Cassius Longinus aus dem Jahre 61 n. Chr.* (Heidelberg, 1988).

13. Tacitus, *Annales*, 14, 43–44.

14. This is now a commonly accepted ratio. See P. Garnsey, "Non-Slave Labour in the Roman World," in Garnsey, ed., *Non-Slave Labour in the Greco-Roman World* (Cambridge, 1980), pp. 34ff., esp. pp. 35, 46; but in the same volume the essays of S. Treggiari, J. E. Skydsgaard, and C. R. Whittaker, pp. 48ff., 65ff., and 73ff., should also be kept in mind. See also K. R. Bradley, "On the Roman Slave Supply and Slavebreeding," in M. Finley, ed., *Classical Slavery* (London, 1987), pp. 42ff.; and C. R. Whittaker, "Circe's Pigs: From Slavery to Serfdom in the Later Roman World," in Finley, ed., *Classical Slavery*, pp. 88ff. But for an argument in favor of dramatically reducing the estimate, see E. Lo Cascio, "La dinamica della popolazione in Italia da Augusto al III secolo," in Ecole Française de Rome, *L'Italie d'Auguste à Dioclétien* (Rome, 1994), pp. 91ff., esp. p. 111. Presuming—as Lo Cascio does—a population (of free men) of close to 12 million, with a density of forty people per square kilometer, it necessarily follows that "the proportion of slaves must be distinctly lower, [. . .] unless we are willing to estimate the total population at a completely unrealistic level" (and according to Lo Cascio, p. 93, the population must nevertheless have reached 14–16 million)—including, we are thus led to presume, 2–4 million slaves. This is still a significant percentage, especially if we accept the high-end estimates (16 million free men and 4 million slaves). Actually, in the absence of incontrovertible evidence, the quantity of slaves as a percentage of the free population cannot be reduced beyond a certain limit (probably around 30 percent) without undermining everything we know about the economy in Italy in the period between the Gracchi and Antoninus Pius. All conjectures about the number of free men must take this threshold of compatibility into account. Lo Cascio's criticism of traditional views is brilliant in many respects, and plausible, and it is likely that the canonical estimates should indeed be revised upward. But the plausibility of the revisions must also be measured by their ability to suggest credible equilibria of production between free men and slaves. See also Lo Cascio, "The Size of the Roman Population:

Beloch and the Mining of the Augustan Census Figures," *Journal of Roman Studies*, 84 (1994): 23ff.

15. I. Biezunska Malowist, *La schiavitù nell'Egitto greco-romano* (Rome, 1984), pp. 323–324. P. M. Fraser, *Ptolemaic Alexandria*, vol. 1 (Oxford, 1973), pp. 90ff., has a higher figure, based on Diodorus, 1, 31, 6–8 and 17, 52, 6 (a difficult text), and on Josephus, 2, 385.

16. As is commonly known, Fogel had begun by applying it to the railroads, in a classic but very controversial study; see R. W. Fogel, *Railroads and American Economic Growth: Essays in Econometric History* (Baltimore, 1964). For some of the implications of his method—particularly the relationship between quantitative measurements and theoretical analysis ("between measurement and theory," as he writes)—see R. W. Fogel, "A Provisional View of the 'New Economic History,'" *American Economic Review*, 54 (1964): 377ff.; idem, "The Reunification of Economic History with Economic Theory," *American Economic Review*, 65 (1965): 92ff.; idem, "The New Economic History, I: Its Findings and Methods," *Economic History Review*, 19 (1966): 642ff.; idem, "The Specification Problem in Economic History," *Journal of Economic History*, 27 (1967): 283ff., reprinted in P. Tamin, ed., *New Economic History* (Middlesex, 1973), pp. 137ff.; and, finally, R. W. Fogel and G. R. Elton, *Which Road to the Past? Two Views of History* (New Haven, 1983). Fogel's writings on slavery will be listed below. See also B. Lance Davis, "Professor Fogel and the New Economic History," *Economic History Review*, 19 (1966): 657ff.; and N. Lamoreaux, "Economic History and the Cliometric Revolution," in A. Molho and G. S. Woods, eds., *Imagined Histories: American Historians Interpret the Past* (Princeton, 1998), pp. 59ff., esp. pp. 63ff.

17. F. L. Olmsted, *A Journey in the Seaboard Slave States* (New York, 1968; orig. pub. 1856); and idem, *The Cotton Kingdom* (New York, 1970; orig. pub. 1861).

18. J. E. Cairns, *The Slave Power: Its Character, Career, and Probable Designs—Being an Attempt to Explain the Real Issues Involved in the American Contest*, ed. Woodman (New York, 1969; orig. pub. 1862).

19. Henri Wallon, *Histoire de l'esclavage dans l'antiquité*, ed. J.-C. Dumont (Paris, 1988; rpt. of 1879 edition), pp. 7ff.

20. Finley makes reference to Fogel once, in *The Ancient Economy* (Berkeley, 1985), pp. 22–23, but only to "The New Economic History" and Fogel's study on railroads. He never mentions Fogel's essays on slavery, one (and perhaps the most important) of which amply predated both the second edition of *The Ancient Economy* (published in 1985), and *Ancient Slavery* (published in 1980). See also M. Finley, "Generalization in Ancient History," in Finley, *The Use and Abuse of History* (rpt. London, 1990), pp. 60ff.

21. Paul, *Epistula Ad Philem.*, 16; I *Ad Cor.*, 7, 20–24; *Ad Ephes.*, 6, 5–9 (and see also, in the New Testament, Matthew, 10, 24; Luke, 17, 7–10; John, 13, 16; 15, 20); Conc. Hisp., canon 1 (*Patrologia Latina* [hereafter abbreviated *PL*], 84, col. 591);

Conc. Tolet IV, canons 67–74 (*PL*, 84, cols. 381–383); Conc. Elib., canon 5 (*PL*, 84, col. 302); Conc. Aurel. I, canons 3, 5, 15 (*PL*, 84, cols. 275–276); Augustine, *De civitate Dei* (ed. Dombart and Kalb), 19, 15; B. D. Shaw, "The Family in Late Antiquity: The Experience of Augustine," *Past and Present*, 115 (1987): 23ff.

22. The concept, as is well known, originated with Marcel Mauss, "Essai sur le don, forme archaïque de l'échange," in idem, *Sociologie et Anthropologie* (Paris, 1950); in English in idem, *The Gift* (New York, 1967), pp. 78ff. It was revised and extended in C. Lévi-Strauss, *Les structures élémentaires de la parenté* (Paris, 1967); in English in idem, *The Elementary Structures of Kinship* (Boston, 1969), p. 52. Important information can also be found in K. R. Bradley, *Slaves and Masters in the Roman Empire: A Study in Social Control* (Brussels, 1984; rpt. New York, 1987), pp. 21ff., 113ff., 139ff.; idem, *Slavery and Society at Rome* (Cambridge, 1994), pp. 10ff., 81ff.; and, from a different point of view, C. Meillassoux, *Anthropologie de l'esclavage: Le ventre de fer et d'argent* (Paris, 1986), esp. pp. 9ff.

23. J. F. Rhodes, *History of the United States from the Compromise of 1850*, Vol. I, *1850–1854* (New York, 1928; orig. pub. 1893).

24. R. Hofstadter, "U. B. Phillips and the Plantation Legend," *Journal of Negro History*, 29 (1944): 109ff.

25. U. B. Phillips, *American Negro Slavery: A Survey of the Supply, Employment, and Control of Negro Labor as Determined by the Plantation Régime* (New York, 1928; orig. pub. 1918). The 1969 Baton Rouge edition has a preface by E. D. Genovese.

26. E. D. Genovese, *The Political Economy of Slavery: Studies in the Economy and Society of the Slave South* (New York, 1967); idem, *The World the Slaveholders Made* (New York, 1969); idem, *In Red and Black: Marxian Explorations in Southern and Afro-American History* (New York, 1971).

27. K. M. Stampp, *The Peculiar Institution: Slavery in the Ante-Bellum South* (New York, 1956; rpt. 1989).

28. A. H. Conrad and J. R. Meyer, *"The Economics of Slavery" and Other Studies in Economic History* (Chicago, 1964). "The Economics of Slavery in the Antebellum South," included in that volume, had already been published in *Journal of Political Economy*, 66 (1958): 95ff., and reprinted in Tamin, ed., *New Economic History*, pp. 339ff. R. W. Fogel and S. L. Engerman, *Time on the Cross: The Economics of American Negro Slavery* (Boston, 1974; rpt. New York, 1989); and idem, *Evidence and Methods: A Supplement* (Boston, 1974). These works were discussed, with sometimes misleading polemics, by P. A. David, H. G. Gutman, R. Sutch, P. Tamin, and G. Wright, in *Reckoning with Slavery: A Critical Study in the Quantitative History of American Negro Slavery*, introd. K. M. Stampp (New York, 1976). R. W. Fogel, *Without Consent or Contract: The Rise and Fall of American Slavery*, 4 vols. (New York, 1989–1992). (The first, "interpretative" volume is entirely Fogel's work; the other three, intended to serve as a "technical foundation," edited with the collaboration of S. L. Engerman, R. L. Manning, and R. A. Galan-

tine, are collective efforts.) S. L. Engerman, "The Effects of Slavery upon the Southern Economy: A Review of a Recent Debate," *Explorations in Entrepreneurial History,* 4 (1967): 71ff., reprinted in Tamin, ed., *The New Economic History,* pp. 398ff.; and S. L. Engerman and E. D. Genovese, eds., *Race and Slavery in the Western Hemisphere: Quantitative Studies* (Princeton, 1975). Schematically speaking, two broad lines of inquiry can be identified, one leading from Stampp to Conrad and Meyer, and the second from Conrad and Meyer to Engerman and Fogel. Helpful for appraising the various positions are H. G. J. Aitken, *Did Slavery Pay? Readings in the Economics of Black Slavery in the United States* (Boston, 1971); and P. J. Parish, *Slavery: History and Historians* (New York, 1989). See also J. D. Harrington, "'Res' or 'Personae': Roman Civil Law's Influence on Southern Slave Law," *Labeo,* 40 (1994): 309ff.

29. The ensuing discussion follows Fogel, *Time on the Cross,* pp. 4ff., 170ff., 181ff., 192ff., 209ff., 223ff.; and idem, *Without Consent or Contract,* vol. 1, pp. 9ff., 154ff., and 389ff.

30. Fogel, *Without Consent or Contract,* vol. 1, p. 9.

31. Ibid., pp. 393ff.

32. Columella, *Res rustica,* 3, 3, 8. See R. Duncan-Jones, *The Economy of the Roman Empire: Quantitative Studies* (Cambridge, 1982), pp. 39–40, 348ff.

33. Pliny, *Historia Naturalis,* 7, 40, 128. If the prosopographic identification of the participants in the transaction is the most obvious, this exchange must have taken place in the first century B.C.

34. Estates ranged in value from the 400 million sesterces of Cn. Cornelius Lentulus (Seneca, *De beneficiis,* 2, 27; Suetonius, *Tiberius,* 49, 1; *Prosopographia Imperii Romani,* C 1379) to the 60 million of Marcus Aquilius Regulus (Pliny, *Epistulae,* 2, 20, 13; *Prosopographia Imperii Romani,* A 1005; Duncan-Jones, *The Economy of the Roman Empire,* pp. 343–344.

35. Strabo, 14, 5, 2 (ed. Meineke).

36. *An Abstract of the Evidence Delivered before a Select Committee of the Commons on the Slave Trade* (Edinburgh, 1792), p. 37 and figs. 5–6. A copy of this text can be found in the John Carter Brown Library, Brown University, Providence, Rhode Island.

37. D., 14, 2, 10, "principium" (Labeo, 1 *Pith. a Paul epit.*), and D., 19, 2, 19, 7 (Ulpian, 32 *Ad edictum*).

38. B. Jacoby, *Fragmente der Griechischen Historiker* (Berlin, 1923; rpt. Leiden, 1954–1960), 115 F 122 = Athenaeus (ed. Kaibel), 6, 88, 265 b–c (but see also F 171 = Athenaeus, 6, 101, 271 c–d); F 40 = Athenaeus, 6, 101, 271e; and F 176 = Athenaeus, 6, 101, 271d, without deleting *doulous* in accordance with Jacoby's isolated suggestion in Jacoby, "Kommentar," *Fragmente,* vol. 2, D, p. 382. An important book here is P. Vidal-Naquet, *Le chasseur noir* (Paris, 1981), pp. 223ff.

39. Athenaeus, *Deipnosophistai,* 6, 84, 263 c–e, with a double citation from

Posidonius (*Fragmente der Griechischen Historiker,* 87 F 8; also in Edelstein and Kidd, eds., *Posidonius I: The Fragments* [1972, 1989] F 60) and Callistratus (*Fragmente der Griechischen Historiker,* 348 F 4).

40. Athenaeus, *Deipnosophistai,* 6, 101–103 and 271–272. See the keen observations in A. Paradiso, *Forme di dipendenza nel mondo greco: Ricerche sul VI libro di Ateneo* (Bari, 1991), esp. pp. 29ff.

41. Also from Athenaeus, 6, 87–88, 265 b–c, by way of Theopompus. See *Fragmente der Griechischen Historiker,* 115 F 122, cited above in n. 38.

42. *Fragmente der Griechischen Historiker,* 566 F 11b = Athenaeus, 6, 103, 272b.

43. Athenaeus, 6, 103, 272b; cf. Polybius, 12, 6, 7–8.

44. Herodotus, 6, 137, 3: In this text—which, in Herodotus' account, was set in the time of the Pelasgian settlement in Attica—there was probably a connection between female housework and the absence of slavery.

45. Polybius, 30, 15 = Strabo, 7, 7, 3; Livy, 45, 34, 5; Plutarch, *Aemilius Paulus,* 29. For other comparisons, see Livy, 26, 40, 13; 27, 16, 7; 41, 28, 8–9. See also W. V. Harris, *War and Imperialism in Republican Rome, 327–70 B.C.* (Oxford, 1979; rpt. 1992), p. 81.

46. Appian, *Gallica,* 4, 2; Plutarch, *Caesar,* 15. Even if the exact number is inaccurate, the order of magnitude is believable. See W. L. Westerman, *The Slave Systems of Greek and Roman Antiquity* (Philadelphia, 1955), p. 63; P. A. Brunt, *Italian Manpower, 225 B.C.–A.D. 14* (Oxford, 1987), pp. 124, 702–703; C. R. Whittaker, "Circe's Pig: From Slavery to Serfdom in the Later Roman World," in M. Finley, ed., *Classical Slavery* (London, 1987), p. 97.

47. Plutarch, *Tiberius Gracchus,* 8–9 = *Oratorum Romanorum Fragmenta,* 13–15.

48. Diodorus, 34–35, 2, 27 (ed. Walton); but see also 2, 1.

49. L. Bove, "Due nuove iscrizioni di Pozzuoli e di Cuma," *Rendiconti della Accademia di Archeologia, Lettere e Belle Arti di Napoli,* 41 (1966): 207ff. (the text and reconstruction are on pp. 210–216) = *Année Epigraphique* (1971): 37–41. See also J. C. Dumont, *Servus: Rome et l'esclavage sous la république* (Rome, 1987), pp. 126ff.; and Y. Thomas, "Vitae necisque potestas: Le père, la cité, la mort," in Ecole Française de Rome, *Du châtiment dans la cité: Supplices corporels et peine de mort dans le monde antique* (Rome, 1984), pp. 499ff.

50. M. Finley, *Ancient Slavery and Modern Ideology* (New York, 1980), p. 65; updated and expanded edition (Princeton, 1998), p. 133. On wage labor in Roman society, see also F. M. De Robertis, *Lavoro e lavoratori nel mondo romano* (Bari, 1963; rpt. New York, 1979), presenting evaluations that are occasionally excessive; and compare D. Nörr's review in *Zeitschrift der Savigny-Stiftung für Rechtsgeschichte, Romanistische Abteilung,* 82 (1965): 67ff. See also P. A. Brunt, "Free Labour and Public Works at Rome," *Journal of Roman Studies,* 70 (1980): 81ff.

51. A. de Tocqueville, *Voyages aux Etats-Unis;* in English, *Journey to America,* ed. J. P. Mayer, trans. G. Lawrence (Garden City, N.Y., 1971), p. 95.

52. Plutarch, *Caius Marius*, 45, 4; Cicero, *De fato*, 3, 5; idem, *De natura deorum*, 2, 34, 88; idem, *Tusculanae disputationes*, 2, 25, 61.

53. L. Canfora, "La rivolta dei dannati della terra," preface to Diodorus Siculus, *La rivolta degli schiavi in Sicilia* (Palermo, 1983), pp. 49ff.

54. Livy, 32, 26, 4–18; 33, 36, 1–3; 39, 29, 8–9; 39, 41, 6–7. M. Capozza, *Movimenti servili nel mondo romano in età repubblicana*, vol. 1: *Dal 501 al 184 a. Cr.* (Rome, 1966).

55. Diodorus, 34–35, 2, 25.

56. Diodorus, 34–35, 2, 18. But according to Livy (*perioke* 56), the number was no higher than 70,000. See P. Green, "The First Sicilian Slave War," *Past and Present*, 20 (1961): 10ff.; M. I. Finley, *Ancient Sicily: To the Arab Conquest* (London, 1968); G. P. Verbrugghe, "Slave Rebellion or Sicily in Revolt?" *Kokalos*, 20 (1974): 46ff. In A. Giardina and A. Schiavone, eds., *Società romana e produzione schiavistica* (Rome, 1981), vol. 1, see: F. Coarelli, "La Sicilia tra la fine della guerra annibalica e Cicerone," pp. 8ff.; M. Mazza, "Terra e lavoratori nella Sicilia tardorepubblicana," pp. 35ff.; A. Fraschetti, "Per una prosopografia dello sfruttamento: Romani e italici in Sicilia (212–44 a. C.)," pp. 53ff. See also K. R. Bradley, *Slavery and Rebellion in the Roman World, 140 b.c.–70 b.c.* (Bloomington, 1989).

57. Appian, *Bella Civilia*, 1, 9, 35–37.

58. Diodorus, 34–35, 2, 46.

59. Sallust, *Bellum Lugurth.*, 5, 1.

60. Athenaeus, 6, 104, 272–273 = *Fragmente der Griechischen Historiker* 183 F 1.

61. In Diodorus—whose sole source for this part was probably Posidonius (see Canfora, "La rivolta," pp. 56–57)—we read that "an abyss between slaves and masters," created "by the maltreatment of the slaves," was the cause of the explosion "of the accumulation of hatred [. . .]: the more cruel and illegal the power of those in command becomes, the more the behavior of the subjected people, who are driven to desperation, turns to ferocity." Diodorus, 34–35, 2, 26 and 33.

62. Diodorus 5, 35–38; 3, 12, 2–6.

63. Lucretius, *De rerum natura*, 6, 813–815: "Nonne vides audisve perire in tempore parvo / quam soleant et quam vitai copia desit, / quos opere in tali cohibet vis magna necessis?" (correcting, with Lachmann, an unacceptable *necessest* in the manuscript tradition; see Codd. Leidd., 30 and 94).

64. Strabo, 3, 2, 9.

65. Thucydides, 7, 27, 5.

66. Diodorus, 34–35, 2, 25. He is continuing to paraphrase Posidonius (we must believe).

67. Important inferences can be gleaned from the account in Athenaeus, 6, 84, 263 c–d = *Fragmente der Griechischen Historiker* 87 F 8 = Edelstein and Kidd, eds.,

Posidonius I, F 60 (cited above, n. 39), in comparison with the episode narrated by Diodorus, 34–35, 2, 20, and repeated in Athenaeus, 12, 59, 542 b = *Fragmente der Griechischen Historiker* 87 F 7 = *Posidonius I,* F 59 (which is felicitous evidence of the dependence of Diodorus on Posidonius). While Helot slavery (of which the Mariandunoi offer a perfect historical example) is, from Posidonius' perspective, "consensual," so to speak, and free of violence, chattel slavery, which is expressively summarized in the episode of Damophilus and in which the victims are branded by their masters, is marked by violence and terror. It is quite likely that the entire eleventh book of the *History* follows this schema. The picture is made complete by another citation from Posidonius in Athenaeus, 6, 105–109, 273a–275b = *Fragmente der Griechischen Historiker* 87 F 59 = *Posidonius I,* Edelstein-Kidd, F 265, F 266, F 267, on the virtues of the ancient Romans (specifically referring to Scipio Africanus), who succeeded in making extremely sparing use of slave labor.

68. The adjective "degenerate" is used by Canfora, "La rivolta dei dannati," p. 61 (but see also idem, *Index,* 11 [1982]: 43ff.), elaborating on K. Reinhardt, *Poseidonios* (Munich, 1921), esp. pp. 19ff. and 31ff.

69. Posidonius dedicated a book to Pompey. See Strabo, 11, 1, 6 (*Posidonius I,* F 79).

70. See, for example, Diodorus, 34–35, 25, 1, which can also be traced to Posidonius.

71. Athenaeus, 6, 91, 266 e–f (another transcription from Posidonius) = *Fragmente der Griechischen Historiker* 87 F 38 = *Posidonius I,* F 51 (but see the whole account, 88–91 and 265b–266f).

72. Appian, *Bella Civilia,* 1, 116, 539.

73. Ibid., 1, 117, 545. See also Plutarch, *Crassus* 8–11; and Lucius Annaeus Florus, *Epitome,* 2, 8. G. Stampacchia, *La tradizione della guerra di Spartaco da Sallustio a Orosio* (Pisa, 1976), esp. pp. 108ff., 149ff.

74. Sallust, *Historiae,* 3, 91.

75. In my opinion, A. Guarino, *Spartaco* (Naples, 1979), pp. 59ff., esp. pp. 75–76, reconstructs correctly.

76. Referred to in Guarino, *Spartaco,* pp. 119ff.

77. Appian, *Bella Civilia,* 1, 116, 541.

78. Ibid., 1, 120, 559.

79. There are hints of this in Appian, *Bella Civilia,* 1, 26, 115; in Orosius, *Historiarum adversus paganos,* 5, 12, 6; and in Lucius Ampelius, *Liber Memorialis,* 26, 2. But Plutarch, *Caius Gracchus,* 16–19, does not mention it.

80. Sallust, *Cat.,* 24, 4 ("servitia urbana sollicitare"), 50, 2 ("servitia sollicitabant"). Although Catiline himself (in 56, 5) refused at the decisive moment to openly enlist the slaves who, not by accident, had flocked to his camp ("servitia repudiabat"), he at least seemed to do it, but only to maintain his image (according to Sallust's account: "alienum suis rationibus existumans videri causam

civium cum servis fugitivis communicavisse"). For other allusions, see ibid., 28, 4; 30, 7; and 39, 6.

81. E. Manni, "L'utopia di Clodio," *Rivista di Filologia e d'Istruzione Classica,* 68 (1940): 161ff., is still useful. More recent works include M. Letruoblen, "Les esclaves dans les bandes armées d'après les discours de Cicéron de 57 à 52," in *Actes du Colloque 1972 sur l'esclavage, Besançon* (Paris, 1974), pp. 235ff.; and F. Favory, "Classes dangereuses et crise de l'Etat dans le discours cicéronien," in *Texte, politique, idéologie: Cicéron* (Paris, 1976), pp. 111ff.

82. Cato, *De agri cultura,* 11, 1–5.

83. Pliny, *Historia Naturalis,* 17, 36, 215.

84. Columella, *Res rustica,* 3, 3, 8.

85. Varro, *Res rustica,* 1, 18, 2 (but this may also have been a vineyard).

86. Cato, *De agri cultura,* 10, 1–5.

87. Columella, *Res rustica,* 1, 7, 4; 1, 8, 8; 2, 12, 7–9; 2, 21, 3; 11, 1, 27–28; 11, 2, 1–101 (cf. Varro, *Res rustica,* 1, 19, 1); Pliny, *Historia Naturalis,* 18, 48, 173; 18, 49, 178; 18, 65, 241.

88. R. Duncan-Jones, *The Economy of the Roman Empire,* pp. 33ff., 39ff., 327ff.

89. A. Carandini, *Schiavi in Italia: Gli strumenti pensanti dei romani fra tarda repubblica e medio impero* (Rome, 1988), pp. 246ff.; 287ff. F. De Martino, *Storia economica di Roma antica,* vol. 2 (Florence, 1979), pp. 227ff., is important. See also K. D. White, "The Productivity of Labour in Roman Agriculture," *Antiquity,* 39 (1965): 102ff.; K. D. White, *Roman Farming* (Ithaca, 1970); J. M. Frayn, *Subsistence Farming in Roman Italy* (London, 1979); J. Percival, *The Roman Villa: An Historical Introduction* (London, 1988), esp. pp. 145ff.; K. Greene, *The Archaeology of the Roman Economy* (Berkeley, rpt. 1990), esp. pp. 67ff.

90. See below, Chapter 11, section 3.

91. Plutarch, *Crassus,* 2.

92. Such historians include (it must be said) Moses Finley, both in *Ancient Slavery* and, especially, in *Ancient Economy.* But in the end, Carandini's objections (*Schiavi in Italia,* pp. 235ff., 291ff.) do more to revive the false schema of primitivism-versus-modernization than to point to a real solution to the interpretative deadlock. See the discussion in part II, section 5 of this chapter.

93. Aristotle, *Politics,* 1, 4 (1253b).

94. Idem, *Nicomachean Ethics,* 8, 11 (1161b).

95. Varro, *Res rustica,* 1, 17, 1.

96. Aristotle, *Politics,* 1, 4 (1253b–1254a).

97. Ibid., 1, 4 (1254a, 7).

98. Jean-Pierre Vernant, "Aspects psychologiques du travail dans la Grèce ancienne," reprinted in Vernant, *Mythe et pensée chez les grecs* (Paris, 1990), pp. 295ff., esp. p. 301.

99. Aristotle, *Politics,* 1, 4 (1253b, 31).

100. Homer, *Iliad,* 18, 376.
101. Aristotle, *Politics,* 1, 4 (1253b, 33–39).
102. See Samuel Butler, *Erewhon, or Over the Range* (London, 1901; orig. pub. 1872), chs. 23 and 24, pp. 235ff., 244ff.
103. M. Finley, "Aristotle and Economic Analysis," *Past and Present,* 47 (1970): 3–25; reprinted in Finley, ed., *Studies in Ancient Society* (London, 1974), pp. 26ff. Karl Polanyi, "Aristotle Discovers the Economy," in K. Polanyi, C. M. Arensberg, and H. W. Pearson, eds., *Trade and Market in the Early Empires: Economies in History and Theory* (Chicago, 1957), pp. 64ff., promises more than he delivers.
104. R. L. Sargent, *The Size of the Slave Population at Athens during the Fifth and Fourth Centuries before Christ* (Urbana, Ill., 1924), pp. 63, 127; A. W. Gomme, *The Population of Athens in the Fifth and Fourth Centuries B.C.* (Oxford, 1933), esp. pp. 20ff.; K. Hopkins, *Conquerors and Slaves* (Cambridge, 1978), p. 101.
105. A. Koyré, "Les Philosophes et la machine," in Koyré, *Etudes d'histoire de la pensée philosophique* (Paris, 1961), pp. 273, 300ff.
106. F 16, *Poetae comici graeci,* ed. R. Kassel and C. Austin, from Athenaeus, 6, 94, 267e–f, along with other citations from comic poets describing analogous situations of spontaneous abundance, but without any specific reference to the absence of slavery (Athenaeus, 6, 94–98, and 267e–270e). One commentary on Athenaeus calls this a "prophecy of the electrical era"; see Athenaeus, *The Deipnosophists,* vol. 3, trans. C. B. Gulick (Cambridge, Mass., 1967), p. 203, note g.
107. Aristotle, *Politics,* 1, 2 (1225b), citing a line from Hesiod (*Works and Days,* 405).
108. Cicero, *De republica,* 3, 25, 37 (see also 22, 33); J.-L. Ferrary, *Philhellénisme et impérialisme: Aspects idéologiques de la conquête romaine du monde hellénistique* (Rome, 1988), pp. 371ff. See below, Chapter 11, section 3.
109. Carandini's argument came to this conclusion as well (*Schiavi in Italia,* pp. 303–304).
110. André Aymard, "Stagnation technique et esclavage" (1959), reprinted in Aymard, *Etudes d'histoire ancienne* (Paris, 1967), pp. 334ff.
111. Aristotle, *Politics,* 1, 4 (1253b, 31–32): *ktema.*
112. Gaius, *Institutiones,* 1, 8–9; 2, 86–91 (= D., 41, 1, 10); Florentinus, 9 *Institutiones,* in D., 1, 5, 4; Marcianus, 1 *Institutiones,* in D., 1, 5, 5. We will return to the two latter texts in Chapter 11, section 3.
113. Herodotus, 2, 167, 1; English translation by G. Rawlinson (New York, 1880), vol. 2, p. 215. This citation comes from the heart of Herodotus' "Egyptian book": all analogies with Egypt are explained in terms of cultural diffusion. See W. W. How and J. A. Wells, *A Commentary on Herodotus,* vol. 1 (Oxford, 1912), p. 250; comments by A. B. Lloyd, in Fondazione Lorenzo Valla, *Erodoto: Le storie* (Milan, 1989), Book 2, pp. 26, 385; also M. Austin and P. Vidal-Naquet, *Economies et sociétés en Grèce ancienne* (Paris, 1972), pp. 11ff.
114. Santo Mazzarino, *Fra Oriente e Occidente: Ricerche di storia greca arcaica* (Flor-

ence, 1947; rpt. Milan, 1989). At present, superficial researches—especially by followers of some American trends—sometimes tend to lend these contacts a spurious anti-Western coloring.

115. Xenophon, *Economics,* ed. S. Pomeroy (Oxford, 1994), 4, 2–3.

116. K. J. Dover, *Greek Popular Morality in the Time of Plato and Aristotle* (Oxford, 1974), pp. 74ff., 114ff., 283ff. See also G. Glotz, *Le travail dans la Grèce ancienne* (Paris, 1920), esp. pp. 193ff.

117. Plato, *Gorgias,* 62 (506d); Socrates is speaking. See also 59 (503e).

118. P.-M. Schuhl, "Remarques sur Platon et la technologie," reprinted in Schuhl, *Etudes platoniciennes* (Paris, 1960), pp. 92–93; idem, "Perché l'antichità classica non ha conosciuto il 'macchinismo'?" reprinted as app. in A. Koyré, *Dal mondo del pressappoco all'universo della precisione* (Turin, 1967), pp. 115ff., esp. pp. 122–123, with very penetrating observations. See also D. Ross, *Plato's Theory of Ideas* (Oxford, 1951), esp. pp. 206ff., 221ff.; M. Isnardi Parente, *Techne: Momenti del pensiero antico da Platone a Epicuro* (Florence, 1966), esp. pp. 97ff.; G. Cambiano, *Platone e le tecniche* (Turin, 1971), esp. pp. 26ff., 170ff.

119. A. Aymard, "Hiérarchie du travail et autarcie individuelle dans la Grèce archaïque" (1943), reprinted in Aymard, *Etudes d'histoire ancienne,* pp. 316ff.

120. Herodotus, 2, 167, 2. On the meaning of Thucydides, 2, 40, 1–2, Aymard's interpretation in "Hiérarchie du travail et autarcie individuelle," p. 319, is correct.

121. The association is suggested by J.-P. Vernant, "Prométhée et la fonction technique" (1952), reprinted in Vernant, *Mythe et pensée chez les grecs,* pp. 263ff., in agreement with L. Séchan, *Le mythe de Prométhée* (Paris, 1951), esp. pp. 4ff. There is an important passage in Plato, *Leges,* 11, 5 (920d-3), on Athena and Hephaestus.

122. Hesiod, *Theogony,* 521–616; idem, *Works and Days,* 42–105.

123. See Aeschylus, *Prometheus Bound.* In addition to these texts the same emphasis should be placed on the Platonic version of the Prometheus myth; see Plato, *Protagoras,* 11–12 (320c–322d). P. Joos, *Tyche, Physis, Techne: Studien zur Thematik frühgriechischer Lebensbetrachtung* (Winterthur, 1955), pp. 54ff.; E. A. Havelock, *The Liberal Temper in Greek Politics* (New Haven, 1957), pp. 91ff.; Cambiano, *Platone e le tecniche,* pp. 13ff.

124. G. Dumézil, *Le festin d'immortalité* (Paris, 1924), esp. pp. 94ff.

125. Vernant, "Prométhée et la fonction technique," pp. 264ff.; J.-P. Vernant, "Le mythe prométhéen chez Hésiode," in idem, *Mythe et société en Grèce ancienne* (Paris, 1981; orig. pub. 1974), pp. 177ff.

126. Homer, *Odyssey,* 5, 243ff., and 23, 189ff.

127. Idem, *Iliad,* 18, 373ff., 469ff.

128. Hesiod, *Works and Days,* 538ff.

129. Also keep in mind the important comments made by P. Veyne, "Mythe et réalité de l'autarcie à Rome," *Revue des études anciennes,* 81 (1979): 261ff.,

esp. 267ff. See also W. E. Heitland, *Agricola: A Study of Agriculture and Rustic Life in the Greco-Roman World from the Point of View of Labour* (Cambridge, 1921), esp. pp. 131ff.

130. Plutarch, *Numa*, 17, 3; on the derivation from Varro, see De Martino, *Storia economica di Roma antica*, vol. 1, p. 153; E. Gabba, "The *Collegia* of Numa: Problems of Method and Political Ideas," in *Journal of Roman Studies*, 74 (1984): 81ff. For a long time, Plutarch's description was considered anachronistic; but see G. Colonna, "La produzione artiginale," in A. Momigliano and A. Schiavone, eds., *Storia di Roma*, vol. 1 (Turin, 1988), p. 309. See also Pliny, *Historia Naturalis*, 34, 1, 1 and 35, 45, 157; and Florus, 1, 1 (= 1, 6, 3).

131. Dionysius of Halicarnassus, 2, 28, 1 and 9, 25, 2. See also Livy, 1, 56, 1.

132. A. E. Gordon, "Note on the Duenos-Vase Inscription in Berlin," *California Studies in Classical Antiquity*, 8 (1975): 53ff.; G. Colonna, "Duenos," *Studi Etruschi*, 47 (1979): 163ff.; and idem, "L'aspetto epigrafico, Appendice: Le iscrizioni strumentali latine del VI e V secolo a. C.," in C. M. Stibbe, et al., *Lapis Satricanus* (The Hague, 1980), pp. 53ff.

133. Pacuvius, *Tragedies*, F 167 (ed. Warmington), but the attribution is uncertain because of textual corruption. See O. Ribbeck, *Tragicorum Romanorum Fragmenta* (Leipzig, 1871), "Pacuvius," note F 32; Nonius Marcellus, *De conpendiosa doctrina* (ed. Lindsay), p. 546, n. 6 (and see also p. 545).

134. Plautus, *Curculio*, 480ff.

135. Varro, *Agatho* (ed. Cèbe), 11 (14); also Nonius Marcellus, *De conpendiosa doctrina* (ed. Lindsay), p. 546.

136. Seneca, *Epistulae* 88, 20–21.

137. Dionysius Lysius, 32. See Finley, *The Ancient Economy*, p. 97; and idem, *Studies in Land and Credit in Ancient Athens* (New Brunswick, 1952), pp. 56ff.

138. Pliny, *Historia Naturalis*, 18, 4, 19–21; English translation by H. Rackham (Cambridge, 1961), pp. 201, 203.

139. G. Agricola, *L'arte de' metalli* (Basel, 1563; reprinted Turin, 1969), p. 22; originally published in Latin as *De re metallica lib. XII* (Basel, 1561), p. 17. But the author (1494–1555), a friend of Erasmus and Melancthon, was actually named Georg Bauer; see E. Garin, *La cultura del Rinascimento* (Bari, 1967), p. 147; and P. Rossi, *Francesco Bacone: Dalla Magia alla scienza* (Turin, 1974), p. 54, n. 5.

140. A. Gara, *Tecnica e tecnologia nelle società antiche* (Rome, 1994), pp. 18ff.

141. F. Krafft, *Dynamische und statische Betrachtungsweise in der antiken Mechanik* (Wiesbaden, 1970), pp. 62ff., asserts that Aristotle is the true author of the work (which is preserved among his writings), but this conjecture is not defensible.

142. G. A. Ferrari, "Meccanica 'allargata,'" in G. Giannantoni and M. Vegetti, eds., *La scienza ellenistica* (Naples, 1984), pp. 242ff., contains a careful examination of the surviving fragments.

143. E. Romano, *La capanna e il tempio: Vitruvio o dell'architettura* (Palermo, 1987), pp. 195ff., includes an analysis of the important text of 10, 1, 4–6 (in which the integration suggested by Valentin Rose in the Leipzig edition of 1899 is accepted).

144. A. G. Drachmann, *The Mechanical Technology of Greek and Roman Antiquity* (Copenhagen, 1963), pp. 22ff.

145. H. W. Pleket, "Technology in the Graeco-Roman World: A Reappraisal," *Talanta*, 5 (1973): 6ff., is an excellent assessment. H. Diels, *Antike Technik* (Berlin, 1924) contains a sampling of the old ideas. See also K. D. White, *Greek and Roman Technology* (Ithaca, N.Y., 1984). F. Kiechle, *Sklavenarbeit und technischer Fortschritt im römischen Reich* (Wiesbaden, 1969), is useful.

146. T. Clifford Allbutt, "Palissy, Bacon and the Revival of Natural Science," *Proceedings of the British Academy*, 6 (1913–1914), pp. 223ff.; Allbutt in part restates A. B. Hanschmann, *B. Palissy und F. Bacon* (Leipzig, 1903). See also Rossi, *Francesco Bacone*, pp. 13–14.

147. Francis Bacon, "De principiis atque originibus secundum fabulas Cupidinis et Coeli: Sive Parmenidis, et Telesii et praecipue Democriti philosophia, tractata in fabula de Cupidine" (1623–1624), in *The Works of Francis Bacon*, ed. Spedding, Hellis, and Heath (London, 1876), vol. 3, pp. 92ff.

148. François Rabelais, *La vie très horrifique du grand Gargantua, père de Pantagruel* (Lyons, 1542), ed. Boulanger (Paris, 1955), pp. 76–77 (ch. 24); English translation by J. Le Clercq, *The Five Books of Gargantua and Pantagruel* (New York, 1944), pp. 78–80.

149. E. Garin, "Il filosofo e il mago," in M. Fumagalli Beonio Brocchieri and E. Garin, *L'intellettuale tra Medioevo e Rinascimento* (Rome, 1994), pp. 75ff.

150. The following studies are of great importance for the understanding of late-medieval concepts of labor: J. Le Goff, "Le temps du travail dans la 'crise' du XIV siècle: Du temps médiéval au temps moderne," *Le Moyen Age*, 69 (1963): 597ff., reprinted in idem, *"Tempo della Chiesa e tempo del mercante" e altri saggi sul lavoro e la cultura nel Medioevo* (Turin, 1977), pp. 25ff.; and idem, *Pour un autre Moyen Age: Temps, travail et culture en Occident—18 Essais* (Paris, 1977). See also L. Febvre, "Travail: Evolution d'un mot et d'une idée" (1948), in Febvre, *Pour une histoire à part entière* (Paris, 1962), pp. 649ff.; and A. I. Gurevich, *Categories of Medieval Culture* (London, 1985; orig. pub. in Russian, 1972), esp. pp. 211ff.

151. For example, C. Cipolla, in a deservedly renowned book, *The Economic History of World Populations* (Harmondsworth, 1962; 5th ed., 1970), pp. 17ff.

152. M. Finley, "Technical Innovation and Economic Progress in the Ancient World," *Economic History Review*, 18 (1965): 29ff.; reprinted in Finley, *Economy and Society in Ancient Greece* (London, 1981; rpt. Harmondsworth, 1983), pp. 176ff.

153. If he did not invent it, he at least described it. See Hero of Alexandria, *Pneumatica,* 2, 6, and 11; A. G. Drachmann, "Ktesibios, Philon and Heron: A Study in Ancient Pneumatics," in *Acta historica scientiarum naturalium et medicinalium,* 4 (1948): 1ff., esp. p. 128; G. Landels, *Engineering in the Ancient World* (London, 1978; rpt. Berkeley, 1981), pp. 26ff.

154. Giovanni Branca, *Le machine: Volume nuovo et di molto artificio da fare effetti maravigliosi tanto Spiritali quanto di animale operatione, arichito di bellissime figure con le dichiarationi a ciascuna di esse in lingua volgare et latina* (Rome, 1629), figs. 1–23 (third series).

155. J.-J. Rousseau, *Oeuvres complètes,* ed. Gagnebin and Raymond (Paris, 1959–1969), vol. 1, p. 101.

156. Drachmann, *Ktesibios, Philon and Heron,* esp. pp. 16ff.

157. Hero of Alexandria, *Dioptra,* 34.

158. Vitruvius, *De architectura,* 10, 9, 5–7. See A. M. Sleeswick, "Archimedes' Odometer and Waterclock," in *Ancient Technology* (Helsinki, 1990); M. J. T. Lewis, "Gearing in the Ancient World," *Endeavour,* 17 (1993): 110ff.

159. Anonymous, *De rebus bellicis,* 17, 3.

160. *De rebus bellicis,* 17, 2.

161. R. J. Forbes, *Studies in Ancient Technology,* vol. 8 (Leiden, 1964), pp. 1ff.; Finley, "Technical Innovation and Economic Progress in the Ancient World," p. 183; F. Franco Repellini, "Tecnologie e macchine," in *Storia di Roma,* vol. 4, p. 331.

162. L. Cracco Ruggini, "Progresso tecnico e manodopera in età imperiale romana," in *Tecnologia, economia e società nel mondo romano* (Como, 1980), pp. 45ff., reconstructs the situation effectively.

163. Ö. Wikander, "Exploitation of Water-Power or Technological Stagnation?" *Scripta Minora Regiae Societatis Humaniorum Litterarum Ludensis,* 3 (1983–1984): 1ff. See also A. G. Drachmann, *Ancient Oil Mills and Presses* (Copenhagen, 1932).

164. F. M. Cornford, *Principium sapientiae: The Origins of Greek Philosophical Thought* (Oxford, 1952), esp. pp. 159ff., is fundamental. See also the varied perspectives of G. E. R. Lloyd, *Magic, Reason, and Experience: Studies in the Origin and Development of Greek Science* (Cambridge, 1979), esp. pp. 59ff., 126ff.; and M. Serres, *Les origines de la géométrie* (Paris, 1993), esp. pp. 71ff.

165. Francis Bacon, "Novum Organum," in Bacon, *Works,* vol. 1 (London, 1879), pp. 185ff. (secs. 77–79); P. Rossi, *Francesco Bacone,* pp. 92ff.; and P. Rossi, *Naufragi senza spettatore: L'idea di progresso* (Bologna, 1995), pp. 24ff.

166. *Die Fragmente der Vorsokratiker,* ed. H. Diels and W. Kranz, 22 B F 123; the source is Themistius, *Orationes,* 5, ed. W. Dindorf (Hildesheim, 1961), p. 69. See G. Colli, *La natura ama nascondersi* (Milan, 1988); this is a fascinating book, although its dominant idea—that "we understand almost nothing about the Greeks of truly vital importance, except what Nietzsche and Burckhardt

have said" (p. 14)—is frequently recast in a deceptively prejudicial way. His reappraisal of the Pre-Socratics subverts, so to speak, Bacon's intuition (a reversal in the polarity of which two major lines of European thought are condensed and reflected). On p. 209 he translates φύσις as "transcendent nature"; this is semantically correct, in all probability, but excessively redundant. Yet in the same passage he correctly speaks of an "unfathomable abyss."

167. *Fragmente der Vorsokratiker,* 22 B, F 54 (from Hippolytus, *Refutatio contra omnes haereses,* 9, 9, p. 241, ed. Wendland). My translation follows Colli, *La natura ama nascondersi,* pp. 207–208.

168. *Fragmente der Vorsokratiker,* 12 A, F 9 (Theophrastus, *Physicorum opiniones,* F 2, in H. Diels, ed., *Doxographi Graeci,* p. 476 = Simplicius, *Physics,* 23, 14). See also A. Maddalena, ed., *Ionici: Testimonianze e frammenti* (Florence, 1963), p. 117.

169. The expression comes from J.-P. Vernant, "La formation de la pensée positive dans la Grèce archaïque" (1957), reprinted in idem, *Mythe et pensée chez les Grecques,* pp. 373ff.

170. Plutarch, *Marcellus,* 14; in English in *Plutarch's Lives,* vol. 5 (Cambridge, Mass., 1917), pp. 469ff.

171. Plutarch, *Marcellus,* 14.

172. Ibid., 16.

173. Ibid., 17.

174. Ibid., 17.

175. Pliny, *Historia Naturalis,* 22, 117; 33, 2–4; 36, 1–3.

176. Ibid., 22, 117.

177. *Fragmente der Vorsokratiker,* 28 B, F 4 (Clement of Alexandria, *Stromateis,* 5, 15); my translation again follows Colli, *La natura ama nascondersi,* p. 171 (who in turn has adopted P. Albertelli, *Gli Eleati: Testimonianze e frammenti* [Bari, 1939], pp. 133–134), as I distance myself from Diels.

178. *Fragmente der Vorsokratiker,* 22 B, F 45 (Diogenes Laertes, 9, 7).

179. I must refer to what I state in *Storia di Roma,* vol. 1, pp. 545ff.

180. P. Rossi, *I filosofi e le macchine, 1400–1700* (Milan, 1974; orig. pub. 1962).

181. C. A. Viano, "Perché non c'è sangue nelle arterie: La cecità epistemologica degli anatomisti antichi," in G. Giannantoni and M. Vegetti, eds., *La scienza ellenistica* (Naples, 1985), pp. 297ff.

182. Vitruvius, *De architectura,* 1, 1.

183. Celsus, *De medicina,* "praefatio," 36 (ed. Marx).

184. A. Carlino, *La fabbrica del corpo: Libri e dissezione nel Rinascimento* (Turin, 1994).

185. Pliny, *Historia Naturalis,* 15, 57 (see also 17, 116). This is an attitude that is not contradicted by 2, 117–118, where, in the image of crossing the sea only for the

sake of financial gain ("lucri, non scientiae, gratia"), an echo of Plato can perhaps be traced. See above, Chapter 8, section 1.

186. The quotation from Posidonius is in Seneca, *Epistulae* 90, 25 (Edelstein and Kidd, eds., F 284).

187. Seneca, *Epistulae,* 90, 23.

188. Athenaeus, 6, 233 d–e (*Fragmente der Griechischen Historiker,* 87 F 48; Edelstein and Kidd, eds., F 240 a). This is a tradition handed down from Zeno of Citium; see *Stoicorum Veterum Fragmenta* (Leipzig, 1903–24), vol. 1, 239 (Athenaeus, 6, 233 b–c).

189. Seneca, *Naturales quaestiones,* 5, 15.

190. K. Reinhardt, *Poseidonios,* pp. 59ff., 135ff., 176ff.; M. Laffranque, *Poseidonios d'Apamée* (Paris, 1964), pp. 153ff., 215ff., 285ff., 369ff.

191. Descartes, *Discours de la méthode* (1637), in *Oeuvres,* vol. 6 (Paris, 1902; rpt. 1965), pp. 61–62; in English in *The Philosophical Works of Descartes* (Cambridge, 1968), vol. 1, pp. 119–120, which reflects the entire tradition of engineering between the Middle Ages and the Renaissance.

192. Thucydides, 1, 71, 3.

193. Libanius, *Epistulae,* 369, 9.

194. Sidonius, *Epistulae,* 8, 2, 2 (in Krush, ed., *Monumenta Germaniae Historica*). See also Diodorus, 1, 2, 6.

195. All of the *Germania* can be read in this light, as a representation of the "other." See M. Corbier, "Produzioni, economie, vie di comunicazione, 600 a. C.–500 d. C," in P. Anderson et al., eds., *Storia d'Europa,* vol. 2, pt. 2 (Turin, 1994), pp. 942–943.

196. Andreas Alföldi, "The Moral Barrier on Rhine and Danube," in E. Birley, ed., *The Congress of Roman Frontier Studies, 1949* (Durham, 1952), pp. 1ff.

197. S. Piggot, *Ancient Europe: From the Beginnings of Agriculture to Classical Antiquity* (Chicago, 1965), pp. 256ff.

198. J. G. D. Clark, *Prehistoric Europe: The Economic Basis* (rpt. Stanford, 1966), esp. pp. 91ff., 171ff., 205ff.; idem, *World History in a New Perspective* (Cambridge, 1977); C. Clark, *World Prehistory* (Cambridge, 1969), esp. pp. 84ff.; C. Renfrew, *The Emergence of Civilization: The Cyclades and the Aegean in the Third Millennium* (London, 1972); J. Guillaine, *Premiers bergers et paysans de l'Occident méditerranéen* (Paris, 1976); D. H. Trumph, *The Prehistory of the Mediterranean* (London, 1980); R. Chapman, *Emerging Complexity: The Later Prehistoric Antiquities of South-East Spain, Iberia, and the West Mediterranean* (Cambridge, 1990); and J. Guillaine, ed., *Pour une archéologie agraire* (Paris, 1991). See also M. I. Finley, *Early Greece: The Bronze and Archaic Ages* (rpt. New York, 1981); and W. H. McNeill, *The Rise of the West* (Chicago, 1963).

199. J. G. D. Clark, "Radiocarbon Dating and Expansion of Farming from the Near

East over Europe," *Proceedings of the Prehistoric Society*, 21 (1965): 58ff.; C. Renfrew, *Before Civilization: The Radiocarbon Revolution and Prehistoric Europe* (Cambridge, 1979).

200. Prodicus of Ceos (*Fragmente der Vorsokratiker*, 84 B, F 5 [Philodemus, *De pietate*, ed. T. Gomperz, 9, 7]; later Perseus, a follower of Zeno of Citium (*Fragmente der Vorsokratiker*, 84 B, F 5; also in *Stoicorum Veterum Fragmenta*, 1, 448, with reference to Cicero, *De natura deorum*, 1, 38, in addition to Philodemus). The reader can also refer to A. Schiavone, *Giuristi e nobili nella Roma repubblicana* (Rome, 1987), pp. 93, 219.

201. Heraclitus, in *Fragmente der Vorsokratiker*, 22 B, F 101 (from Plutarch, *Moralia, adversus Colotem*, 20).

202. Again Heraclitus, in *Fragmente der Vorsokratiker*, 22 B, F 115 (from J. Stobaios, *Florilegium*, ed., Hensel, 1, 180a).

203. Bruno Snell, *Die Entdeckung des Geistes: Studien zur Entstehung des europäischen Denkens bei den Griechen* (Hamburg, 1955), esp. pp. 7ff.; in English in idem, *The Discovery of the Mind* (Oxford, 1953), pp. vff.

204. Vernant, *Mythe et pensée chez les grecs*, p. 373. But it must be said that his "esprit" reflects more the thinking of Ignace Meyerson than the historicism of Snell.

205. I am persuaded by the recent hypothesis according to which the first alphabetization of Greek was devised not for commercial reasons but for the sake of poetic memorization. See A. Johnston, "The Extent and the Use of Literacy: The Archeological Evidence," in R. Hägg, ed., *The Greek Renaissance of the Eighth Century b.c.: Tradition and Innovation* (Stockholm, 1983), pp. 63ff.; and B. B. Powell, "Why Was the Greek Alphabet Invented? The Epigraphical Evidence," *Classical Antiquity*, 8 (1989): 321ff.

206. Neither of the two interpretations that are now quasi-classic avoid the pitfalls of determinism, although they take different routes. See B. Farrington, *Greek Science* (Harmondsworth, 1953), esp. pp. 33ff.; and G. Thomson, *The First Philosophers*, in *Studies in Ancient Greek Society*, vol. 2 (London, 1955), esp. pp. 140ff.

207. D. Musti, "I Greci e l'Italia," in *Storia di Roma*, vol. 1, pp. 39ff.; L. Canfora, "Roma, 'città greca,'" *Quaderni di storia*, 39 (1994): 5ff.

208. This very effective expression is found in Veyne, "Mythe et réalité de l'autarcie à Rome," p. 278.

209. We must not forget, however, the brief but chilling interlude constituted by the massive use of forced labor in the Nazi war economy.

210. This argument was made in two famous essays. See Marc Bloch, "Comment et pourquoi finit l'esclavage antique?" (1947); and idem, "Liberté et servitude personelles au Moyen Age, particulièrement en France: Contribution à une

étude des classes" (1933). Both are reprinted in Bloch, *Mélanges historiques,* vol. 1 (Paris, 1963), pp. 261ff., 286ff.

10. Ancient and Modern Work

1. Aristotle, *Politics,* 1, 4 (1254a); in English in *"The Politics" and "The Constitution of Athens,"* trans. J. Barnes (Cambridge, 1996), p. 15. Cf. Aristotle, *Nicomachean Ethics,* 5, 6 (1134b).

2. Julian's opinion is reported by Sextus Caecilius Africanus, 3 *Quaestiones,* in *Digesta* (hereafter abbreviated "D."), 50, 16, 207. See also *Corpus Inscriptionum Latinarum,* 6, 2, 9632; and Ulpian, 29 *Ad edictum,* in D., 14, 4, 1, 1.

3. The text is Cicero, *De republica,* 3, 25, 37; see Chapter 9 above. See also A. Schiavone, "Legge di natura o convenzione sociale? Aristotele, Cicerone, Ulpiano sulla schiavitù-merce," in M. Moggi and G. Cordiano, eds., *Schiavi e dipendenti nell'ambito dell'"oikos" e della "familia": Atti del XXII Colloquio Girea, Pontignano (Siena), 19–20 novembre 1995* (1997), pp. 173ff.; and P. Garnsey, *Ideas of Slavery from Aristotle to Augustine* (Cambridge, 1996), pp. 23ff., 107ff.

4. G. W. F. Hegel, *Phänomenologie des Geistes,* ed. Lasson-Hoffmeister (Hamburg, 1952), pp. 146–149; in English in *Phenomenology of Spirit,* trans. A. V. Miller (Oxford, 1977), pp. 115–118, with slight modifications.

5. A. Kojève, *Introduction à la lecture de Hegel,* ed. R. Queneau (Paris, 1947; rpt. 1976), p. 27.

6. Ibid., p. 25.

7. K. Marx, *Das Kapital: Erster Band,* in Marx, *Werke,* vol. 23 (Berlin, 1975), pp. 562, n. 28; in English in *Capital: A Critique of Political Economy,* ed. S. Moore and E. Aveling (New York, 1906), p. 591 and note.

8. M. Finley, *The Ancient Economy* (Berkeley, 1985), p. 65 and n. 6.

9. P. Sraffa, *Production of Commodities by Means of Commodities: Prelude to a Critique of Economic Theory* (rpt. Cambridge, 1975), pp. 6ff. ("production with a surplus"). The arguments developed here in Chapter 10 depend in various ways on P. Garegnani, *Marx e gli economisti classici: Valore e distribuzione nelle teorie del sovrappiù* (Turin, 1981), esp. pp. 5ff., 80ff., 91ff.; and on C. Napoleoni, *Discorso sull'economia politica* (Turin, 1985), esp. pp. 24ff. and 74ff.

10. K. Marx, *Grundrisse der Kritik der politischen Ökonomie* (Berlin, 1974), p. 592. In English in Marx, *Grundrisse: Foundations of the Critique of Political Economy,* trans. Martin Nicolaus (New York, 1973), p. 704.

11. This remark comes from Max Weber, "Agrarverhältnisse im Altertum," in Weber, *Gesammelte Aufsätze zur Sozial- und Wirtschaftsgeschichte* (Tübingen, 1924), p. 258; English translation, p. 342. See also Finley, *The Ancient Economy,* pp. 35ff.; and idem, *Ancient Slavery and Modern Ideology* (New York, 1980), pp. 132ff. (up-

dated and expanded edition Princeton, 1998, pp. 200ff.). On the themes touched on in this paragraph but considered from a different point of view, see P. Garnsey, *Social Status and Legal Privilege in the Roman Empire* (Oxford, 1970). Of little value is J. Gagé, *Les classes sociales dans l'empire romain* (Paris, 1964).

11. A Blind Alley between Economics and Politics

1. The same phenomenon is discussed in a different context in S. J. Gould, *Wonderful Life: The Burgess Shale and the Nature of History* (New York, 1989). This is a splendid book that has much to teach all historians.

2. Emilio Gabba, "Dallo stato-città allo stato municipale," in A. Schiavone, ed., *Storia di Roma*, vol. 2, part 1 (Turin, 1990), pp. 697ff.; idem, "Rome and Italy: The Social War," in *Cambridge Ancient History*, 2nd ed., vol. 9 (Cambridge, 1994), pp. 104ff.; and idem, *Italia romana* (Como, 1994), pp. 14ff. See also E. Badian, "Roman Politics and Italians," in *Dialoghi di Archeologia*, 4–5 (1971): 373ff.; and P. A. Brunt, "Italian Aims at the Time of Social War," *Journal of Roman Studies*, 55 (1965): 90ff., reprinted in Brunt, *"The Fall of the Roman Republic" and Other Essays* (Oxford, 1988), pp. 93ff. (but see also pp. 144ff. and 240ff.). F. De Martino, *Storia della costituzione romana*, vol. 3 (Naples, 1973), pp. 32ff., is still important.

3. To the works already cited we must now add W. V. Harris, "Between Archaic and Modern: Some Current Problems in the History of the Roman Economy," in W. V. Harris, ed., *The Inscribed Economy: Production and Distribution in the Roman Empire in the Light of "Instrumentum Domesticum"* (Ann Arbor, 1993), pp. 11ff., which makes important comments. See also P. Herz, *Studien zur römischen Wirtschaftsgesetzgebung: Die Lebensmittelversorgung* (Stuttgart, 1988), esp. pp. 24ff., 55ff., 208ff.

4. Ettore Lepore, *Il princeps ciceroniano e gli ideali politici della tarda repubblica* (Naples, 1954). Lepore returned to this subject near the end of his life, with two dense essays written for the *Storia di Roma*: "La crisi della 'nobilitas': Fra reazione e riforma," and "La decisione politica e l'auctoritas' senatoria," vol. 2, part 1, pp. 737ff. and 760ff, respectively.

5. "Concordia ordinum": the expression is not literally a Ciceronian topos (but see *Pro Cluentio*, 55, 152; *In Catalinam*, 4, 15; and *Epistulae ad Atticum*, 1, 17, 10; 1, 17, 8; 1, 18, 3, and 2, 3, 4)—a point that in truth Lepore does not explain clearly (see pp. 13ff.)—yet the program of action it denoted was certainly at the heart of the consulate in the year 63. See also H. Strasbuger, *Concordia ordinum* (Leipzig, 1931), pp. 12ff., 38ff.

6. Livy, 6, 42, 12; Plutarch, *Camillus*, 42; Pliny, *Historia Naturalis*, 33, 6, 19. See A. Momigliano, "Camillus and Concord" (1942), reprinted in Momigliano, *Secondo contributo alla storia degli studi classici* (Rome, 1960), pp. 89ff.

7. See, for example, Cicero, *In Verrem*, 1, 12, 36.

8. This is found verbatim—"consensu bonorum omnium"—in Cicero, *De domo sua,* 35, 94 (also in his *Pro Sestio,* 12, 27). "Consensio bonorum omnium" occurs in his *De haruspicum responso,* 21, 45; "causa omnium bonorum" in his *Pro Sulla,* 3, 9; and "coniunctio omnium bonorum" in ibid., 10, 29. The entire texts of *Pro Sestio* and *De legibus* are important for Ciceronian theory. Other evidence, although presented in a somewhat disorderly manner, can be found in Lepore, *Il princeps ciceroniano,* pp. 168ff., esp. p. 171 and notes 247–249. I have translated "omnes boni," which occurs very frequently in Cicero (for example, *In Catalinam,* 4, 11, 22; *Pro Flacco,* 2, 3; *Epistulae ad Atticum,* 1, 20, 2; 2, 18, 1; 2, 19, 4; etc.), with "all good landholding citizens," and not simply with "honorable" or "decent," as is the common practice, because I believe that the latter terms do not convey the nuance of property, or in any case of patrimony, that is present in the Latin expression and that decisively connotes Cicero's perspective socially and ideologically.

9. "Innumerabiles": Cicero, *Pro Sestio,* 45, 97.

10. "Ex tota Italia": Cicero, *Pro Sulla,* 8, 24.

11. Cicero, *De legibus,* 2, 5.

12. A rigorous and powerful synthesis of this depiction can be found in the essays of E. Gabba now collected in his *Italia romana,* esp. pp. 11ff., 63ff., 105ff., and 133ff. Moreover, Gabba himself does not hesitate to link the results of his own research with Cicero's program (p. 161), presented in terms that are fairly similar to those proposed by Lepore in his day. See also W. Eck, *Die staatliche Organisation Italiens in der hohen Kaiserzeit* (Munich, 1979); and the collective work *Les "bourgeoises" municipales italiennes aux IIe et Ie siècles avant J.-C.* (Paris, 1983). H. Hill, *The Roman Middle Class in the Republican Period* (Oxford, 1952), pp. 45ff., is not very useful.

13. "Res novae": Sallust, *Cat.,* 28, 4.

14. Antonio La Penna, *Sallustio e la "rivoluzione" romana* (Milan, 1968), pp. 68ff.

15. S. Mazzarino, *Il pensiero storico classico,* vol. 2, part 1 (Bari, 1966), pp. 368, 371.

16. Sallust, *Bellum Lugurth.,* 5, 2.

17. Mazzarino, *Il pensiero storico classico,* vol. 2, part 1, p. 368. (See also, on a different occasion, Mazzarino, *Trattato di storia romana,* vol. 2 [Rome, 1962], pp. 139ff.) All of the best historians on the subject are in agreement on the use of this word, from Lepore (*Il princeps ciceroniano,* pp. 190–191, where he also speaks of "the spirit of capitalism") to Gabba (*Italia romana,* p. 16). They were perhaps influenced by a choice of Max Weber—see, for example, "Agrarverhältnisse im Altertum," in Weber, *Gesammelte Aufsätze zur Sozial- und Wirtschaftsgeschichte* (Tübingen, 1924), p. 253; in English in Weber, *The Agrarian Sociology of Ancient Civilizations* (London, 1976; rpt. 1998), pp. 334–335. We usually attribute to Mommsen the tendency to boldly modernize the Roman and Italic society of the late republican era, and he certainly did this. But we must not lose sight of the fact that throughout his *Römische Geschichte* he laid parallel emphasis on the

effects of slavery on Roman society. As he wrote, "If we try to imagine a London with the slave population of New Orleans, with the police of Constantinople, with the nonindustrial character of modern Rome, and agitated by politics after the fashion of the Paris of 1848, we will acquire an approximate idea of the republican glory whose departure Cicero and his associates in their sulky letters deplore." See T. Mommsen, *Römische Geschichte* (Munich, 1976), vol. 5, p. 178; in English in Mommsen, *The History of the Roman Republic*, abridged ed. (New York, 1908), p. 499. This is an extraordinary vision of Rome, suspended between Marx and Rostovtzeff.

18. Gabba, "Considerazioni politiche ed economiche sullo sviluppo urbano in Italia nei secoli II e I a. C." (reprinted in Gabba, *Italia romana*, p. 109), is quite correct.

19. A. Giardina, "L'identità incompiuta dell'Italia romana," in Ecole Française de Rome, *L'Italie d'Auguste à Dioclétien* (Rome, 1994), esp. pp. 29ff.; reprinted in Giardina, *L'Italia Romana: Storie di una identità incompiuta* (Rome, 1997), pp. 28ff. See also Mazzarino, *Il pensiero storico classico,* vol. 2, part 1, p. 212, where he speaks of an "Italian revolution" during the period between the Gracchi and Caesar—although his reference to Ronald Syme, *The Roman Revolution* (London, 1951; orig. pub. 1939), is neither lucid nor justified in the given context.

20. F. Braudel, *Civilisation matérielle, économie et capitalisme: XVe–XVIIIe siècle,* vol. 3 of *Les temps du monde* (Paris, 1979), pp. 538ff.; in English in Braudel, *Civilization and Capitalism,* vol. 3 of *The Perspective of the World* (New York, 1984), pp. 620ff.

21. For what follows on this subject, see also A. Schiavone, *Giuristi e nobili nella Roma repubblicana* (Rome, 1987), pp. 118ff.

22. In the closing years of the second century B.C., at the latest, the Roman government promulgated the praetorial edicts *De excercitoria actione, De institoria actione, De peculio et de in rem verso*—recorded by Servius and Alfenus (*Digesta* [hereafter abbreviated "D."], 15, 3, 16)—and *De tributoria actione* (all of which are known to us indirectly through the jurisprudential reports of the Julian version of the edict: *Edictum Perpetuum,* pp. 257ff., ed. Otto Lenel), which delineates the central points of the juridical regulations pertaining to commercial activities administered "per servos." For matters concerning jurisprudence, see the careful analysis in A. Di Porto, *Impresa collettiva e schiavo 'manager' in Roma antica, II sec. a. C.–II sec. d. C.* (Milan, 1984), esp. pp. 31ff., 63ff., 169ff. (But here again excessive emphasis is occasionally placed on signs of modernization.) The venerable work by W. W. Buckland, *The Roman Law of Slavery* (Cambridge, 1908; rpt. 1970) is still a classic. See also R. H. Barrow, *Slavery in the Roman Empire* (London, 1928); and T. Wiedermann, *Slavery* (Oxford, 1987). W. Blair, *An Inquiry into the State of Slavery amongst the Romans, from the Earliest Period till the Establishment of the Lombards in Italy* (Edinburgh, 1833; rpt. Detroit, 1970),

is old but remains of some use. See also M. Finley, ed., *Slavery in Classical Antiquity: Views and Controversies* (Cambridge, 1968).

23. Servius (D., 15, 1, 9, 2–3; cited by Ulpian); Servius-Alfenus (D., 15, 3, 16); Tubero (D., 15, 1, 5, 4; cited by Celsus-Ulpian); Labeo (D., 15, 1, 6; cited by Celsus).

24. Alfenus, 2 *Digestorum*, in D., 15, 3, 16.

25. For the most part these were measures taken by Antoninus Pius, mentioned by the jurists: *Collatio*, 3, 3, 5–6; Ulpian, 8 *De officio proconsulis*, in D., 1, 6, 2 = *Coll.*, 3, 3, 1–3 = *Institutiones Iustiniani*, 1, 8, 2; Gaius, 1, 53 = *Institutiones Iustiniani*, 1, 8, 2 (but see also *Scriptores historiae Augustae: Vita Hadriani*, 18, 7). See De Martino, *Storia della costituzione romana*, vol. 4, part 1 (Naples, 1974), pp. 340ff.; F. Casavola, "Potere imperiale e stato delle persone tra Adriano e Antonino Pio," reprinted in Casavola, *Giuristi adrianei* (Naples, 1980), pp. 199ff., esp. pp. 223ff.; K. R. Bradley, *Slaves and Masters in the Roman Empire: A Study in Social Control* (Brussels, 1984; rpt. New York, 1987), pp. 113ff.

26. Galen, *De cognoscendis curandisque animi morbis* (ed. Kühn), 4 (p. 18).

27. Florentinus, 9 *Institutiones*, in D., 1, 5, 4 (= *Institutiones Iustiniani*, 1, 3, 1–3); Tryphoninus, 7 *Disputationum*, in D., 12, 6, 64; Marcianus, 1 *Institutionum*, in D., 1, 5, 5 "principium," 2 (and see idem, 2 *Reg.* in D., 49, 16, 11); Ulpian, 1 *Institutionum*, in D., 1, 1, 4 (= *Institutiones Iustiniani*, 1, 5, "principium"). But also keep in mind Ulpian, 43 *Ad Sabinum*, in D., 50, 17, 32: "quod attinet ad ius civile, servi pro nullis habentur." We have already discussed Cicero.

28. Gabba, "Il problema dell'"unità' dell'Italia romana"; reprinted in Gabba, *Italia romana*, p. 28.

29. Giardina, "L'identità incompiuta dell'Italia romana," p. 5; reprinted in Giardina, *L'Italia romana*.

30. Tacitus, *Annales*, 11, 24. Claudius' speech is also in *Corpus Inscriptionum Latinarum*, 13, 1, 1, 1668 = *Inscriptiones Latinae Selectae*, 212 = *Fontes Iuris Romani Ante Iustiniani*, ed. S. Riccobono (1940), vol. 1, no. 43. The relationship between the two versions poses rather delicate problems, but it is certain that Tacitus—although he was familiar with the original text—"omits, transposes, and adds." See R. Syme, *Tacitus* (Oxford, 1958), p. 318. See also M. T. Griffin, "The Lyons Tablet and Tacitean Hindsight," *Classical Quarterly*, 32 (1982): 404ff.

31. R. Syme, *The Augustan Aristocracy* (London, 1986), p. 43.

32. Mommsen, *Römische Geschichte*, vols. 3–5 (I–III); and especially idem, *Römische Forschungen*, vols. 1–2 (Berlin, 1864–1879).

33. M. Gelzer, *Die Nobilität der römische Republik* (Leipzig, 1912).

34. R. Syme, *The Roman Revolution*.

35. Sallust, *Historiae*, 4, 69, 18.

36. Aristotle, *Politics*, 1, 2 (1252a); see also 1, 5 (1254a).

37. This expression refers to a category that goes back to the political thought of An-

tonio Gramsci. He used it to explain certain aspects of contemporary Italian history (the Risorgimento, for example), but he did not seem to exclude its broader application. See A. Gramsci, *Quaderni del carcere,* ed. Gerratana, vol. 3 (Turin, 1975), p. 1774.

38. Syme, *The Augustan Aristocracy,* p. 36.

39. Augustus, *Res gestae,* 5, 25, 2 (ed. Malcovati).

40. Appian, *Bella civilia,* 2, 106 (also 124 and 145).

41. De Martino presents a good interpretation in *Storia della costituzione romana,* vol. 4, part 1, p. 110.

42. Augustus, *Res gestae,* 6, 34, 1.

43. From Volusius Maecianus, *De lege Rhodia,* in D., 14, 2, 9. (The manuscript of the *Florentina,* which reads *"Ex lege Rhodia,"* has been amended according to Otto Lenel's suggestion in *Palingenesia,* vol. 1, p. 588.) See V. Marotta, *Multa de iure sanxit: Aspetti della politica del diritto di Antonino Pio* (Milan, 1988), pp. 73ff.

44. M. Weber, "Die sozialen Gründe des Untergangs der antiken Kultur" (1896), reprinted in Weber, *Gesammelte Aufsätze zur Sozial- und Wirtschaftsgeschichte,* pp. 229ff.; English translation, pp. 389ff. Also idem, "Agrarverhältnisse im Altertum," esp. pp. 78–79, 242ff., 271ff.; English translation, pp. 63–64, 323ff., 358ff. See E. Lo Cascio, "Weber e il capitalismo antico," in M. Losito and P. Schiera, eds., *Max Weber e le scienze sociali del suo tempo* (Bologna, 1988), pp. 401ff.; L. Capogrossi Colognesi, *Economie antiche e capitalismo moderno: La sfida di Max Weber* (Rome, 1990); and J. R. Love, *Antiquity and Capitalism: Max Weber and the Sociological Foundations of Roman Civilization* (London, 1991).

45. Weber, "Agrarverhältnisse im Altertum," p. 276; English translation, p. 364.

46. Cyprian, *Ad Demetrianum,* 3–5 (ed. Simonetti), cited in S. Mazzarino, *La fine del mondo antico* (1959; rpt. Milan, 1988), pp. 43–44; in English in *The Treatises of Cyprian,* trans. E. Wallis, vol. 5 of *Fathers of the Third Century* (Grand Rapids, Mich., 1971), pp. 458–459. See also P. Ørsted, *Roman Imperial Economy and Romanization* (Copenhagen, 1985), p. 373.

47. D. S. Potter, *Prophecy and History in the Crisis of the Roman Empire: A Historical Commentary on the Thirteenth Sibylline Oracle* (Oxford, 1990). See also the work of G. Alföldi, now in Alföldi, *Die Krise des römischen Reichs: Geschichte, Geschichtsschreibung und Geschichtsbetrachtung* (Stuttgart, 1989).

48. The expression "government without bureaucracy," in P. Garnsey and R. Saller, *The Roman Empire: Economy, Society, and Culture* (London, 1978), pp. 20ff., is well chosen: the ancient Chinese empire employed twenty times as many functionaries, proportionally speaking. See F. Millar, *The Emperor in the Roman World, 31 B.C.–A.D. 337* (Ithaca, N.Y., rpt. 1992), esp. pp. 59ff., 363ff.; and A. Lintott, *Imperium Romanum: Politics and Administration* (London, 1993), pp. 5ff. On later developments, see also D. Kagan, ed., *Decline and Fall of the Roman Empire: Why Did It Collapse?* (Boston, 1962); A. H. M. Jones, *The Later Ro-*

man Empire, 284–602: A Social, Economic, and Administrative Survey (Baltimore, 1964; rpt. 1992), vol. 1, pp. 37ff., 321ff.; A. H. M. Jones, *The Roman Economy: Studies in Ancient Economic and Administrative History* (Oxford, 1974), pp. 168ff., 177ff., 193ff.; F. Millar, *The Roman Empire and Its Neighbours* (London, 1967); M. Finley, *Aspects of Antiquity: Discoveries and Controversies* (London, 1968), pp. 153ff.; F. De Martino, *Storia della costituzione romana*, vol. 5 (Naples, 1975), pp. 253ff.; R. MacMullen, *The Roman Government's Response to Crisis*, A.D. *235–337* (New Haven, Conn., 1976); and R. MacMullen, *Corruption and the Decline of Rome* (New Haven, Conn., 1988), esp. pp. 58ff., 171ff.; G. W. Bowersock, "The Dissolution of the Roman Empire," in N. Yoffee and G. L. Cowgill, eds., *The Collapse of Ancient States and Civilizations* (Tucson, Ariz., 1988), pp. 165ff. See also T. Spagnuolo Vigorita, "Cittadini e sudditi tra secondo e terzo secolo," A. Giardina, "La formazione dell'Italia provinciale," and F. Grelle, "La forma dell'Impero"—all in *Storia di Roma*, vol. 3, part 1 (Turin, 1993), pp. 5ff., 51ff., and 69ff., respectively. A book that remains important is S. Mazzarino, *Aspetti sociali del quarto secolo* (Rome, 1951). See also S. N. Eisenstadt, *The Political Systems of Empires* (New York, 1967); C. Cipolla, ed., *The Economic Decline of Empires* (London, 1970); M. W. Doyle, *Empires* (Ithaca, N.Y., 1986), esp. pp. 82ff., 123ff.

49. I have discussed this subject elsewhere. See *Storia di Roma*, vol. 2, part 3, pp. 57ff.; and Schiavone, *Linee di storia del pensiero giuridico romano* (Turin, 1995), pp. 221ff.

12. How History Works

1. The phrase comes from Milan Kundera, *Les testaments trahis* (Paris, 1993); in English in Kundera, *Testaments Betrayed* (New York, 1995), p. 77.

2. K. Marx, *Grundrisse der Kritik der politischen Ökonomie* (Berlin, 1974), pp. 387–388. In English in Marx, *Grundrisse: Foundations of the Critique of Political Economy,* trans. Martin Nicolaus (New York, 1973), p. 488.

3. "Kindische": *Grundrisse,* p. 387.

4. Strabo, 2, 5, 5.

5. I am elaborating on Kundera again here. See Milan Kundera, *La Lenteur* (Paris, 1995); in English in Kundera, *Slowness,* trans. Linda Asher (New York, 1996), p. 38.

6. Marx, *Grundrisse,* p. 387; English translation, p. 488.

7. Ibid., p. 387; English translation, p. 488. This is clearly a Hegelian motif.

8. Seneca, *Epistulae,* 24, 25: "libido moriendi" and "faciendi videndique satietas" (24, 26).

9. Weber's conclusion remains unsatisfying. See Max Weber, "Agrarverhältnisse im Altertum," in Weber, *Gesammelte Aufsätze zur Sozial- und Wirtschaftsgeschichte*

(Tübingen, 1924), pp. 277–278; in English in Weber, *The Agrarian Sociology of Ancient Civilizations* (London, 1976; rpt. 1998), p. 365. The very polarization of "ancient" and "modern" is inherent in Western history alone. Jacques Le Goff's comments are quite correct; see Le Goff, "Antico/moderno," in *Enciclopedia Einaudi*, R. Romano, ed., vol. 1 (Turin, 1977), pp. 678ff., reprinted in Le Goff, *Storia e memoria* (Turin, 1986), pp. 133ff.

10. See S. Settis, "Continuità, distanza, conoscenza: Tre usi dell'antico," in Settis, ed., *Memoria dell'antico nell'arte italiana*, vol. 3 (Turin, 1986), pp. 373ff. This essay provides a good reconstruction of the significance of the rupture, encapsulated in the high medieval image of the "fracta Urbs."

11. See R. Mondolfo, *Figure e idee della filosofia del Rinascimento* (Florence, 1955), pp. 233ff.; H. Baron, "The Querelle of the Ancient and Modern as a Problem for Renaissance Scholarship," in P. O. Kristeller and P. Wiesner, eds., *Renaissance Essays* (New York, 1968), pp. 95ff.; R. Foster Jones, *Ancients and Moderns: A Study in the Rise of Scientific Movement in Seventeenth Century England* (Berkeley, 1965); and P. Rossi, *Naufragi senza spettatore: L'idea di progresso* (Bologna, 1995), pp. 69ff.

12. See E. Garin, *Medioevo e Rinascimento* (Bari, 1954), esp. pp. 121ff.; F. A. Yates, *Giordano Bruno and the Hermetic Tradition* (London, 1964), esp. pp. 1ff.; and D. P. Walker, *The Ancient Theology* (London, 1972). G. Preti, *Retorica e logica: Le due culture* (Turin, 1968), remains important, esp. pp. 61ff.

13. R. K. Merton, *On the Shoulders of Giants* (Orlando, Fla., 1985).

14. The thread goes from Herodotus (3, 80–82), to Plato (*Politicus*, 31 [291 d–e]), to Aristotle, who stabilized the schema (*Politics*, 3, 7 [1279 a–b]), to Polybius, who restates Aristotle but adds a theory of history (6, 3–4; but see also 6, 9 and 6, 57); then to Machiavelli (*Discorsi*, Book 1, chapter 2), who relies on Polybius but transforms his concept of cyclicity from a simple naturalistic progression to a far more complex process (my interpretation goes further than Garin's; see Eugenio Garin, "Polibio e Machiavelli," reprinted in Garin, *Machiavelli fra politica e storia* [Turin, 1993], pp. 3ff.); and finally to Hobbes (*Leviathan*, ed. Macpherson [Harmondsworth, 1968], ch. 19), who relies on Aristotle. L. Canfora, "La tipologia costituzionale," *Quaderni di storia*, 37 (1993): 19ff., contains useful ideas, although they do not concur with what I have outlined here.

15. N. Machiavelli, *Discorsi sopra la prima deca di Tito Livio*, ed. Vivanti (Turin, 1983), pp. 506–507 (book 3, ch. 43); in English in *The Discourses of Niccolò Machiavelli*, trans. L. J. Walker (New Haven, 1950), vol. 1, p. 575.

16. Ecclesiastes 3 15.

17. Machiavelli, *Discorsi*, p. 8 (Book 1, "Proemio"); English translation, p. 206.

18. N. Machiavelli, "Del modo di trattare i popoli della Valdichiana ribellati," in Machiavelli, *Tutte le opere*, ed. Martelli (Florence, 1971), p. 14b.

19. For example, in F. Guicciardini, *Ricordi*, ed. R. Spongano (Florence, 1951), p. 87

(C 76), but see also p. 121 (C 110); in English in Guicciardini, *Selected Writings*, trans. Margaret Grayson (London, 1965), pp. 23, 30.

20. E. Garin, "Aspetti del pensiero di Machiavelli," in Garin, *Dal Rinascimento all'Illuminismo* (Pisa, 1970), pp. 43ff., esp. p. 73.

21. Galileo Galilei, *Dialogo sopra i due massimi sistemi del mondo* (1632), ed. Sosio (Turin, 1970), p. 140; in English in Galileo, *Dialogue Concerning the Two Chief World Systems,* trans. S. Drake (Berkeley, 1953), p. 113, slightly modified.

22. Garin, "Polibio e Machiavelli," p. 18.

23. "Imitare" is a verb used by Machiavelli—for example, in the *Discorsi,* Book 1, "Proemio," pp. 8 and 9; English translation, pp. 205–206.

24. Galileo, *Dialogo,* p. 139; English translation, p. 112.

25. Machiavelli, *Discorsi,* pp. 146–147 (book 1, ch. 39); English translation, p. 302.

26. Bacon, *The Works of Francis Bacon,* ed. Spedding, Hellis, and Heath (London, 1876), vol. 3, p. 535.

Index

REVEALING ANTIQUITY

G. W. Bowersock, General Editor